I have nothing new to teach the world
Truth and nonviolence are as old as the hills

Harijan, March 28, 1936

M.K. Gandhi

MAHATMA GANDHI

ALL MEN
ARE BROTHERS

AUTOBIOGRAPHICAL REFLECTIONS

Compiled and Edited by
Krishna Kripalani

Introduction by
Sarvepalli Radhakrishnan

CONTINUUM · New York

1980
The Continuum Publishing Corporation
815 Second Avenue, New York, NY 10017
Copyright © 1980 by The Continuum Publishing Corporation.
All rights reserved. No part of this book may be reproduced, stored
in a retrieval system, or transmitted, in any form or by any means,
electronic, mechanical, photocopying, recording, or otherwise, without the written permission of The Continuum Publishing Corporation.

Printed in the United States of America

First published by UNESCO
and The Columbia University Press © 1958.

Library of Congress Catalog Number 79-56684

ISBN 0-8264-0003-5
Previously ISBN 0-8164-9237-9

The extracts from Gandhi's works are reproduced by permission of
the Navajivan Trust Ahmedabad-14, India.

CONTENTS

Pictures on page 1 and following pages 14, 48, 84, 108, and 156

INTRODUCTION

A great teacher appears once in a while. Several centuries may pass by without the advent of such a one. That by which he is known is his life. He first lives and then tells others how they may live likewise. Such a teacher was Gandhi. These Selections from his speeches and writings compiled with great care and discrimination by Sri Krishna Kripalani will give the reader some idea of the workings of Gandhi's mind, the growth of his thoughts and the practical techniques which he adopted.

Gandhi's life was rooted in India's religious tradition with its emphasis on a passionate search for truth, a profound reverence for life, the ideal of nonattachment and the readiness to sacrifice all for the knowledge of God. He lived his whole life in the perpetual quest of truth: 'I live and move and have my being in the pursuit of this goal.'

A life which has no roots, which is lacking in depth of background is a superficial one. There are some who assume that when we see what is right we will do it. It is not so. Even when we know what is right it does not follow that we will choose and do right. We are overborne by powerful impulses and do wrong and betray the light in us. 'In our present state we are, according to the Hindu doctrine, only partly human; the lower part of us is still animal; only the conquest of our lower instincts by love can slay the animal in us.' It is by a process of trial and error, self-search and austere discipline that the human being moves step by painful step along the road to fulfilment.

Gandhi's religion was a rational and ethical one. He would not accept any belief which did not appeal to his reason or any injunction which did not commend to his conscience.

If we believe in God, not merely with our intellect but with our whole being, we will love all mankind without any distinction of race or class, nation or religion. We will work for the unity of mankind. 'All my actions have their rise in my inalienable love of mankind.' 'I have known no distinction between relatives and strangers, countrymen and foreigners, white and coloured, Hindus and Indians of other faiths whether Mussulmans, Parsees, Christians or Jews. I may say that my heart has been incapable of making any such distinctions.' 'By a long process of prayerful discipline I have ceased for over forty years to hate anybody.' All men are brothers and no human being should be a stranger to another. The welfare of all, *sarvodaya*, should be our aim. God is the common bond that unites all human beings. To break this bond even with our greatest enemy is to tear God himself to pieces. There is humanity even in the most wicked.[1]

This view leads naturally to the adoption of nonviolence as the best means for solving all problems, national and international. Gandhi affirmed that he was not a visionary but a practical idealist. Nonviolence is meant not merely for saints and sages but for the common people also. 'Nonviolence is the law of our species, as violence is the law of the brute. The spirit lies dormant in the brute and he knows no law but that of physical might. The dignity of man requires obedience to a higher law—to the strength of the spirit.'

Gandhi was the first in human history to extend the principle of nonviolence from the individual to the social and political plane. He entered politics for the purpose of experimenting with nonviolence and establishing its validity.

'Some friends have told me that truth and nonviolence have no place in politics and worldly affairs. I do not agree. I have no use for them as a means of individual salvation. Their introduction and application in everyday life has been my experiment all along.' 'For me, politics bereft of religion are absolute dirt, ever to be shunned. Politics concerns nations and that which concerns the welfare of nations must be one of the concerns of a man who is religiously inclined, in other words, a seeker after God and Truth. For me God and Truth are convertible terms, and if any one told me that God was a God of untruth or a God of torture I would decline to worship Him. Therefore, in politics also we have to establish the Kingdom of Heaven.'

In the struggle for India's independence, he insisted that we should adopt civilized methods of nonviolence and suffering. His stand for the freedom of India was not based on any hatred for Britain. We must hate the sin but not the sinner. 'For me patriotism is the same as humanity. I am patriotic because I am human and humane. I will not hurt England or Germany to serve India.' He believed that he rendered a service to the British in helping them to do the right thing

1. See. *Mahā-bhārata: asādhuś caiva puruso labhate śilam ekadā*, xii.259 11.

by India. The result was not only the liberation of the Indian people but an increase in the moral resources of mankind.

In the present nuclear context, if we wish to save the world, we should adopt the principles of nonviolence. Gandhi said: 'I did not move a muscle, when I first heard that an atom bomb had wiped out Hiroshima. On the contrary I said to myself: "Unless now the world adopts nonviolence, it will spell certain suicide for mankind".' In any future conflict we cannot be certain that neither side will deliberately use nuclear weapons. We have the power to destroy in one blinding flash all that we have carefully built up across the centuries by our endeavour and sacrifice. By a campaign of propaganda we condition men's minds for nuclear warfare. Provocative remarks fly about freely. We use aggression even in words; harsh judgements, ill-will, anger, are all insidious forms of violence.

In the present predicament when we are not able to adjust ourselves to the new conditions which science has brought about, it is not easy to adopt the principles of nonviolence, truth and understanding. But on that ground we should not give up the effort. While the obstinacy of the political leaders puts fear into our hearts, the common sense and conscience of the peoples of the world give us hope.

With the increased velocity of modern changes we do not know what the world will be a hundred years hence. We cannot anticipate the future currents of thought and feeling. But years may go their way, yet the great principles of *satya* and *ahimsā*, truth and nonviolence, are there to guide us. They are the silent stars keeping holy vigil above a tired and turbulent world. Like Gandhi we may be firm in our conviction that the sun shines above the drifting clouds.

We live in an age which is aware of its own defeat and moral coarsening, an age in which old certainties are breaking down, the familiar patterns are tilting and cracking. There is increasing intolerance and embitterment. The creative flame that kindled the great human society is languishing. The human mind in all its baffling strangeness and variety produces contrary types, a Buddha or a Gandhi, a Nero or a Hitler. It is our pride that one of the greatest figures of history lived in our generation, walked with us, spoke to us, taught us the way of civilized living. He who wrongs no one fears no one. He has nothing to hide and so is fearless. He looks everyone in the face. His step is firm, his body upright, and his words are direct and straight. Plato said long ago: 'There always are in the world a few inspired men whose acquaintance is beyond price.'

New Delhi
15 August 1958   S. Radhakrishnan

At the time of writing this introduction, Professor Sarvepalli Radhakrishnan was Vice-President of India and later President.

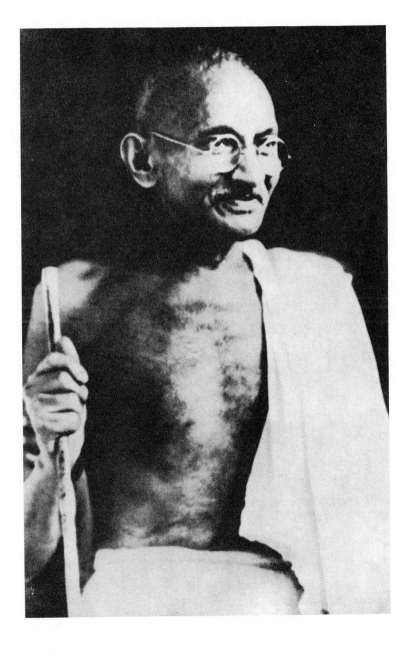

Portrait of Gandhi, 1944   (Photo Keystone)

I AUTOBIOGRAPHICAL

It is not my purpose to attempt a real autobiography. I simply want to tell the story of my numerous experiments with truth, and as my life consists of nothing but those experiments, it is true that the story will take the shape of an autobiography. But I shall not mind, if every page of it speaks only of my experiments. *1*

An Autobiography

My experiments in the political field are now known, not only to India, but to a certain extent to the 'civilized' world. For me, they have not much value; and the title of 'Mahatma' that they have won for me has, therefore, even less. Often the title has deeply pained me; and there is not a moment I can recall when it may be said to have tickled me. But I should certainly like to narrate my experiments in the spiritual field which are known only to myself, and from which I have derived such power as I possess for working in the political field. If the experiments are really spiritual, then there can be no room for self-praise. They can only add to my humility. The more I reflect and look back on the past, the more vividly do I feel my limitations. *2*

An Autobiography

What I want to achieve—what I have been striving and pining to

For this chapter Krishna Kripalani has edited Gandhi's *Autobiography* and has added selections from his other writings providing a brief yet complete autobiography. Gandhi's *An Autobiography, The Story of My Experiments with Truth* was written between 1920 and 1925 and originally appeared serially in *Young India. An Autobiography* concludes in 1921, twenty seven years before Gandhi's death. The selections added here by the editor have been identified and dated. Readers interested in a more detailed account of Gandhi's life should read *MAHATMA, Life of Mohandas Karamchand Gandhi* by D. G. Tendular in eight volumes or one of the biographies listed in the Select Bibliography, p. 174.

achieve these thirty years—is self-realization, to see God face to face, to attain *Moksha*. I live and move and have my being in pursuit of this goal. All that I do by way of speaking and writing, and all my ventures in the political field, are directed to this same end. But as I have all along believed that what is possible for one is possible for all, my experiments have not been conducted in the closet, but in the open; and I do not think that this fact detracts from their spiritual value. There are some things which are known only to oneself and one's Maker. These are clearly incommunicable. The experiments I am about to relate are not such. But they are spiritual, or rather moral; for the essence of religion is morality. *3*   *An Autobiography*

Far be it from me to claim any degree of perfection for these experiments. I claim for them nothing more than does a scientist who, though he conducts his experiments with the utmost accuracy, forethought and minuteness, never claims any finality about his conclusions, but keeps an open mind regarding them. I have gone through deep self-introspection, searched myself through and through, and examined and analysed every psychological situation. Yet I am far from claiming any finality or infallibility about my conclusions. One claim I do indeed make and it is this. For me they appear to be absolutely correct, and seem for the time being to be final. For if they were not, I should base no action on them. But at every step I have carried out the process of acceptance or rejection and acted accordingly. *4*   *An Autobiography*

My life is one indivisible whole, and all my activities run into one another, and they all have their rise in my insatiable love of mankind. *5*   *The Harijan, March 2, 1934*

The Gandhis belong to the *Baniā* caste and seem to have been originally grocers. But for three generations, from my grandfather, they have been prime ministers in several Kathiawad States. . . . My grandfather must have been a man of principle. State intrigues compelled him to leave Porbandar, where he was *Diwān*, and to seek refuge in Junagadh. There he saluted the *Nawāb* with the left hand. Someone, noticing the apparent discourtesy, asked for an explanation, which was given thus: 'The right hand is already pledged to Porbandar.'   *6*   *An Autobiography*

My father was a lover of his clan, truthful, brave and generous, but short-tempered. To a certain extent he might have been even given to carnal pleasures. For he married for the fourth time when he was over forty. But he was incorruptible and had earned a name for strict impartiality in his family as well as outside. *7*   *An Autobiography*

Autobiographical

The outstanding impression my mother has left on my memory is that of saintliness. She was deeply religious. She would not think of taking her meals without her daily prayers. . . . She would take the hardest vows and keep them without flinching. Illness was no excuse for relaxing them. *8*   *An Autobiography*

Of these parents I was born at Porbandar. . . . I passed my childhood in Porbandar. I recollect having been put to school. It was with some difficulty that I got through the multiplication tables. The fact that I recollect nothing more of those days than having learnt, in company with other boys, to call our teacher all kinds of names, would strongly suggest that my intellect must have been sluggish, and my memory raw. *9*   *An Autobiography*

I used to be very shy and avoided all company. My books and my lessons were my sole companions. To be at school at the stroke of the hour and to run back home as soon as the school closed—that was my daily habit. I literally ran back, because I could not bear to talk to anybody. I was even afraid lest anyone should poke fun at me. *10*   *An Autobiography*

There is an incident which occurred at the examination during my first year at the high school and which is worth recording. Mr. Giles, the Educational Inspector, had come on a visit of inspection. He had set us five words to write as a spelling exercise. One of the words was 'kettle.' I had mis-spelt it. The teacher tried to prompt me with the point of his boot, but I would not be prompted. It was beyond me to see that he wanted me to copy the spelling from my neighbour's slate, for I had thought that the teacher was there to supervise us against copying. The result was that all the boys, except myself, were found to have spelt every word correctly. Only I had been stupid. The teacher tried later to bring this stupidity home to me, but without effect. I never could learn the art of 'copying.' *11*
                                    An Autobiography

It is my painful duty to have to record here my marriage at the age of thirteen. As I see the youngsters of the same age about me who are under my care, and think of my own marriage, I am inclined to pity myself and to congratulate them on having escaped my lot. I can see no moral argument in support of such a preposterously early marriage. *12*   *An Autobiography*

I do not think it [marriage] meant to me anything more than the prospect of good clothes to wear, drum beating, marriage processions,

rich dinners and a strange girl to play with. The carnal desire came
later. *13*   *An Autobiography*

And oh! that first night. Two innocent children all unwittingly hurled
themselves into the ocean of life. My brother's wife had thoroughly
coached me about my behaviour on the first night. I do not know
who had coached my wife. I have never asked her about it, nor am I
inclined to do so now. The reader may be sure that we were too
nervous to face each other. We were certainly too shy. How was I to
talk to her, and what was I to say? The coaching could not carry me
far. But no coaching is really necessary in such matters. . . . We gradually began to know each other, and to speak freely together. We were
the same age. But I took no time in assuming the authority of a
husband. *14*   *An Autobiography*

I must say I was passionately fond of her. Even at school I used to
think of her, and the thought of nightfall and our subsequent meeting was ever haunting me. Separation was unbearable. I used to keep
her awake till late in the night with my idle talk. If with this devour-
ing passion there had not been in me a burning attachment to duty, I
should either have fallen a prey to disease and premature death, or
have sunk into a burdensome existence. But the appointed tasks had
to be gone through every morning, and lying to anyone was out of
the question. It was this last thing that saved me from many a pit-
fall. *15*   *An Autobiography*

I had not any high regard for my ability. I used to be astonished
whenever I won prizes and scholarships. But I very jealously guarded
my character. The least little blemish drew tears from my eyes. When
I merited, or seemed to the teacher to merit, a rebuke, it was unbearable for me. I remember having once received corporal punishment. I
did not so much mind the punishment, as the fact that it was considered my desert. I wept piteously. *16*   *An Autobiography*

Amongst my few friends at the high school I had, at different times,
two who might be called intimate. One of these friendships . . . I
regard as a tragedy in my life. It lasted long. I formed it in the spirit
of a reformer. *17*   *An Autobiography*

I have seen since that I had calculated wrongly. A reformer cannot
afford to have close intimacy with him whom he seeks to reform.
True friendship is an identity of souls rarely to be found in this
world. Only between like natures can friendship be altogether worthy
and enduring. Friends react on one another. Hence in friendship there
is very little scope for reform. I am of opinion that all exclusive

Autobiographical

intimacies are to be avoided; for man takes in vice far more readily than virtue. And he who would be friends with God must remain alone, or make the whole world his friend. I may be wrong, but my effort to cultivate an intimate friendship proved a failure. *18*

An Autobiography

This friend's exploits cast a spell over me. He could run long distances and extraordinarily fast. He was an adept in high and long jumping. He could put up with any amount of corporal punishment. He would often display his exploits to me and, as one is always dazzled when he sees in others the qualities that he lacks himself, I was dazzled by this friend's exploits. This was followed by a strong desire to be like him. I could hardly jump or run. Why should not I also be as strong as he? *19*

An Autobiography

I was a coward. I used to be haunted by the fear of thieves, ghosts, and serpents. I did not dare to stir out of doors at night. Darkness was a terror to me. It was almost impossible for me to sleep in the dark, as I would imagine ghosts coming from one direction, thieves from another and serpents from a third. I could not therefore bear to sleep without a light in the room. *20*

An Autobiography

My friend knew all these weaknesses of mine. He would tell me that he could hold in his hand live serpents, could defy thieves and did not believe in ghosts. And all this was, of course, the result of eating meat. *21*

An Autobiography

All this had its due effect on me. . . . It began to grow on me that meat-eating was good, that it would make me strong and daring, and that, if the whole country took to meat-eating, the English could be overcome. *22*

An Autobiography

Whenever I had occasion to indulge in these surreptitious feasts, dinner at home was out of the question. My mother would naturally ask me to come and take my food and want to know the reason why I did not wish to eat. I would say to her 'I have no appetite today; there is something wrong with my digestion.' It was not without compunction that I devised these pretexts. I knew I was lying, and lying to my mother. I also knew that if my mother and father came to know of my having become a meat-eater, they would be deeply shocked. This knowledge was gnawing at my heart.

Therefore I said to myself: Though it is essential to eat meat, and also essential to take up food 'reform' in the country, yet deceiving and lying to one's father and mother is worse than not eating meat. In their lifetime, therefore, meat-eating must be out of the question.

When they are no more and I have found my freedom, I will eat meat openly, but until that moment arrives I will abstain from it.

This decision I communicated to my friend, and I have never since gone back to meat. *23*   *An Autobiography*

My friend once took me to a brothel. He sent me in with the necessary instructions. It was all pre-arranged. The bill had already been paid. I went into the jaws of sin, but God in His infinite mercy protected me against myself. I was almost struck blind and dumb in this den of vice. I sat near the woman on her bed, but I was tongue-tied. She naturally lost patience with me, and showed me the door, with abuses and insults. I then felt as though my manhood had been injured, and wished to sink into the ground for shame. But I have ever since given thanks to God for having saved me. I can recall four more similar incidents in my life, and in most of them my good fortune, rather than any effort on my part, saved me. From a strictly ethical point of view, all these occasions must be regarded as moral lapses; for the carnal desire was there, and it was as good as the act. But from the ordinary point of view, a man who is saved from physically committing sin is regarded as saved. And I was saved only in that sense. *24*   *An Autobiography*

As we know that a man often succumbs to temptation, however much he may resist it, we also know that Providence often intercedes and saves him in spite of himself. How all this happens—how far a man is free and how far a creature of circumstances—how far free-will comes into play and where fate enters on the scene—all this is a mystery and will remain a mystery. *25*   *An Autobiography*

One of the reasons of my differences with my wife was undoubtedly the company of this friend. I was both a devoted and a jealous husband, and this friend fanned the flame of my suspicions about my wife. I never could doubt his veracity. And I have never forgiven myself the violence of which I have been guilty in often having pained my wife by acting on his information. Perhaps only a Hindu wife could tolerate these hardships, and that is why I have regarded woman as an incarnation of tolerance. *26*   *An Autobiography*

The canker of suspicion was rooted out only when I understood *ahiṃsā* in all its bearings. I saw then the glory of *brahmacharya* and realized that the wife is not the husband's bondslave, but his companion and his helpmate, and an equal partner in all his joys and sorrows—as free as the husband to choose her own path. Whenever I think of those dark days of doubts and suspicions, I am filled with loathing of my folly and my lustful cruelty, and I deplore my blind devotion to my friend.   *27*   *An Autobiography*

From my sixth or seventh year up to my sixteenth I was at school, being taught all sorts of things except religion. I may say that I failed to get from the teachers what they could have given me without any effort on their part. And yet I kept on picking up things here and there from my surroundings. The term 'religion' I am using in its broadest sense, meaning thereby self-realization or knowledge of self. *28*   *An Autobiography*

But one thing took deep root in me—the conviction that morality is the basis of things, and that truth is the substance of all morality. Truth became my sole objective. It began to grow in magnitude every day, and my definition of it also has been ever widening.   *29*
An Autobiography

I regard untouchability as the greatest blot on Hinduism. This idea was not brought home to me by my bitter experiences during the South African struggle. It is not due to the fact that I was once an agnostic. It is equally wrong to think that I have taken my views from my study of Christian religious literature. These views date as far back as the time when I was neither enamoured of, nor was acquainted with, the Bible or the followers of the Bible.

I was hardly yet twelve when this idea had dawned on me. A scavenger named Uka, an untouchable, used to attend our house for cleaning latrines. Often I would ask my mother why it was wrong to touch him, why I was forbidden to touch him. If I accidentally touched Uka, I was asked to perform the ablutions, and though I naturally obeyed, it was not without smilingly protesting that untouchability was not sanctioned by religion, that it was impossible that it should be so. I was a very dutiful and obedient child and so far as it was consistent with respect for parents, I often had tussles with them on this matter. I told my mother that she was entirely wrong in considering physical contact with Uka as sinful.   *30*
Mahatma, Tendular, Vol. II, Speech at the Depressed Classes Conference,
Ahmedabad, April 13, 1921

I passed the matriculation examination in 1887.   *31 An Autobiography*

My elders wanted me to pursue my studies at college after the matriculation. There was a college in Bhavnagar as well as in Bombay, and as the former was cheaper, I decided to go there and join the Samaldas College. I went, but found myself entirely at sea. Everything was difficult. I could not follow, let alone take interest in, the professors' lectures. It was no fault of theirs. The professors in that college were regarded as first-rate. But I was so raw. At the end of the first term, I returned home. *32* *An Autobiography*

A shrewd and learned Brahmin, an old friend and adviser of the family . . . happened to visit us during my vacation. In conversation with my mother and elder brother, he inquired about my studies. Learning that I was at Samaldas College, he said: 'The times are changed. . . . I would far rather that you sent him to England. My son Kevalram says it is very easy to become a barrister. In three years' time he will return. Also expenses will not exceed four to five thousand rupees. Think of that barrister who has just come back from England. How stylishly he lives! He could get the diwanship for the asking. I would strongly advise you to send Mohandas to England this very year. *33* *An Autobiography*

My mother was sorely perplexed. . . . Someone had told her that young men got lost in England. Someone else had said that they took to meat; and yet another that they could not live there without liquor. 'How about all this?' she asked me. I said: 'Will you not trust me? I shall not lie to you. I swear that I shall not touch any of those things. If there were any such danger, would Joshiji let me go?' . . . I vowed not to touch wine, woman and meat. This done, my mother gave her permission. *34* *An Autobiography*

Before the intention of coming to London for the sake of study was actually formed, I had a secret design in my mind of coming here to satisfy my curiosity of knowing what London was. *35*
From the London Diary, November 12, 1888

At the age of eighteen I went to England. . . . Everything was strange —the people, their ways, and even their dwellings. I was a complete novice in the matter of English etiquette and continually had to be on my guard. There was the additional inconvenience of the vegetarian vow. Even the dishes that I could eat were tasteless and insipid. I thus found myself between Scylla and Charybdis. England I could not bear, but to return to India was not to be thought of. Now that I had come, I must finish the three years, said the inner voice. *36* *An Autobiography*

The landlady was at a loss to know what to prepare for me. . . . The friend[1] continually reasoned with me to eat meat, but I always pleaded my vow and then remained silent. . . . One day the friend began to

1. A gentleman with whom he stayed in Richmond for a month.

read to me Bentham's *Theory of Utility*. I was at my wits' end. The language was too difficult for me to understand. He began to expound it. I said: 'Pray excuse me. These abstruse things are beyond me. I admit it is necessary to eat meat. But I cannot break my vow. I cannot argue about it.' *37*   *An Autobiography*

I would trot ten or twelve miles each day, go into a cheap restaurant and eat my fill of bread, but would never be satisfied. During these wanderings I once hit on a vegetarian restaurant in Farringdon Street. The sight of it filled me with the same joy that a child feels on getting a thing after its own heart. Before I entered I noticed books for sale exhibited under a glass window near the door. I saw among them Salt's *Plea for Vegetarianism*. This I purchased for a shilling and went straight to the dining room. This was my first hearty meal since my arrival in England. God had come to my aid.

I read Salt's book from cover to cover and was very much impressed by it. From the date of reading this book, I may claim to have become a vegetarian by choice. I blessed the day on which I had taken the vow before my mother. I had all along abstained from meat in the interests of truth and of the vow I had taken, but had wished at the same time that every Indian should be a meat-eater, and had looked forward to being one myself freely and openly some day, and to enlisting others in the cause. The choice was now made in favour of vegetarianism, the spread of which henceforth became my mission. *38*   *An Autobiography*

A convert's enthusiasm for his new religion is greater than that of a person who is born in it. Vegetarianism was then a new cult in England, and likewise for me, because, as we have seen, I had gone there a convinced meat-eater, and was intellectually converted to vegetarianism later. Full of the neophyte's zeal for vegetarianism, I decided to start a vegetarian club in my locality, Bayswater. I invited Sir Edwin Arnold, who lived there, to be vice-president. Dr. Oldfield who was editor of *The Vegetarian* became president. I myself became the secretary. *39*   *An Autobiography*

I was elected to the Executive Committee of the Vegetarian Society, and made it a point to attend every one of its meetings, but I always felt tongue-tied. . . . Not that I never felt tempted to speak. But I was at a loss to know how to express myself. . . . This shyness I retained throughout my stay in England. Even when I paid a social call the presence of half a dozen or more people would strike me dumb. *40*
An Autobiography

I must say that, beyond occasionally exposing me to laughter, my constitutional shyness has been no disadvantage whatever. In fact I can see that, on the contrary, it has been all to my advantage. My hesitancy in speech, which was once an annoyance, is now a pleasure. Its greatest benefit has been that it has taught me the economy of words. *41* *An Autobiography*

There was a great exhibition at Paris in 1890. I had read about its elaborate preparation, and I also had a keen desire to see Paris. So I thought I had better combine two things in one and go there at this juncture. A particular attraction of the exhibit was the Eiffel Tower, constructed entirely of iron, and nearly 1,000 feet high. There were of course many other things of interest, but the tower was the chief one, inasmuch as it had been supposed till then that a structure of that height could not safely stand. *42* *An Autobiography*

I remember nothing of the exhibition excepting its magnitude and variety. I have fair recollection of the Eiffel Tower as I ascended it twice or thrice. There was a restaurant on the first platform, and just for the satisfaction of being able to say that I had had my lunch at a great height, I threw away seven shillings on it.

The ancient churches of Paris are still in my memory. Their grandeur and their peacefulness are unforgettable. The wonderful construction of Notre Dame and the elaborate decoration of the interior with its beautiful sculptures cannot be forgotten. I felt then that those who expended millions on such divine cathedrals could not but have the love of God in their hearts. *43* *An Autobiography*

I must say a word about the Eiffel Tower. I do not know what purpose it serves today. But I then heard it greatly disparaged as well as praised. I remember that Tolstoy was the chief among those who disparaged it. He said that the Eiffel Tower was a monument of man's folly, not of his wisdom. Tobacco, he argued, was the worst of all intoxicants, inasmuch as a man addicted to it was tempted to commit crimes which a drunkard never dared to do; liquor made a man mad, but tobacco clouded his intellect and made him build castles in the air. The Eiffel Tower was one of the creations of a man under such influence. There is no art about the Eiffel Tower. In no way can it be said to have contributed to the real beauty of the exhibition. Men flocked to see it and ascended it as it was a novelty and of unique dimensions. It was the toy of the exhibition. So long as we are children we are attracted by toys, and the tower was a good demonstration of the fact that we are all children attracted by trinkets. That may be claimed to be the purpose served by the Eiffel Tower. *44* *An Autobiography*

Autobiographical

I passed my examinations, was called to the Bar on the tenth of June 1891, and enrolled in the High Court on the eleventh. On the twelfth I sailed for home. *45*   *An Autobiography*

My elder brother had built high hopes on me. The desire for wealth and name and fame was great in him. He had a big heart, generous to a fault. This, combined with his simple nature, had attracted to him many friends, and through them he expected to get me briefs. He had also assumed that I should have a swinging practice and had, in that expectation, allowed the household expenses to become top-heavy. He had also left no stone unturned in preparing the field for my practice. *46*   *An Autobiography*

But it was impossible for me to get along in Bombay for more than four or five months, there being no income to square with the ever-increasing expenditure.

    This was how I began life. I found the barrister's profession a bad job—much show and little knowledge. I felt a crushing sense of my responsibility. *47*   *An Autobiography*

Disappointed, I left Bombay and went to Rajkot where I set up my own office. Here I got along moderately well. Drafting applications and memorials brought me in on an average Rs.300 a month. *48*
An Autobiography

In the meantime a Meman firm from Porbandar wrote to my brother making the following offer: 'We have business in South Africa. Ours is a big firm, and we have a big case there in the Court, our claim being £40,000. It has been going on for a long time. We have engaged the services of the best *vakils* and barristers. If you sent your brother there, he would be useful to us and also to himself. He would be able to instruct our counsel better than ourselves. And he would have the advantage of seeing a new part of the world, and of making new acquaintances.' *49*   *An Autobiography*

This was hardly going there as a barrister. It was going as a servant of the firm. But I wanted somehow to leave India. There was also the tempting opportunity of seeing a new country, and of having new experience. Also I could send £105 to my brother and help in the expenses of the household. I closed with the offer without any higgling, and got ready to go to South Africa. *50*   *An Autobiography*

When starting for South Africa I did not feel the wrench of separation which I had experienced when leaving for England. My mother was now no more. I had gained some knowledge of the world and of travel abroad, and going from Rajkot to Bombay was no unusual affair.

This time I only felt the pang of parting with my wife. Another baby had been born to us since my return from England. Our love could not yet be called free from lust, but it was getting gradually purer. Since my return from Europe, we had lived very little together; and as I had now become her teacher, however indifferent, and helped her to make certain reforms we both felt the necessity of being more together, if only to continue the reforms. But the attraction of South Africa rendered the separation bearable. *51*

An Autobiography

The port of Natal is Durban also known as Port Natal. Abdulla Sheth was there to receive me. As the ship arrived at the quay and I watched the people coming on board to meet their friends, I observed that the Indians were not held in much respect. I could not fail to notice a sort of snobbishness about the manner in which those who knew Abdulla Sheth behaved towards him, and it stung me. Abdulla Sheth had got used to it. Those who looked at me did so with a certain amount of curiosity. My dress marked me out from other Indians. I had a frockcoat and a turban. *52*   *An Autobiography*

On the second or third day of my arrival, he took me to see the Durban court. There he introduced me to several people and seated me next to his attorney. The magistrate kept staring at me and finally asked me to take off my turban. This I refused to do and left the court. *53*

An Autobiography

On the seventh or eighth day after my arrival, I left Durban (for Pretoria). A first class seat was booked for me. . . . The train reached Maritzburg, the capital of Natal, at about 9 p.m. Beddings used to be provided at this station. A railway servant came and asked me if I wanted one. 'No,' said I, 'I have one with me.' He went away. But a passenger came next, and looked me up and down. He saw that I was a 'coloured' man. This disturbed him. Out he went and came in again with one or two officials. They all kept quiet, when another official came to me and said, 'Come along, you must go to the van compartment.'

'But I have a first class ticket,' said I.

'That doesn't matter,' rejoined the other. 'I tell you, you must go to the van compartment.'

'I tell you, I was permitted to travel in this compartment at Durban, and I insist on going on in it.'

'No, you won't,' said the official. 'You must leave this compartment, or else I shall have to call a police constable to push you out.'

Gandhi at the time he was a barrister in South Africa

'Yes, you may. I refuse to get out voluntarily.'

The constable came. He took me by the hand and pushed me out. My luggage was also taken out. I refused to go to the other compartment and the train steamed away. I went and sat in the waiting room, keeping my hand-bag with me, and leaving the other luggage where it was. The railway authorities had taken charge of it.

It was winter, and winter in the higher regions of South Africa is severely cold. Maritzburg being at a high altitude, the cold was extremely bitter. My overcoat was in my luggage, but I did not dare to ask for it lest I should be insulted again, so I sat and shivered. There was no light in the room. A passenger came in at about midnight and possibly wanted to talk to me. But I was in no mood to talk.

I began to think of my duty. Should I fight for my rights or go back to India, or should I go on to Pretoria without minding the insults, and return to India after finishing the case? It would be cowardice to run back to India without fulfilling my obligation. The hardship to which I was subjected was superficial—only a symptom of the deep disease of colour prejudice. I should try, if possible, to root out the disease and suffer hardships in the process. Redress for wrongs I should seek only to the extent that would be necessary for the removal of the colour prejudice.

So I decided to take the next available train to Pretoria. *54*
An Autobiography

My first step was to call a meeting of all the Indians in Pretoria and to present to them a picture of their condition in the Transvaal. *55*
An Autobiography

My speech at this meeting may be said to have been the first public speech in my life. I went fairly prepared with my subject, which was about observing truthfulness in business. I had always heard the merchants say that truth was not possible in business. I did not think so then, nor do I now. Even today there are merchant friends who contend that truth is inconsistent with business. Business, they say, is a very practical affair, and truth a matter of religion; and they argue that practical affairs are one thing, while religion is quite another. Pure truth, they hold, is out of the question in business, one can speak it only so far as is suitable. I strongly contested the position in my speech and awakened the merchants to a sense of their duty, which was twofold. Their responsibility to be truthful was all the greater in a foreign land, because the conduct of a few Indians was the measure of that of the millions of their fellow-countrymen. *56*
An Autobiography

The consequences of the regulation regarding the use of footpaths were rather serious for me. I always went out for a walk through President Street to an open plain. President Kruger's house was in this street—a very modest, unostentatious building, without a garden, and not distinguishable from other houses in its neighbourhood. The houses of many of the millionaires in Pretoria were far more pretentious, and were surrounded by gardens. Indeed President Kruger's simplicity was proverbial. Only the presence of a police patrol before the house indicated that it belonged to some official. I nearly always went along the footpath past this patrol without the slightest hitch or hindrance.

Now the man on duty used to be changed from time to time. Once one of these men, without giving me the slightest warning, without even asking me to leave the footpath, pushed and kicked me into the street. I was dismayed. Before I could question him as to his behaviour, Mr. Coates, who happened to be passing the spot on horseback, hailed me and said:

'Gandhi, I have seen everything. I shall gladly be your witness in court if you proceed against the man. I am very sorry you have been so rudely assaulted.'

'You need not be sorry,' I said. 'What does the poor man know? All coloured people are the same to him. He no doubt treats Negroes just as he has treated me. I have made it a rule not to go to court in respect of any personal grievance. So I do not intend to proceed against him.' *57*   *An Autobiography*

The incident deepened my feeling for the Indian settlers. . . . I thus made an intimate study of the hard condition of the Indian settlers, not only by reading and hearing about it, but by personal experience. I saw that South Africa was no country for a self-respecting Indian, and my mind became more and more occupied with the question as to how this state of things might be improved. *58*   *An Autobiography*

The year's stay in Pretoria was a most valuable experience in my life. Here it was that I had opportunities of learning public work and acquired some measure of my capacity for it. Here it was that the religious spirit within me became a living force, and here too I acquired a true knowledge of legal practice. *59*   *An Autobiography*

I realized that the true function of a lawyer was to unite parties riven asunder. The lesson was so indelibly burnt into me that a large part of my time during the twenty years of practice as a lawyer was occupied in bringing about private compromises of hundreds of cases. I lost nothing thereby—not even money, certainly not my soul. *60*
An Autobiography

Autobiographical

The heart's earnest and pure desire is always fulfilled. In my own experience I have often seen this rule verified. Service of the poor has been my heart's desire, and it has always thrown me amongst the poor and enabled me to identify myself with them.   *61*

An Autobiography

I had put in scarcely three or four months' practice, and the Congress[1] also was still in its infancy, when a Tamil man in tattered clothes, head-gear in hand, two front teeth broken and his mouth bleeding, stood before me trembling and weeping. He had been heavily belaboured by his master. I learnt all about him from my clerk, who was a Tamilian. Balasundaram—as that was the visitor's name— was serving his indenture under a well-known European resident of Durban. The master, getting angry with him, had lost self-control, and had beaten Balasundaram severely, breaking two of his teeth.

I sent him to a doctor. In those days only white doctors were available. I wanted a certificate from the doctor about the nature of the injury Balasundaram had sustained. I secured the certificate, and straightaway took the injured man to the magistrate, to whom I submitted his affidavit. The magistrate was indignant when he read it, and issued a summons against the employer.   *62   An Autobiography*

Balasundaram's case reached the ears of every indentured labourer, and I came to be regarded as their friend. I hailed this connexion with delight. A regular stream of indentured labourers began to pour into my office, and I got the best opportunity of learning their joys and sorrows.   *63*

An Autobiography

It has always been a mystery to me how men can feel themselves honoured by the humiliation of their fellow-beings.   *64*

An Autobiography

If I found myself entirely absorbed in the service of the community, the reason behind it was my desire for self-realization. I had made the religion of service my own, as I felt that God could be realized only through service. And service for me was the service of India, because it came to me without my seeking, because I had an aptitude for it. I had gone to South Africa for travel, for finding an escape from Kathiawad intrigues and for gaining my own livelihood. But as I have said, I found myself in search of God and striving for self-realization.   *65   An Autobiography*

---

1. Natal Indian Congress organized by Gandhi to agitate against the Bill in the Natal Legislative Assembly to disfranchise Indians.

Hardly ever have I known anybody to cherish such loyalty as I did to the British Constitution. I can see now that my love of truth was at the root of this loyalty. It has never been possible for me to simulate loyalty or, for that matter, any other virtue. The National Anthem used to be sung at every meeting that I attended in Natal. I then felt that I must also join in the singing. Not that I was unaware of the defects in British rule, but I thought that it was on the whole acceptable. In those days I believed that British rule was on the whole beneficial to the ruled.

The colour prejudice that I saw in South Africa was, I thought, quite contrary to British traditions, and I believed that it was only temporary and local. I therefore vied with Englishmen in loyalty to the throne. With careful perseverance I learnt the tune of the 'national anthem' and joined in the singing whenever it was sung. Whenever there was an occasion for the expression of loyalty without fuss or ostentation, I readily took part in it.

Never in my life did I exploit this loyalty, never did I seek to gain a selfish end by its means. It was for me more in the nature of an obligation, and I rendered it without expecting a reward. *66*

An Autobiography

By now I had been three years in South Africa. I had got to know the people and they had got to know me. In 1896 I asked permission to go home for six months, for I saw that I was in for a long stay there. I had established a fairly good practice, and could see that people felt the need of my presence. So I made up my mind to go home, fetch my wife and children, and then return and settle out there. *67* *An Autobiography*

This was my first voyage with my wife and children. . . . I believed, at the time of which I am writing, that in order to look civilized, our dress and manners had as far as possible to approximate to the European standard. Because, I thought, only thus could we have some influence, and without influence it would not be possible to serve the community. . . . I therefore determined the style of dress for my wife and children. . . . The Parsis used then to be regarded as the most civilized people amongst Indians, and so, when the complete European style seemed to be unsuited, we adopted the Parsi style. . . . In the same spirit and with even more reluctance they adopted the use of knives and forks. When my infatuation for these signs of civilization wore away, they gave up the knives and forks. After having become long accustomed to the new style, it was perhaps no less irksome for them to return to the original mode. But I can see today that we feel all the freer and lighter for having cast off the tinsel of 'civilization.' *68* *An Autobiography*

Autobiographical

The ship cast anchor in the port of Durban on the eighteenth or nineteenth of December. *69*   *An Autobiography*

Our ship was ordered to be put in quarantine until the twenty-third day of our sailing from Bombay. But this quarantine order had more than health reasons behind it.

The white residents of Durban had been agitating for our repatriation, and the agitation was one of the reasons for the order. . . . The real object of the quarantine was thus to coerce the passengers into returning to India by somehow intimidating them or the agent company. For now threats began to be addressed to us also: 'If you do not go back, you will surely be pushed into the sea. But if you consent to return, you may even get your passage money back.' I constantly moved amongst my fellow passengers cheering them up. *70*   *An Autobiography*

At last ultimatums were served on the passengers and me. We were asked to submit, if we would escape with our lives. In our reply the passengers and I both maintained our right to land at Port Natal, and intimated our determination to enter Natal at any risk.

At the end of twenty-three days the ships were permitted to enter the harbour, and orders permitting the passengers to land were passed. *71*   *An Autobiography*

As soon as we landed, some youngsters recognized me and shouted 'Gandhi, Gandhi.' About half a dozen men rushed to the spot and joined in the shouting. . . . As we went ahead, the crowd continued to swell, until it became impossible to proceed farther. . . . Then they pelted me with stones, brickbats and rotten eggs. Someone snatched away my turban, whilst other began to batter and kick me. I fainted and caught hold of the front railings of a house and stood there to get my breath. But it was impossible. They came upon me boxing and battering. The wife of the Police Superintendent, who knew me, happened to be passing by. The brave lady came up, opened her parasol, though there was no sun then, and stood between the crowd and me. This checked the fury of the mob, as it was difficult for them to deliver blows on me without harming Mrs. Alexander. *72*
An Autobiography

The late Mr. Chamberlain, who was then Secretary of State for the Colonies, cabled asking the Natal Government to prosecute my assailants. Mr. Escombe sent for me, expressed his regret for the injuries I had sustained, and said: 'Believe me, I cannot feel happy over the least little injury done to your person. . . . If you can identify the assailants, I am prepared to arrest and prosecute them. Mr. Chamberlain also desires me to do so.'

To which I gave the following reply:

'I do not want to prosecute anyone. It is possible that I may be able to identify one or two of them, but what is the use of getting them punished? Besides, I do not hold the assailants to blame. They were given to understand that I had made exaggerated statements in India about the whites in Natal and calumniated them. If they believed these reports, it is no wonder that they were enraged. The leaders and, if you will permit me to say so, you are to blame. You could have guided the people properly, but you also believed Reuter and assumed that I must have indulged in exaggeration. I do not want to bring anyone to book. I am sure that, when the truth becomes known, they will be sorry for their conduct.' *73*

An Autobiography

On the day of landing, as soon as the yellow flag was lowered, a representative of *The Natal Advertiser* had come to interview me. He had asked me a number of questions, and in reply I had been able to refute every one of the charges that had been levelled against me. . . . This interview and my refusal to prosecute the assailants produced such a profound impression that the Europeans of Durban were ashamed of their conduct. The press declared me to be innocent and condemned the mob. Thus the lynching ultimately proved to be a blessing for me, that is, for the cause. It enhanced the prestige of the Indian community in South Africa and made my work easier. *74*

An Autobiography

My profession progressed satisfactorily, but that was far from satisfying me. . . . I was still ill at ease. I longed for some humanitarian work of a permanent nature. . . . So I found time to serve in the small hospital. This meant two hours every morning, including the time taken in going to and from the hospital. This work brought me some peace. It consisted in ascertaining the patient's complaints, laying the facts before the doctor and dispensing the prescriptions. It brought me in close touch with suffering Indians, most of them indentured Tamil, Telugu or North Indian men.

The experience stood me in good stead, when during the Boer War I offered my services for nursing the sick and wounded soldiers. *75*

An Autobiography

The birth of the last child put me to the severest test. The travail came on suddenly. The doctor was not immediately available, and some time was lost in fetching the midwife. Even if she had been on the spot, she could not have helped delivery. I had to see through the safe delivery of the baby. *76*   *An Autobiography*

I am convinced that for the proper upbringing of children the parents ought to have a general knowledge of the care and nursing of babies. At every step I have seen the advantages of my careful study of the subject. My children would not have enjoyed the general health that they do today, had I not studied the subject and turned my knowledge to account. We labour under a sort of superstition that the child has nothing to learn during the first five years of its life. On the contrary the fact is that the child never learns in after life what it does in its first five years. The education of the child begins with conception. *77*   *An Autobiography*

The couple who realize these things will never have sexual union for the fulfilment of their lust, but only when they desire issue. I think it is the height of ignorance to believe that the sexual act is an independent function necessary like sleeping or eating. The world depends for its existence on the act of generation, and as the world is the playground of God and a reflection of His glory, the act of generation should be controlled for the ordered growth of the world. He who realizes this will control his lust at any cost, equip himself with the knowledge necessary for the physical, mental and spiritual well-being of his progeny, and give the benefit of that knowledge to posterity. *78*   *An Autobiography*

After full discussion and mature deliberation, I took the vow (of *brahmacharya*) in 1906. I had not shared my thoughts with my wife until then, but only consulted her at the time of taking the vow. She had no objection. But I had great difficulty in making the final resolve. I had not the necessary strength. How was I to control my passions? The elimination of carnal relationship with one's wife seemed then a strange thing. But I launched forth with faith in the sustaining power of God.

As I look back upon the twenty years of the vow, I am filled with pleasure and wonderment. The more or less successful practice of self-control had been going on since 1901. But the freedom and joy that came to me after taking the vow had never been experienced before 1906. Before the vow I had been open to being overcome by temptation at any moment. Now the vow was a sure shield against temptation. *79*   *An Autobiography*

But if it was a matter of ever-increasing joy, let no one believe that it was an easy thing for me. Even when I am past fifty-six years, I realize how hard a thing it is. Every day I realize more and more that it is like walking on the sword's edge, and I see every moment the necessity for eternal vigilance.

Control of the palate is the first essential in the observance of the vow. I found that complete control of the palate made the observance very easy, and so I now pursued my dietetic experiments not merely from the vegetarian's but also from the *brachmachari's* point of view. *80*   *An Autobiography*

I know it is argued that the soul has nothing to do with what one eats or drinks, as the soul neither eats nor drinks; that it is not what you put inside from without, but what you express outwardly from within, that matters. There is no doubt some force in this. But rather than examine this reasoning, I shall content myself with merely declaring my firm conviction that, for the seeker who would live in fear of God and who would see Him face to face, restraint in diet both as to quantity and quality is as essential as restraint in thought and speech. *81*   *An Autobiography*

I had started on a life of ease and comfort, but the experiment was short-lived. Although I had furnished the house with care, yet it failed to have any hold on me. So no sooner had I launched forth on that life, than I began to cut down expenses. The washerman's bill was heavy, and as he was besides by no means noted for his punctuality, even two to three dozen shirts and collars proved insufficient for me. Collars had to be changed daily and shirts, if not daily, at least every alternate day. This meant a double expense which appeared to me unnecessary. So I equipped myself with a washing outfit to save it. I bought a book on washing, studied the art and taught it also to my wife. This no doubt added to my work, but its novelty made it a pleasure.

I shall never forget the first collar that I washed myself. I had used more starch than necessary, the iron had not been made hot enough, and for fear of burning the collar I had not pressed it sufficiently. The result was that, though the collar was fairly stiff, the superfluous starch continually dropped off it. I went to court with the collar on, thus inviting the ridicule of brother barristers, but even in those days I could be impervious to ridicule. *82 An Autobiography*

In the same way, as I freed myself from slavery to the washerman, I threw off dependence on the barber. All people who go to England learn there at least the art of shaving, but none, to my knowledge, learn to cut their own hair. I had to learn that too. I once went to an English hair-cutter in Pretoria. He contemptuously refused to cut my hair. I certainly felt hurt, but immediately purchased a pair of clippers and cut my hair before the mirror. I succeeded more or less

Autobiographical

in cutting the front hair, but I spoiled the back. The friends in the court shook with laughter.

'What's wrong with your hair, Gandhi? Rats have been at it?'

'No. The white barber would not condescend to touch my black hair,' said I, 'so I preferred to cut it myself, no matter how badly.' The reply did not surprise the friends.

The barber was not at fault in having refused to cut my hair. There was every chance of his losing his custom, if he should serve black men. *83*   *An Autobiography*

When the war [Boer] was declared, my personal sympathies were all with the Boers, but I believed then that I had yet no right, in such cases, to enforce my individual convictions. I have minutely dealt with the inner struggle regarding this in my history of the *Satyāgraha* in South Africa, and I must not repeat the argument here. I invite the curious to turn to those pages. Suffice it to say that my loyalty to the British rule drove me to participation with the British in that war. I felt that, if I demanded rights as a British citizen, it was also my duty, as such, to participate in the defence of the British Empire. I held then that India could achieve her complete emancipation only within and through the British Empire. So I collected together as many comrades as possible, and with very great difficulty got their services accepted as an ambulance corps. *84*   *An Autobiography*

Thus service of the Indians in South Africa ever revealed to me new implications of truth at every stage. Truth is like a vast tree, which yields more and more fruit the more you nurture it. The deeper the search in the mine of truth the richer the discovery of the gems buried there, in the shape of openings for an ever greater variety of service. *85*   *An Autobiography*

Man and his deed are two distinct things. Whereas a good deed should call forth approbation and a wicked deed disapprobation, the doer of the deed, whether good or wicked, always deserves respect or pity as the case may be. 'Hate the sin and not the sinner' is a precept which, though easy enough to understand is rarely practised, and that is why the poison of hatred spreads in the world.

This *ahiṃsā* is the basis of the search for truth. I am realizing every day that the search is vain unless it is founded on *ahiṃsā* as the basis. It is quite proper to resist and attack a system, but to resist and attack its author is tantamount to resisting and attacking oneself. For we are all tarred with the same brush, and are children of one and the same Creator, and as such the divine powers within us are infinite. To slight a single human being is to slight those divine powers, and thus to harm not only that being but with him the whole world. *86*   *An Autobiography*

A variety of incidents in my life have conspired to bring me in close contact with people of many creeds and many communities, and my experience with all of them warrants the statement that I have known no distinction between relatives and strangers, countrymen and foreigners, white and coloured, Hindus and Indians of other faiths, whether Mussulmans, Parsis, Christians or Jews. I may say that my heart has been incapable of making any such distinctions. *87*
An Autobiography

I am not a profound scholar of Sanskrit. I have read the *Vedas* and the *Upanishads* only in translations. Naturally, therefore, mine is not a scholarly study of them. My knowledge of them is in no way profound, but I have studied them as I should do as a Hindu and I claim to have grasped their true spirit. By the time I had reached the age of twenty-one, I had studied other religions also.

There was a time when I was wavering between Hinduism and Christianity. When I recovered my balance of mind, I felt that to me salvation was possible only through the Hindu religion and my faith in Hinduism grew deeper and more enlightened.

But even then I believed that untouchability was no part of Hinduism; and that, if it was, such Hinduism was not for me. *88*
Mahatma, Tendular, Vol. II, Speech at the Depressed Classes Conference,
Ahmedabad, April 13, 1921

I understand more clearly today what I read long ago about the inadequacy of all autobiography as history. I know that I do not set down in this story all that I remember. Who can say how much I must give and how much omit in the interests of truth? And what would be the value in a court of law of the inadequate *ex parte* evidence being tendered by me of certain events in my life? If some busybody were to cross-examine me on the chapters already written, he could probably shed much more light on them, and if it were a hostile critic's cross-examination, he might even flatter himself for having shown up 'the hollowness of many of my pretensions.'

I therefore wonder for a moment whether it might not be proper to stop writing these chapters. But so long as there is no prohibition from the voice within, I must continue the writing. I must follow the sage maxim that nothing once begun should be abandoned unless it is proved to be morally wrong. *89*   *An Autobiography*

In the very first month of *Indian Opinion*,[1] I realized that the sole

1. A journal founded by Gandhi in South Africa.

aim of journalism should be service. The newspaper press is a great power, but just as an unchained torrent of water submerges whole countrysides and devastates crops, even so an uncontrollable pen serves but to destroy. If the control is from without, it proves more poisonous than want of control. It can be profitable only when exercised from within. If this line of reasoning is correct, how many of the journals in the world would stand the test? But who would stop those that are useless? And who should be the judge? The useful and the useless must, like good and evil generally, go on together, and man must make his choice. *90*   *An Autobiography*

This [*Unto This Last*] was the first book of Ruskin I had ever read. During the days of my education I had read practically nothing outside textbooks, and after I launched into active life I had very little time for reading. I cannot therefore claim much book knowledge. However, I believe I have not lost much because of this enforced restraint. On the contrary, the limited reading may be said to have enabled me thoroughly to digest what I did read. Of these books, the one that brought about an instantaneous and practical transformation in my life was *Unto This Last*. I translated it later into Gujarati, entitling it *Sarvodaya* (the welfare of all).

I believe that I discovered some of my deepest convictions reflected in this great book of Ruskin, and that is why it so captured me and made me transform my life. A poet is one who can call forth the good latent in the human breast. Poets do not influence all alike, for everyone is not evolved in an equal measure. *91*

An Autobiography

Even after I thought I had settled down in Johannesburg, there was to be no settled life for me. Just when I felt that I should be breathing in peace, an unexpected event happened. The papers brought the news of the outbreak of the Zulu 'rebellion' in Natal. I bore no grudge against the Zulus, they had harmed no Indian. I had doubts about the 'rebellion' itself. But I then believed that the British Empire existed for the welfare of the world. A genuine sense of loyalty prevented me from even wishing ill to the Empire. The rightness or otherwise of the 'rebellion' was therefore not likely to affect my decision. Natal had a Volunteer Defence Force, and it was open to it to recruit more men. I read that this force had already been mobilized to quell the 'rebellion.' *92*   *An Autobiography*

On reaching the scene of the 'rebellion' I saw that there was nothing there to justify the name of 'rebellion.' There was no resistance that one could see. The reason why the disturbance had been magnified into a rebellion was that a Zulu chief had advised non-payment of a new tax imposed on his people, and had assagaied a sergeant who had gone to collect the tax. At any rate my heart was with the Zulus, and I was delighted, on reaching headquarters, to hear that our main work was to be the nursing of the wounded Zulus. The medical officer in charge welcomed us. He said the white people were not willing nurses for the wounded Zulus, that their wounds were festering, and that he was at his wits' end. He hailed our arrival as a godsend for those innocent people, and he equipped us with bandages, disinfectants, etc., and took us to the improvised hospital. The Zulus were delighted to see us. The white soldiers used to peep through the railings that separated us from them and tried to dissuade us from attending to the wounds. And as we would not heed them, they became enraged and poured unspeakable abuse on the Zulus. *93*   *An Autobiography*

The wounded in our charge were not wounded in battle. A section of them had been taken prisoners as suspects. The general had sentenced them to be flogged. The flogging had caused severe sores. These, being unattended to, were festering. The others were Zulu friendlies. Although these had badges given them to distinguish them from the 'enemy' they had been shot at by the soldiers by mistake. *94*
An Autobiography

The Zulu 'rebellion' was full of new experiences and gave me much food for thought. The Boer War had not brought home to me the horrors of war with anything like the vividness that the 'rebellion' did. This was no war but a man-hunt, not only in my opinion, but also in that of many Englishmen with whom I had occasion to talk. To hear every morning reports of soldiers' rifles exploding like crackers in innocent hamlets, and to live in the midst of them was a trial. But I swallowed the bitter draught, especially as the work of my Corps consisted only in nursing the wounded Zulus. I could see that but for us the Zulus would have been uncared for. This work, therefore, eased my conscience. *95*   *An Autobiography*

I was anxious to observe *brahmacharya* in thought, word and deed, and equally anxious to devote the maximum of time to the *Satyā-graha* struggle and fit myself for it by cultivating purity. I was therefore led to make further changes and to impose greater restraints upon myself in the matter of food. The motive for the previous changes had been largely hygienic, but the new experiments were made from a religious standpoint.

Fasting and restriction in diet now played a more important part in my life. Passion in man is generally co-existent with a hankering after the pleasures of the palate. And so it was with me. I have encountered many difficulties in trying to control passion as well as taste, and I cannot claim even now to have brought them under complete subjection. I have considered myself to be a heavy eater. What friends have thought to be my restraint has never appeared to me in that light. If I had failed to develop restraint to the extent that I have, I should have descended lower than the beasts and met my doom long ago. However, as I had adequately realized my shortcomings, I made great efforts to get rid of them, and thanks to this endeavour I have all these years pulled on with my body and put in with it my share of work. *96*   *An Autobiography*

I began with a fruit diet, but from the standpoint of restraint I did not find much to choose between a fruit diet and a diet of food grains. I observed that the same indulgence of taste was possible with the former as with the latter, and even more, when one got accustomed to it. I therefore came to attach greater importance to fasting or having only one meal a day on holidays. And if there was some occasion for penance or the like, I gladly utilized it too for the purpose of fasting.

But I also saw that, the body now being drained more effectively, the food yielded greater relish and appetite grew keener. It dawned upon me that fasting could be made as powerful a weapon of indulgence as of restraint. Many similar later experiences of mine as well as of others can be adduced as evidence of this startling fact. I wanted to improve and train my body, but as my chief object now was to achieve restraint and a conquest of the palate, I selected first one food and then another, and at the same time, restricted the amount. But the relish was after me, as it were. As I gave up one thing and took up another, this latter afforded me a fresher and greater relish than its predecessor. *97*   *An Autobiography*

Experience has taught me, however, that it was wrong to have dwelt upon the relish of food. One should eat not in order to please the palate, but just to keep the body going. When each organ of sense subserves the body and through the body the soul, its special relish disappears, and then alone does it begin to function in the way nature intended it to do.

Any number of experiments is too small and no sacrifice is too great for attaining this symphony with nature. But unfortunately the current is nowadays flowing strongly in the opposite direction. We are not ashamed to sacrifice a multitude of other lives in decorating the perishable body and trying to prolong its existence for a few fleeting moments, with the result that we kill ourselves, both body and soul. *98*   *An Autobiography*

My first experience of jail life was in 1908. I saw that some of the regulations that the prisoners had to observe were such as should be voluntarily observed by a *brahmachari*, that is, one desiring to practise self-restraint. Such, for instance, was the regulation requiring the last meal to be finished before sunset. Neither the Indian nor the African prisoners were allowed tea or coffee. They could add salt to the cooked food if they wished, but they might not have anything for the mere satisfaction of the palate.   *99*   *An Autobiography*

Ultimately these restrictions were modified, though not without much difficulty, but both were wholesome rules of self-restraint. Inhibitions imposed from without rarely succeed, but when they are self-imposed, they have a decidedly salutary effect. So, immediately after release from jail, I imposed on myself the two rules. As far as was then possible I stopped taking tea, and finished my last meal before sunset. Both these now require no effort in the observance. *100*   *An Autobiography*

Fasting can help to curb animal passion, only if it is undertaken with a view to self-restraint. Some of my friends have actually found their animal passion and palate stimulated as an after-effect of fasts. That is to say, fasting is futile unless it is accompanied by an incessant longing for self-restraint.   *101*   *An Autobiography*

Fasting and similar discipline is, therefore, one of the means to the end of self-restraint, but it is not all, and if physical fasting is not accompanied by mental fasting, it is bound to end in hypocrisy and disaster.   *102*   *An Autobiography*

On Tolstoy Farm[1] we made it a rule that the youngsters should not be asked to do what the teachers did not do, and therefore, when they were asked to do any work, there was always a teacher cooperating and actually working with them. Hence whatever the youngsters learnt, they learnt cheerfully.   *103*   *An Autobiography*

Of textbooks, about which we hear so much, I never felt the want. I do not even remember having made much use of the books that were available. I did not find it at all necessary to load the boys with quantities of books. I have always felt that the true textbook for the pupil is his teacher. I remember very little that my teachers taught me from books, but I have even now a clear recollection of the things they taught me independently of books.

1. Tolstoy Farm and the Phoenix Colony were the two settlements or *Ashrams* founded by Gandhi in South Africa where he and his co-workers lived a life of self-discipline and service.

Autobiographical

Children take in much more and with less labour through their ears than through their eyes. I do not remember having read any book from cover to cover with my boys. But I gave them, in my own language, all that I had digested from my reading of various books, and I dare say they are still carrying a recollection of it in their minds. It was laborious for them to remember what they learnt from books, but what I imparted to them by word of mouth they could repeat with the greatest ease. Reading was a task for them, but listening to me was a pleasure, when I did not bore them by failure to make my subject interesting. And from the questions that my talks prompted them to put, I had a measure of their power of understanding. *104*   *An Autobiography*

Just as physical training was to be imparted through physical exercise, even so the training of the spirit was possible only through the exercise of the spirit. And the exercise of the spirit entirely depended on the life and character of the teacher. The teacher had always to be mindful of his p's and q's, whether he was in the midst of his boys or not. *105*   *An Autobiography*

It would be idle for me, if I were a liar, to teach boys to tell the truth. A cowardly teacher would never succeed in making his boys valiant, and a stranger to self-restraint could never teach his pupils the value of self-restraint. I saw, therefore, that I must be an eternal object-lesson to the boys and girls living with me. They thus became my teachers, and I learnt I must be good and live straight if only for their sakes. I may say that the increasing discipline and restraint I imposed on myself at Tolstoy Farm was mostly due to those wards of mine.

One of them was wild, unruly, given to lying, and quarrelsome. On one occasion he broke out most violently. I was exasperated. I never punished my boys, but this time I was very angry. I tried to reason with him. But he was adamant and even tried to overreach me. At last I picked up a ruler lying at hand and delivered a blow on his arm. I trembled as I struck him. I dare say he noticed it. This was an entirely novel experience for them all. The boy cried out and begged to be forgiven. He cried not because the beating was painful to him; he could, if he had been so minded, have paid me back in the same coin, being a stoutly built youth of seventeen; but he realized my pain in being driven to this violent resource. Never again after this incident did he disobey me. But I still repent that violence. I am afraid I exhibited before him that day not the spirit, but the brute, in me.

I have always been opposed to corporal punishment. I remember only one occasion on which I physically punished one of my sons. I have therefore never until this day been able to decide whether I was right or wrong in using the ruler. Probably it was improper, for it was prompted by anger and a desire to punish. Had it been an expression only of my distress, I should have considered it justified. But the motive in this case was mixed. *106*   *An Autobiography*

Cases of misconduct on the part of the boys often occurred after this, but I never resorted to corporal punishment. Thus in my endeavor to impart spiritual training to the boys and girls under me, I came to understand better and better the power of the spirit. *107*
An Autobiography

In those days I had to move between Johannesburg and Phoenix. Once when I was in Johannesburg I received tidings of the moral fall of two of the inmates of the *āshram*. News of an apparent failure or reverse in the *Satyāgraha* struggle would not have shocked me, but this news came upon me like a thunderbolt. The same day I took the train for Phoenix. *108*   *An Autobiography*

During the journey my duty seemed clear to me. I felt that the guardian or teacher was responsible, to some extent at least, for the lapse of his ward or pupil. So my responsibility regarding the incident in question became clear to me as daylight. My wife had already warned me in the matter, but being of a trusting nature, I had ignored her caution. I felt that the only way the guilty parties could be made to realize my distress and the depth of their own fall would be for me to do some penance. So I imposed upon myself a fast for seven days and a vow to have only one meal a day for a period of four months and a half. *109*   *An Autobiography*

My penance pained everybody, but it cleared the atmosphere. Everyone came to realize what a terrible thing it was to be sinful, and the bond that bound me to the boys and girls became stronger and truer. *110*   *An Autobiography*

I never resorted to untruth in my profession, and . . . a large part of my legal practice was in the interest of public work, for which I charged nothing beyond out-of-pocket expenses, and these too I sometimes met myself. . . . As a student I had heard that the lawyer's profession was a liar's profession. But this did not influence me, as I had no intention of earning either position or money by lying. . . . My principle was put to the test many a time in South Africa. Often I knew that my opponents had tutored their witnesses, and if I only encouraged my client or his witnesses to lie, we could win the case. But I always resisted the temptation. I remember only one occasion, when, after having won a case, I suspected that my client had deceived me. In my heart of hearts I always wished that I should win only if my client's case was right. In fixing my fees I do not recall every having made them conditional on my winning the case. Whether my client won or lost, I expected nothing more nor less than my fees.

I warned every new client at the outset that he should not expect me to take up a false case or to coach the witnesses, with the result that I built up such a reputation that no false cases used to come to me. Indeed some of my clients would keep their clean cases for me, and take the doubtful ones elsewhere. *111*   *An Autobiography*

During my professional work it was also my habit never to conceal my ignorance from my clients or my colleagues. Wherever I felt myself at sea, I would advise my client to consult some other counsel. This frankness earned me the unbounded affection and trust of my clients. They were always willing to pay the fee whenever consultation with senior counsel was necessary. This affection and trust served me in good stead in my public work. *112*   *An Autobiography*

At the conclusion of the *Satyāgraha* struggle in 1914, I received Gokhale's instruction to return home via London. . . . War was declared on the fourth of August. We reached London on the sixth. *113*   *An Autobiography*

I felt that Indians residing in England ought to do their bit in the war. English students had volunteered to serve in the army, and Indians might do no less. A number of objections were taken to this line of argument. There was, it was contended, a world of difference between the Indians and the English. We were slaves and they were masters. How could a slave cooperate with the master in the hour of the latter's need? Was it not the duty of the slave, seeking to be free, to make the master's need his opportunity? This argument failed to appeal to me then. I knew the difference of status between an Indian and an Englishman, but I did not believe that we had been quite reduced to slavery. I felt then that it was more the fault of individual British officials than of the British system, and that we could convert them by love. If we would improve our status through the help and co-operation of the British, it was our duty to win their help by standing by them in their hour of need. Though the system was faulty, it did not seem to me to be intolerable, as it does today. But if, having lost my faith in the system, I refuse to co-operate with the British Government today, how could those friends then do so, having lost their faith not only in the system but in the officials as well? *114*   *An Autobiography*

I thought that England's need should not be turned into our opportunity, and that it was more becoming and far-sighted not to press our demands while the war lasted. I therefore adhered to my advice and invited those who would enlist as volunteers. *115*

An Autobiography

All of us recognized the immorality of war. If I was not prepared to prosecute my assailant, much less should I be willing to participate in a war, especially when I knew nothing of the justice or otherwise of the cause of the combatants. Friends of course knew that I had previously served in the Boer War, but they assumed that my views had since undergone a change.

As a matter of fact the very same line of argument that persuaded me to take part in the Boer War had weighed with me on this occasion. It was quite clear to me that participation in war could never be consistent with *ahiṃsā*. But it is not always given to one to be equally clear about one's duty. A votary of truth is often obliged to grope in the dark. *116* *An Autobiography*

By enlisting men for ambulance work in South Africa and in England, and recruits for field service in India, I helped not the cause of war, but I helped the institution called the British Empire in whose ultimate beneficial character I then believed. My repugnance to war was as strong then as it is today; and I could not then have and would not have shouldered a rifle. But one's life is not a single straight line; it is a bundle of duties very often conflicting. And one is called upon continually to make one's choice between one duty and another. As a citizen not then, and not even now, a reformer leading an agitation against the institution of war, I had to advise and lead men who believed in war but who from cowardice or from base motives, or from anger against the British Government, refrained from enlisting. I did not hesitate to advise them that so long as they believed in war and professed loyalty to the British constitution they were in duty bound to support it by enlistment. . . . I do not believe in retaliation, but I did not hesitate to tell the villagers near Bettia four years ago that they who knew nothing of *ahiṃsā* were guilty of cowardice in failing to defend the honour of their womenfolk and their property by force of arms. And I have not hesitated . . . only recently to tell the Hindus that if they do not believe in out-and-out *ahiṃsā* and cannot practise it they will be guilty of a crime against their religion and humanity if they failed to defend by force of arms the honour of their women against a kidnapper who chooses to take away their women. And all this advice and my previous practice I hold to be not only consistent with my profession of the religion of *ahiṃsā* out-and-out, but a direct result of it. To state that noble

doctrine is simple enough; to know it and to practise it in the midst
of a world full of strife, turmoil and passions is a task whose difficulty I realize more and more day by day. And yet the conviction
too that without it life is not worth living is growing daily deeper.
117   *Young India, November 5, 1925*

There is no defence for my conduct weighed only in the scales of
ahiṃsā, I draw no distinction between those who wield the weapons
of destruction and those who do Red Cross work. Both participate in
war and advance its cause. Both are guilty of the crime of war. But
even after introspection during all these years, I feel that in the
circumstances in which I found myself I was bound to adopt the
course I did both during the Boer War and the Great European War
and for that matter the so-called Zulu 'Rebellion' of Natal in 1906.

Life is governed by a multitude of forces. It would be smooth
sailing, if one could determine the course of one's actions only by
one general principle whose application at a given moment was too
obvious to need even a moment's reflection. But I cannot recall a
single act which could be so easily determined.

Being a confirmed war resister I have never given myself training
in the use of destructive weapons in spite of opportunities to take
such training. It was perhaps thus that I escaped direct destruction of
human life. But so long as I lived under a system of government
based on force and voluntarily partook of the many facilities and
privileges it created for me, I was bound to help that government to
the extent of my ability when it was engaged in a war unless I
non-cooperated with that government and renounced to the utmost of
my capacity the privileges it offered me.

Let me take an illustration. I am a member of an institution which
holds a few acres of land whose crops are in imminent peril from
monkeys. I believe in the sacredness of all life and hence I regard it a
breach of *ahiṃsā* to inflict any injury on the monkeys. But I do not
hesitate to instigate and direct an attack on the monkeys in order to
save the crops. I would like to avoid this evil. I can avoid it by
leaving or breaking up the institution. I do not do so, because I do
not expect to be able to find a society where there will be no
agriculture and therefore no destruction of some life. In fear and
trembling, in humility and penance, I therefore participate in the
injury inflicted on the monkeys, hoping some day to find a way out.

Even so did I participate in the three acts of war. I could not, it
would be madness for me to, sever my connexions with the society
to which I belong. And on those three occasions I had no thought of
non-cooperating with the British Government. My position regarding
the government is totally different today and hence I should not
voluntarily participate in its wars and I should risk imprisonment and

even the gallows if I was forced to take up arms or otherwise take part in its military operations.

But that still does not solve the riddle. If there was a national government, whilst I should not take any direct part in any war I can conceive occasions when it would be my duty to vote for the military training of those who wish to take it. For I know that all its members do not believe in nonviolence to the extent I do. It is not possible to make a person or a society nonviolent by compulsion.

Nonviolence works in a most mysterious manner. Often a man's actions defy analysis in terms of nonviolence; equally often his actions may wear the appearance of violence when he is absolutely nonviolent in the highest sense of the term and is subsequently found so to be. All I can then claim for my conduct is that it was in the instances cited actuated in the interests of nonviolence. There was no thought of sordid national or other interest. I do not believe in the promotion of national or any other interest at the sacrifice of some other interest.

I may not carry my argument any further. Language at best is but a poor vehicle for expressing one's thoughts in full. For me nonviolence is not a mere philosophical principle. It is the rule and the breath of my life. I know I fail often, sometimes consciously, more often unconsciously. It is a matter not of the intellect but of the heart. True guidance comes by constant waiting upon God, by utmost humility, self-abnegation, by being ever ready to sacrifice one's self. Its practice requires fearlessness and courage of the highest order. I am painfully aware of my failings.

But the Light within me is steady and clear. There is no escape for any of us save through truth and nonviolence. I know that war is wrong, is an unmitigated evil. I know too that it has got to go. I firmly believe that freedom won through bloodshed or fraud is no freedom. Would that all the acts alleged against me were found to be wholly indefensible rather than that by any act of mine nonviolence was held to be compromised or that I was ever thought to be in favour of violence or untruth in any shape or form! Not violence, not untruth but nonviolence, Truth is the law of our being.   *118*

Young India, September 13, 1928

I am conscious of my own limitations. That consciousness is my only strength. Whatever I might have been able to do in my life has proceeded more than anything else out of the realization of my own limitations.   *119*   *Young India, November 13, 1924*

I am used to misrepresentation all my life. It is the lot of every public worker. He has to have a tough hide. Life would be burdensome if every misrepresentation has to be answered and cleared. It is a rule of life with me never to explain misrepresentations except when the cause required correction. This rule has saved much time and worry. *120*   *Young India, May 27, 1926*

The only virtue I want to claim is truth and nonviolence. I lay no claim to superhuman powers. I want none. I wear the same corruptible flesh that the weakest of my fellow beings wears and am liable to err as any. My services have many limitations, but God has up to now blessed them in spite of the imperfections.

For, confession of error is like a broom that sweeps away dirt and leaves the surface cleaner than before. I feel stronger for my confession. And the cause must prosper for the retracing. Never has man reached his destination by persistence in deviation from the straight path. *121*   *Young India, February 16, 1922*

The mahatma I leave to his fate. Though a non-cooperator I shall gladly subscribe to a Bill to make it criminal for anybody to call me mahatma and to touch my feet. Where I can impose the law myself, at the *āshram*, the practice is criminal. *122 Young India, March 17, 1927*

The time has now come to bring these chapters to a close. . . . My life from this point onward has been so public that there is hardly anything about it that people do not know. . . . My life has been an open book. I have no secrets and I encourage no secrets. *123*
An Autobiography

My uniform experience has convinced me that there is no other God than Truth. And if every page of these chapters does not proclaim to the reader that the only means for the realization of Truth is *ahiṃsā*, I shall deem all my labour in writing these chapters to have been in vain. And, even though my efforts in this behalf may prove fruitless, let the readers know that the vehicle, not the great principle, is at fault. *124*   *An Autobiography*

Ever since my return to India I have had the experiences of the dormant passions lying hidden within me. The knowledge of them has made me feel humiliated though not defeated. The experiences and experiments have sustained me and given me great joy. But I know that I have still before me a difficult path to traverse. I must reduce myself to zero. So long as a man does not of his own free will put himself last among his fellow creatures, there is no salvation for him. *Ahiṃsā* is the farthest limit of humility. *125   An Autobiography*

I have become literally sick of the adoration of the unthinking multitude. I would feel certain of my ground if I was spat upon by them.

Then there would be no need for confession of Himalayan and other miscalculations, no retracing, no re-arranging. *126*

Young India, March 2, 1922

I have no desire for prestige anywhere. It is furniture required in courts of kings. I am a servant of Mussulmans, Christians, Parsis and Jews as I am of Hindus. And a servant is in need of love, not prestige. That is assured to me so long as I remain a faithful servant. *127* *Young India, March 26, 1925*

Somehow or other I dread a visit to Europe and America. Not that I distrust the peoples of these great continents any more than I distrust my own, but I distrust myself. I have no desire to go to the West in search of health or for sightseeing. I have no desire to deliver public speeches. I detest being lionized. I wonder if I shall ever again have the health to stand the awful strain of public speaking and public demonstrations. If God ever sent me to the West, I should go there to penetrate the hearts of the masses, to have quiet talks with the youth of the West and have the privilege of meeting kindred spirits— lovers of peace at any price save that of truth.

But I feel that I have as yet no message to deliver personally to the West. I believe my message to be universal but as yet I feel that I can best deliver it through my work in my own country. If I can show visible success in India, the delivery of the message becomes complete. If I came to the conclusion that India had no use for my message, I should not care to go elsewhere in search of listeners even though I still retained faith in it. If I ventured out of India, I should do so because I have faith, though I cannot demonstrate it to the satisfaction of all, that the message is being received by India, be it ever so slowly.

Thus whilst I was hesitatingly carrying on the correspondence with friends who had invited me, I saw that there was need for me to go to Europe, if only to see Romain Rolland. Owing to my distrust of myself over a general visit, I wanted to make my visit to that wise man of the West the primary cause of my journey to Europe. I, therefore, referred my difficulty to him and asked him in the frankest manner possible whether he would let me make my desire to meet him the primary cause of my visit to Europe. He says that in the name of truth itself, he will not think of letting me go to Europe if a visit to him is to be the primary cause. He will not let me interrupt my labours here for the sake of our meeting. Apart from this visit I felt within me no imperative call. I regret my decision but it seems to be the correct one. For whilst there is no urge within to go to Europe, there is an incessant call within for so much to do here. *128* *Mahatma, Vol. II, Circa April, 1928*

Autobiographical

I hold myself to be incapable of hating any being on earth. By a long course of prayerful discipline, I have ceased for over forty years to hate anybody. I know this is a big claim. Nevertheless, I make it in all humility. But I can and do hate evil wherever it exists. I hate the system of government that the British people have set up in India. I hate the ruthless exploitation of India even as I hate from the bottom of my heart the hideous system of untouchability for which millions of Hindus have made themselves responsible. But I do not hate the domineering Englishmen as I refuse to hate the domineering Hindus. I seek to reform them in all the loving ways that are open to me. *129*   *Young India, August 6, 1928*

Some days back a calf having been maimed lay in agony in the *āshram*. Whatever treatment and nursing was possible was given to it. The surgeon whose advise was sought in the matter declared the case to be past help and past hope. The suffering of the animal was so great that it could not even turn its side without excruciating pain.

In these circumstances I felt that humanity demanded that the agony should be ended by ending life itself. The matter was placed before the whole *āshram*. At the discussion, a worthy neighbour vehemently opposed the ideal of killing even to end pain. The ground of his opposition was that one has no right to take life which one cannot create. His argument seemed to me to be pointless here. It would have point, if the taking of life was actuated by self-interest. Finally in all humility but with the clearest of convictions I got in my presence a doctor kindly to administer the calf a quietus by means of a poison injection. The whole thing was over in less than two minutes.

I knew that public opinion especialy in Ahmedabad would not approve of my action and that it would read nothing but *himsā* in it. But I know too that performance of one's duty should be independent of public opinion. I have all along held that one is bound to act according to what to one appears to be right, though it may appear wrong to others. And experience has shown that that is the only correct course. That is why the poet has sung: 'The pathway of love is the ordeal of fire, the shrinkers turn away from it.' The pathway of *ahimsā*, that is, of love, one has often to tread all alone.

The question may legitimately be put to me: Would I apply to human beings the principle I have enunciated in connexion with the calf? Would I like it to be applied in my own case? My reply is 'Yes'; the same law holds good in both cases. The law, 'as with one so with all,' admits of no exceptions, or the killing of the calf was wrong and violent. In practice, however, we do not cut short the sufferings of our ailing dear ones by death because, as a rule, we have always means at our disposal to help them and they have the capacity to think and decide for themselves. But supposing that in the case of an ailing friend, I am unable to render any aid and recovery is out of the question and the patient is lying in an unconscious state in the throes of agony, then I would not see any *himsā* in putting an end to his suffering by death.

Just as a surgeon does not commit *himsā* but practises the purest *ahimsā* when he wields his knife, one may find it necessary, under certain imperative circumstances, to go a step further and sever life from the body in the interest of the sufferer. It may be objected that whereas the surgeon performs his operation to save the life of the patient, in the other case we do just the reverse. But on a deeper analysis it will be found that the ultimate object sought to be served in both the cases is the same, namely, to relieve the suffering soul within from pain. In the one case you do it by severing the diseased portion from the body, in the other you do it by severing from the soul the body that has become an instrument of torture to it. In either case it is the relief of the soul from pain that is aimed at, the body without the life within being incapable of feeling either pleasure or pain. Other circumstances can be imagined in which not to kill would spell *himsā*, while killing would be *ahimsā*. Suppose, for instance, that I find my daughter, whose wish at the moment I have no means of ascertaining, is threatened with violation and there is no way by which I can save her, then it would be the purest form of *ahimsā* on my part to put an end to her life and surrender myself to the fury of the incensed ruffian.

The trouble with our votaries of *ahimsā* is that they have made of *ahimsā* a blind fetish and put the greatest obstacle in the way of the spread of true *ahimsā* in our midst. The current—and, in my opinion, mistaken—view of *ahimsā* has drugged our conscience and rendered us insensible to a host of other and more insidious forms of *himsā* like harsh words, harsh judgements, ill will, anger, spite and lust of cruelty; it has made us forget that there may be far more *himsā* in the slow torture of men and animals, the starvation and exploitation to which they are subjected out of selfish greed, the wanton humiliation and oppression of the weak and the killing of their self-respect that we witness all around us today than in mere benevolent taking of life. Does any one doubt for a moment that it would have been far more humane to have summarily put to death those who in the infamous lane of Amritsar were made by their torturers to crawl on their bellies like worms? If anyone desires to retort by saying that these people themselves today feel otherwise, that they are none the worse for crawling, I shall have no hesitation in telling him that he does not know even the elements of *ahimsā*. There arise occasions in a man's life when it becomes his imperative duty to meet them by laying down his life; not to appreciate this fundamental fact of man's estate is to betray an ignorance of the foundation of *ahiṃsā*. For instance, a votary of truth would pray to God to give him death to save him from a life of falsehood. Similarly a votary of *ahiṃsā* would on bent knees implore his enemy to put him to death rather than humiliate him or make him do things unbecoming the dignity of a human being. As the poet has sung: 'The way of the Lord is meant for heroes, not for cowards.'

It is this fundamental misconception about the nature and the scope of *ahiṃsā*, this confusion about the relative values, that is responsible for our mistaking mere non-killing for *ahiṃsā* and for the fearful amount of *hiṃsā* that goes on in the name of *ahiṃsā* in our country. *130*   *"The Fiery Ordeal," Young India, 1928*

Truth to me is infinitely dearer than the 'mahatmaship,' which is purely a burden. It is my knowledge of my limitations and my nothingness which has so far saved me from the oppressiveness of 'mahatmaship.' I am painfully aware of the fact that my desire to continue life in the body evolves me in constant *hiṃsā*, that is why I am becoming growingly indifferent to this physical body of mine. For instance, I know that in the act of respiration I destroy innumerable invisible germs floating in the air. But I do not stop breathing. The consumption of vegetables involves *hiṃsā* but I cannot give them up. Again, there is *hiṃsā* in the use of antiseptics yet I cannot bring myself to discard the use of disinfectants like the kerosene, to rid myself of the mosquito pest and the like. I suffer snakes to be killed in the *āshram* when it is impossible to catch and put them out of harm's way. I even tolerate the use of the stick to drive the bullocks in the *āshram*. Thus there is no end of *hiṃsā* which I directly and indirectly commit. And now I find myself confronted with this monkey problem. Let me assure the reader that I am in no hurry to take the extreme step of killing them. In fact I am not sure that I would at all be able finally to kill the monkeys even though they may destroy all the crop in the *āshram*. If as a result of this confession of mine, friends choose to give me up as lost I would be sorry, but nothing will induce me to try to conceal my imperfections in the practice of *ahiṃsā*. All I claim for myself is that I am ceaselessly trying to understand the implications of great ideals like *ahiṃsā* and to practise them in thought, word and deed and that not without a certain measure of success, as I think. But I know that I have a long distance yet to cover in this direction. *131*

"The Fiery Ordeal," Young India, 1928

I am a poor mendicant. My earthly possessions consist of six spinning wheels, prison dishes, a can of goat's milk, six homespun loin-cloths

and towels, and my reputation which cannot be worth much.[1]   *132*
Mahatma, Vol. III, September 11, 1931

When I found myself drawn into the political coil, I asked myself what was necessary for me, in order to remain untouched by immorality, by untruth, by what is known as political gain. I came definitely to the conclusion that, if I had to serve the people in whose midst my life was cast and of whose difficulties I was a witness from day to day, I must discard all wealth, all possession.

I cannot tell you with truth that, when this belief came to me, I discarded everything immediately. I must confess to you that progress at first was slow. And now, as I recall those days of struggle, I remember that it was also painful in the beginning. But, as days went by, I saw that I had to throw overboard many other things which I used to consider as mine, and a time came when it became a matter of positive joy to give up those things. One after another then, by almost geometric progression, things slipped away from me. And, as I am describing my experiences, I can say a great burden fell off my shoulders, and I felt that I could now walk with ease and do my work also in the service of my fellow men with great comfort and still greater joy. The possession of anything then became a troublesome thing and a burden.

Exploring the cause of that joy, I found that if I kept anything as my own, I had to defend it against the whole world. I found that there were many people who did not have the thing, although they wanted it; and I would have to seek police assistance also if some hungry famine-stricken people, finding me in a lonely place, wanted not only to divide the thing with me but to dispossess me. And I said to myself: if they want it and would take it, they do so not from any malicious motive, but they would do it because theirs was a greater need than mine.

And I said to myself: possession seems to me to be a crime; I can only possess certain things when I know that others, who also want to possess similar things, are able to do so. But we know—every one of us can speak from experience—that such a thing is an impossibility. Therefore, the only thing that can be possessed by all is non-possession, not to have anything whatsoever. Or, in other words, a willing surrender. . . . Therefore, having that absolute conviction in me, such must be my constant desire that this body also may be surrendered at the will of God, and while it is at my disposal, must be used not for dissipation, not for self-indulgence, not for pleasure, but merely for service and service the whole of your waking hours.

1. To the customs official at Marseille, 11 September 1931.

Autobiographical

And if this is true with reference to the body, how much more with reference to clothing and other things that we use?

And those who have followed out this vow of voluntary poverty to the fullest extent possible—to reach absolute perfection is an impossibility, but the fullest possible for a human being—those who have reached the ideal of that state, testify that when you dispossess yourself of everything you have, you really possess all the treasures of the world. *133*   *Speech at the Guild Hall,*
London, September 27, 1931

From my youth upward I learnt the art of estimating the value of scriptures on the basis of their ethical teaching. Miracles had no interest for me. The miracles said to have been performed by Jesus, even if I had believed them literally, would not have reconciled me to any teaching that did not satisfy universal ethics. Somehow, words of religious teachers have for me, as I presume for the millions, a living force which the same words uttered by ordinary mortals do not possess.

Jesus, to me, is a great world teacher among others. He was to the devotees of his generation no doubt 'the only begotten son of God.' Their belief need not be mine. He affects my life no less because I regard him as one among the many begotten sons of God. The adjective 'begotten' has a deeper and possibly a grander meaning than its spiritual birth. In his own times he was the nearest to God.

Jesus atoned for the sins of those who accepted his teachings, by being an infallible example to them. But the example was worth nothing to those who never troubled to change their own lives. A regenerate outgrows the original taint, even as purified gold outgrows the original alloy.

I have made the frankest admission of many sins. But I do not carry their burden on my shoulders. If I am journeying godward, as I feel I am, it is safe with me. For I feel the warmth of the sunshine of His presence. My austerities, fastings and prayers are, I know, of no value, if I rely upon them for reforming me. But they have an inestimable value, if they represent, as I hope they do, the yearnings of a soul, striving to lay his weary head in the lap of his Maker. *134*
Harijan, April 18, 1936

An English friend has been at me for the past thirty years trying to persuade me that there is nothing but damnation in Hinduism and I must accept Christianity. When I was in jail I got from separate sources no less than three copies of *Life of Sister Therese*, in the hope that I should follow her example and accept Jesus as the only begotten son of God and my Saviour. I read the book prayerfully but I could not accept even St. Therese's testimony. I must say I have an open mind, if indeed at this stage and age of my life I can be said to have an open mind on this question. Anyway, I claim to have an open mind in this sense that if things were to happen to me as they did to Saul before he became Paul, I should not hesitate to be converted. But today I rebel against orthodox Christianity, as I am convinced that it has distorted the message of Jesus. He was an Asiatic whose message was delivered through many media and when it had the backing of a Roman emperor, it became an imperialist faith as it remains to this day. Of course, there are noble but rare exceptions, but the general trend is as I have indicated. *135*

Mahatma, Vol. III, Conversation with Sir C. V. Raman
and Professor Rahm, May, 1936

My mind is narrow. I have not read much literature. I have not seen much of the world. I have concentrated upon certain things in life and beyond that I have no other interest. *136*

Mahatma, Vol. VI., Press Conference, September 28, 1944,
following the conclusion of the Gandhi-Jinnah talks

I have not the shadow of a doubt that any man or woman can achieve what I have, if he or she would make the same effort and cultivate the same hope and faith. *137*   *Harijan, October 3, 1936*

I fancy I know the art of living and dying nonviolently. But I have yet to demonstrate it by one perfect act. *138*

Mahatma Gandhi, The Last Phase
by Pyarelal, September, 1947

There is no such thing as 'Gandhism' and I do not want to leave any sect after me. I do not claim to have originated any new principle or doctrine. I have simply tried in my own way to apply the eternal truths to our daily life and problems. There is, therefore, no question of my leaving any code like the code of Manu. There can be no comparison between that great law-giver and me. The opinions I have formed and the conclusions I have arrived at are not final, I may change them tomorrow. I have nothing new to teach the world. Truth and nonviolence are as old as the hills. All I have done is to try experiments in both on as vast a scale as I could do. In doing so, I have sometimes erred and learnt by my errors. Life and its problems have thus become to me so many experiments in the practice of truth and nonviolence. By instinct, I have been truthful, but not nonviolent. As a Jain *muni* once rightly said, I was not so much a votary of *ahiṃsā*, as I was of truth, and I put the latter in the first place and the former in the second. For, as he put it, I was capable of sacrificing nonviolence for the sake of truth. In fact, it was in course of my pursuit of truth that I discovered nonviolence. Our scriptures have declared that there is no *dharma* higher than truth. But nonviolence, they say, is the highest duty. The word *dharma*, in my opinion, has different connotations as used in the two aphorisms.

Well, all my philosophy, if it may be called by that pretentious name, is contained in what I have said. But, you will not call it 'Gandhism'; there is no 'ism' about it. And no elaborate literature or propaganda is needed about it. The scriptures have been quoted against my position, but I have held faster than ever to the position that truth may not be sacrificed for anything whatsoever. Those who believe in the simple truths I have laid down can propagate them only by living them. People have laughed at my spinning wheel, and an acute critic observed that when I died the wheels would serve to make the funeral pyre. That, however, has not shaken my firm faith in the spinning wheel. How am I to convince the world by means of books that the whole of my constructive programme is rooted in nonviolence? My life alone can demonstrate it. *139*

Mahatma, Vol. IV, Meeting of the Gandhi Seva Sangh,
February 29 to March 6, 1936

You have given me a teacher in Thoreau, who furnished me through his essay on the 'Duty of Civil Disobedience' scientific confirmation of what I was doing in South Africa. Great Britain gave me Ruskin, whose *Unto This Last* transformed me overnight from a lawyer and city dweller into a rustic living away from Durban on a farm, three miles from the nearest railway station; and Russia gave me in Tolstoy a teacher who furnished a reasoned basis for my nonviolence. Tolstoy blessed my movement in South Africa when it was still in its infancy and of whose wonderful possibilities I had yet to learn. It was he who had prophesied in his letter to me that I was leading a movement which was destined to bring a message of hope to the downtrodden people of the earth. So you will see that I have not approached the present task in any spirit of enmity to Great Britain and the West. After having imbibed and assimilated the message of *Unto This Last*, I could not be guilty of approving fascism or nazism, whose cult is suppression of the individual and his liberty. *140*

Mahatma, Vol. VI,
"To American Friends," August 3, 1942

I have no secrets of my own in this life. I have owned my weaknesses. If I were sensually inclined, I would have the courage to make the confession. It was when I developed detestation of the sensual connexion even with my own wife and had sufficiently tested myself that I took the vow of *brachmacharya* in 1906, and that for the sake of better dedication to the service of the country. From that day, began my open life.... And from that day when I began *brahmacharya*, our freedom began. My wife became a free woman, free from my authority as her lord and master, and I became free from my slavery to my own appetite which she had to satisfy. No other woman had any attraction for me in the same sense that my wife had. I was too loyal to her as husband and too loyal to the vow I had taken before my mother to be slave to any other woman. But the manner in which my *bramacharya* came to me irresistibly drew me to woman as the mother of man.... My *brahmacharya* knew nothing of the orthodox laws governing its observance. I framed my own rules as occasion necessitated. But I have never believed that all contact with woman was to be shunned for the due observance of *brahmacharya*. That restraint which demands abstention from all contact, no matter how innocent, with the opposite sex is a forced growth, having little or no vital value. Therefore, the natural contacts for service were never restrained. And I found myself enjoying the confidence of many sisters, European and Indian, in South Africa. And when I invited the Indian sisters in South Africa to join the civil resistance movement, I found myself one of them. I discovered that I was specially fitted to serve the womankind. To cut the—for me enthralling—story short, my return to India found me in no time one with India's women. The easy access I had to their hearts was an agreeable revelation to me. Muslim sisters never kept purdah before me here, even as they did not in South Africa. I sleep in the *āshram* surrounded by women, for they feel safe with me in every respect. It should be remembered that there is no privacy in the Segaon *Āshram*.

If I were sexually attracted towards women, I have courage enough, even at this time of life, to become a polygamist. I do not believe in free love—secret or open. Free open love I have looked upon as dog's love. Secret love is besides cowardly. *141*

Mahatma, Vol. V.,
"My Life," October - November 1939

'You have failed to take even your son with you,' wrote a correspondent. 'May it not, therefore, be well for you to rest content with putting your own house in order?'

This may be taken to be a taunt, but I do not take it so. For the question had occurred to me, before it did to anyone else. I am a believer in previous births and rebirths. All our relationships are the result of the *saṃskārs* we carry from our previous births. God's laws are inscrutable and are the subject of endless search. No one will fathom them.

This is how I regard the case of my own son. I regard the birth of a bad son to me as the result of my evil past, whether of this life or previous. My first son was born, when I was in a state of infatuation. Besides, he grew up whilst I was myself growing and whilst I knew myself very little. I do not claim to know myself fully even today, but I certainly know myself better than I did then. For years he remained away from me, and his upbringing was not entirely in my hands. That is why, he has always been at a loose end. His grievance against me has always been that I sacrificed him and his brothers at the altar of what I wrongly believed to be the public good. My other sons have laid more or less the same blame at my door, but with a good deal of hesitation, and they have generously forgiven me. My eldest son was the direct victim of experiments—radical changes in my life—and so he cannot forget what he regards as my blunders. Under the circumstances I believe I am myself the cause of the loss of my son, and have, therefore, learnt patiently to bear it. And yet, it is not quite correct to say that I have lost him. For it is my constant prayer that God may make him see the error of his ways and forgive me my shortcomings, if any, in serving him. It is my firm faith that man is by nature going higher, and so I have not at all lost the hope that, some day, he will wake up from his slumber and ignorance. Thus, he is part of my field of the experiments in nonviolence. When or whether I shall succeed, I have never bothered to know. It is enough for my satisfaction that I do not slacken my efforts in doing what I know to be my duty. *142   Harijan, July 1940*

I read a newspaper cutting sent by a correspondent to the effect that a temple has been erected where my image is being worshipped. This I consider to be a gross form of idolatry. The person who has erected the temple has wasted his resources by misusing them, the villagers who are drawn there are misled, and I am being insulted in that the whole of my life has been caricatured in that temple. The meaning that I have given to worship is distorted. The worship of the *charkhā* lies in plying it for a living, or as a sacrifice for ushering in *swarāj*. Gita is worshipped not by a parrot-like recitation but by following its teaching. Recitation is good and proper only as an aid to action according to its teaching. A man is worshipped only to the extent that he is followed not in his weaknesses, but in his strength. Hinduism is degraded when it is brought down to the level of the worship of the image of a living being. No man can be said to be good before his death. After death too, he is good for the person who believes him to have possessed certain qualities attributed to him. As a matter of fact, God alone knows a man's heart. And hence, the safest thing is not to worship any person, living or dead, but to worship perfection which resides only in God, known as Truth. The question then certainly arises, as to whether possession of photographs is not a form of worship, carrying no merit with it. I have said as much before now in my writings. Nevertheless, I have tolerated the practice, as it has become an innocent though a costly fashion. But this toleration will become ludicrous and harmful, if I were to give directly or indirectly the slightest encouragement to the practice above described. It would be a welcome relief, if the owner of the temple removed the image and converted the building into a spinning centre, where the poor will card and spin for wages, and the others for sacrifice and all will be wearers of *khaddar*. This will be the teaching of the Gita in action, and true worship of it and me. *143*

"A Temple to Gandhiji," Harijan, April, 1946

My imperfections and failures are as much a blessing from God as my successes and my talents, and I lay them both at His feet. Why should He have chosen me, an imperfect instrument, for such a mighty experiment? I think He deliberately did so. He had to serve the poor dumb ignorant millions. A perfect man might have been their despair. When they found that one with their failings was marching on towards *ahiṃsā*, they too had confidence in their own capacity. We should not have recognized a perfect man if he had come as our leader, and we might have driven him to a cave. Maybe he who follows me will be more perfect and you will be able to receive his message. *144*   *Harijan, July 21, 1940*

I did not move a muscle, when I first heard that an atom bomb had wiped out Hiroshima. On the contrary I said to myself, 'Unless now the world adopts nonviolence, it will spell certain suicide for mankind.' *145*   *Mahatma Gandhi, The Last Phase, 1945*

I do not sit in judgement upon the world for its many misdeeds. Being imperfect myself and needing toleration and charity, I tolerate the world's imperfections till I find or create an opportunity for fruitful expostulation. *146 Mahatma, Vol. I, Part of Gandhi's explanation of his participation in World War I, given "some years later."*

When I have become incapable of evil and when nothing harsh or haughty occupies, be it momentarily, my thought-world, then, and not till then, my nonviolence will move all the hearts of all the world. *147*   *Young India, July 2, 1925*

If one has completely merged oneself with Him, he should be content to leave good and bad, success and failure to Him and be careful for nothing. I feel I have not attained that state, and, therefore, my striving is incomplete. *148*

Mahatma Gandhi, The Last Phase, September, 1947

Autobiographical

There is a stage in life when a man does not need even to proclaim his thoughts much less to show them by outward action. Mere thoughts act. They attain that power. Then it can be said of him that his seeming inaction constitutes his action. . . . My striving is in that direction. *149* *Harijan, October 26, 1947*

I would love to attempt an answer to a question which has been addressed to me from more than one quarter of the globe. It is: How can you account for the growing violence among your own people on the part of political parties for the furtherance of political ends? Is this the result of the thirty years of nonviolent practice for ending the British rule? Does your message of nonviolence still hold good for the world? I have condensed the sentiments of my correspondents in my own language.

In reply I must confess my bankruptcy, not that of nonviolence. I have already said that the nonviolence that was offered during the past thirty years was that of the weak. Whether it is a good enough answer or not is for the others to judge. It must be further admitted that such nonviolence can have no play in the altered circumstances. India has no experience of the nonviolence of the strong. It serves no purpose for me to continue to repeat that the nonviolence of the strong is the strongest force in the world. The truth requires constant and extensive demonstration. This I am now endeavouring to do to the best of my ability. What if the best of my ability is very little? May I not be living in a fool's paradise? Why should I ask the people to follow me in the fruitless search? These are pertinent questions. My answer is quite simple. I ask nobody to follow me. Everyone should follow his or her own inner voice. If he or she has no ears to listen to it, he or she should do the best he or she can. In no case, should he or she imitate others sheeplike.

One more question has been and is being asked. If you are certain that India is going the wrong way, why do you associate with the wrongdoers? Why do you not plough your own lonely furrow and have faith that if you are right, your erstwhile friends and your followers will seek you out? I regard this as a very fair question. I must not attempt to argue against it. All I can say is that my faith is as strong as ever. It is quite possible that my technique is faulty. There are old and tried precedents to guide one in such a complexity. Only, no one should act mechanically. Hence, I can say to all my counsellors that they should have patience with me and even share my belief that there is no hope for the aching world except through the narrow and straight path of nonviolence. Millions like me may fail to prove the truth in their own lives, that would be their failure, never of the eternal law. *150* *Mahatma, VIII, June 15, 1947*

The partition has come in spite of me. It has hurt me. But it is the way in which the partition has come that has hurt me more. I have pledged myself to do or die in the attempt to put down the present conflagration. I love all mankind as I love my own countrymen, because God dwells in the heart of every human being, and I aspire to realize the highest in life through the service of humanity. It is true that the nonviolence that we practised was the nonviolence of the weak, i.e., no nonviolence at all. But I maintain that this was not what I presented to my countrymen. Nor did I present to them the weapon of nonviolence because they were weak or disarmed or without military training, but because my study of history has taught me that hatred and violence used in howsoever noble a cause only breed their kind and instead of bringing peace jeopardize it. Thanks to the tradition of our ancient seers, sages and saints, if there is a heritage that India can share with the world, it is this gospel of forgiveness and faith which is her proud possession. I have faith that in time to come, India will pit that against the threat of destruction which the world has invited upon itself by the discovery of the atom bomb. The weapon of truth and love is infallible, but there is something wrong in us, its votaries, which has plunged us into the present suicidal strife. I am, therefore, trying to examine myself. *151*

Mahatma Gandhi, The Last Phase, June 9, 1947

I have passed through many an ordeal in my life. But perhaps this is to be the hardest. I like it. The fiercer it becomes, the closer is the communion with God that I experience and the deeper grows my faith in His abundant grace. So long as it persists, I know it is well with me. *152*   *Mahatma Gandhi, The Last Phase, June 9, 1947*

If I were a perfect man, I own, I should not feel the miseries of neighbours as I do. As a perfect man I should take note of them, prescribe a remedy, and compel adoption by the force of unchallengeable Truth in me. But as yet I only see as through a glass darkly and therefore have to carry conviction by slow and laborious processes, and then, too, not always with success. . . . I would be less human if, with all my knowledge of the avoidable misery pervading the land . . . I did not feel with and for all the suffering of the dumb millions of India. *153*   *Young India, November 17, 1921*

I want to declare to the world that, whatever may be said to the contrary, and although I might have forfeited the regard and even the trust of many in the West—and I bow my head low—but even for their friendship or their love, I must not suppress that voice within, call it conscience, call it the prompting of my inner basic nature. There is something within me impelling me to cry out my agony. I

Last rites of Mahatma Gandhi. Huge crowds following the procession of Gandhi's ashes through the streets of Bombay on their way to the sea, 1948   (Photo Keystone)

have known exactly what it is. That something in me which never deceives me tells me now: 'You have to stand against the whole world although you may have to stand alone. You have to stare the world in the face although the world may look at you with bloodshot eyes. Do not fear. Trust that little thing in you which resides in the heart and says: Forsake friends, wife, all; but testify to that for which you have lived and for which you have to die.' *154*

From My Nonviolence, *by M. K. Gandhi*

My soul refuses to be satisfied so long as it is a helpless witness of a single wrong or a single misery. But it is not possible for me, a weak, frail, miserable being, to mend every wrong or to hold myself free of blame for all the wrong I see. The spirit in me pulls one way, the flesh in me pulls in the opposite direction. There is freedom from the action of these two forces but that freedom is attainable only by slow and painful stages. I cannot attain freedom by a mechanical refusal to act, but only by intelligent action in a detached manner. This struggle resolves itself into an incessant crucifixion of the flesh so that the spirit may become entirely free. *155*

Young India, November 17, 1921

I believe in the message of truth delivered by all the religious teachers of the world. And it is my constant prayer that I may never have a feeling of anger against my traducers, that even if I fall a victim to an assassin's bullet, I may deliver up my soul with the remembrance of God upon my lips. I shall be content to be written down an impostor if my lips utter a word of anger or abuse against my assailant at the last moment. *156*   *From a prayer discourse, summer of 1947*

Have I that nonviolence of the brave in me? My death alone will show that. If someone killed me and I died with prayer for the assassin on my lips, and God's remembrance and consciousness of His living presence in the sanctuary of my heart, then alone would I be said to have had the nonviolence of the brave. *157*

Prayer speech, June 16, 1947

I do not want to die ... of a creeping paralysis of my faculties—a defeated man. An assassin's bullet may put an end to my life. I would welcome it. But I would love, above all, to fade out doing my duty with my last breath. *158*   *Private Conversation, February 1947*

I am not aching for martyrdom, but if it comes in my way in the prosecution of what I consider to be the supreme duty in defense of the faith I hold ... I shall have earned it. *159*   *Harijan, June 29, 1934*

Assaults have been made on my life in the past, but God has spared me till now, and the assailants have repented for their action. But if someone were to shoot me in the belief that he was getting rid of a rascal, he would kill not the real Gandhi, but the one that appeared to him a rascal. *160*   *The Bombay Chronicle, August 9, 1942*

If I die of a lingering illness, nay even by as much as a boil or a pimple, it will be your duty to proclaim to the world, even at the risk of making people angry with you, that I was not the man of God that I claimed to be. If you do that it will give my spirit peace. Note down this also that if someone were to end my life by putting a bullet through me—as someone tried to do with a bomb the other day—and I met his bullet without a groan, and breathed my last taking God's name, then alone would I have made good my claim.[1]
161   *January 29, 1948, to an attendant*

If anybody tried to take out my body in a procession after I died, I would certainly tell them—if my corpse could speak—to spare me and cremate me where I had died. *162*   *September 3, 1947*

After I am gone, no single person will be able completely to represent me. But a little bit of me will live in many of you. If each puts the cause first and himself last, the vacuum will to a large extent be filled. *163*   *Oral tradition, "Gandhiji used to say to us"*

I do not want to be reborn. But if I have to be reborn, I should be born an untouchable, so that I may share their sorrows, sufferings, and affronts levelled at them, in order that I may endeavour to free myself and them from that miserable condition. *164*
Young India, May 4, 1921

1. This was uttered on the night of 29 January 1948, less than twenty hours before he was shot.

II RELIGION AND TRUTH

By religion, I do not mean formal religion, or customary religion, but that religion which underlies all religions, which brings us face to face with our Maker. *1*

Quoted from M. K. Gandhi,
by J. J. Dake, published in 1909

Let me explain what I mean by religion. It is not the Hindu religion which I certainly prize above all other religions, but the religion which transcends Hinduism, which changes one's very nature, which binds one indissolubly to the truth within and which ever purifies. It is the permanent element in human nature which counts no cost too great in order to find full expression and which leaves the soul utterly restless until it has found itself, known its Maker and appreciated the true correspondence between the Maker and itself. *2*

Young India, May 12, 1920

I have not seen Him, neither have I known Him. I have made the world's faith in God my own, and as my faith is ineffaceable, I regard that faith as amounting to experience. However, as it may be said that to describe faith as experience is to tamper with truth, it may perhaps be more correct to say that I have no word for characterizing my belief in God. *3*

An Autobiography

There is an indefinable mysterious Power that pervades everything. I feel it, though I do not see it. It is this unseen Power which makes itself felt and yet defies all proof, because it is so unlike all that I perceive through my senses. It transcends the senses. But it is possible to reason out the existence of God to a limited extent. *4*

Young India, October 11, 1928

I do dimly perceive that whilst everything around me is ever-changing, ever-dying, there is underlying all that change a Living Power that is changeless, that holds all together, that creates, dissolves, and re-creates. That informing Power or Spirit is God. And since nothing else I see merely through the senses can or will persist, He alone is. 5   *Young India, October 11, 1925*

And is this Power benevolent or malevolent? I see it as purely benevolent. For I can see that in the midst of death life persists, in the midst of untruth truth persists, in the midst of darkness light persists. Hence I gather that God is Life, Truth, Light. He is Love. He is the Supreme God. 6   *Young India, October 11, 1925*

I know, too, that I shall never know God if I do not wrestle with and against evil even at the cost of life itself. I am fortified in the belief by my own humble and limited experience. The purer I try to become the nearer to God I feel myself to be. How much more should I be near to Him when my faith is not a mere apology, as it is today, but has become as immovable as the Himalayas and as white and bright as the snows on their peaks? 7
Young India, October 11, 1925

This belief in God has to be based on faith which transcends reason. Indeed, even the so-called realization has at bottom an element of faith without which it cannot be sustained. In the very nature of things it must be so. Who can transgress the limitations of his being? I hold that complete realization is impossible in this embodied life. Nor is it necessary. A living immovable faith is all that is required for reaching the full spiritual height attainable by human beings. God is not outside this earthly case of ours. Therefore, exterior proof is not of much avail, if any at all. We must ever fail to perceive Him through the senses, because He is beyond them. We can feel Him, if we will but withdraw ourselves from the senses. The divine music is incessantly going on within ourselves, but the loud senses drown the delicate music, which is unlike and infinitely superior to anything we can perceive or hear with our senses. 8   *Harijan, June 13, 1936*

But He is no God who merely satisfies the intellect, if He ever does. God to be God must rule the heart and transform it. He must express Himself in every the smallest act of His votary. This can only be done through a definite realization more real than the five senses can ever produce. Sense perceptions can be, often are, false and deceptive, however real they may appear to us. Where there is realization outside the senses it is infallible. It is proved not by extraneous evidence but in the transformed conduct and character of those who

have felt the real presence of God within. Such testimony is to be
found in the experiences of an unbroken line of prophets and sages
in all countries and climes. To reject this evidence is to deny oneself.
9   *Young India, October 11, 1928*

To me God is Truth and Love; God is ethics and morality; God is
fearlessness. God is the source of Light and Life and yet He is above
and beyond all these. God is conscience. He is even the atheism of
the atheist.... He transcends speech and reason.... He is a personal
God to those who need His personal presence. He is embodied to
those who need His touch. He is the purest essence. He simply *is* to
those who have faith. He is all things to all men. He is in us and yet
above and beyond us.... He is long-suffering. He is patient but He is
also terrible.... With Him ignorance is no excuse. And withal He is
ever forgiving for He always gives us the chance to repent. He is the
greatest democrat the world knows, for He leaves us 'unfettered' to
make our own choice between evil and good. He is the greatest
tyrant ever known, for He often dashes the cup from our lips and
under the cover of free will leaves us a margin so wholly inadequate
as to provide only mirth for Himself.... Therefore Hinduism calls it
all His sport. *10*   *Young India, March 5, 1925*

To see the universal and all-pervading Spirit of Truth face to face one
must be able to love the meanest of creation as oneself. And a man
who aspires after that cannot afford to keep out of any field of life.
That is why my devotion to truth has drawn me into the field of
politics; and I can say without the slightest hesitation, and yet in all
humility, that those who say that religion has nothing to do with
politics do not know what religion means. *11*   *An Autobiography*

Identification with everything that lives is impossible without self-
purification; without self-purification the observance of the law of
ahiṃsā must remain an empty dream; God can never be realized by
one who is not pure of heart. Self-purification therefore must mean
purification in all walks of life. And purification being highly infectious, purification of oneself necessarily leads to the purification of
one's surroundings. *12*   *An Autobiography*

But the path of self-purification is hard and steep. To attain to perfect purity one has to become absolutely passion-free in thought,
speech and action; to rise above the opposing currents of love and
hatred, attachment and repulsion. I know that I have not in me as
yet that triple purity, in spite of constant, ceaseless striving for it.
That is why the world's praise fails to move me, indeed it very often
stings me. To conquer the subtle passions seems to me to be far

harder than the physical conquest of the world by the force of arms.
13   *An Autobiography*

I am but a poor struggling soul yearning to be wholly good—wholly truthful and wholly nonviolent in thought, word and deed; but ever failing to reach the ideal which I know to be true. It is a painful climb, but the pain of it is a positive pleasure to me. Each step upward makes me feel stronger and fit for the next. *14*
Young India, April 19, 1925

I am endeavouring to see God through service of humanity, for I know that God is neither in heaven, nor down below, but in every one. *15*   *Young India, August 4, 1927*

Indeed religion should pervade every one of our actions. Here religion does not mean sectarianism. It means a belief in ordered moral government of the universe. It is not less real because it is unseen. This religion transcends Hinduism, Islam, Christianity, etc. It does not supersede them. It harmonizes them and gives them reality. *16*
Harijan, February 10, 1940

Religions are different roads converging to the same point. What does it matter that we take different roads, so long as we reach the same goal? In reality, there are as many religions as there are individuals.
17   *Indian Home Rule, 1909*

If a man reaches the heart of his own religion, he has reached the heart of the others too. *18*   *Indian Home Rule, 1909*

So long as there are different religions, every one of them may need some distinctive symbol. But when the symbol is made into a fetish and an instrument of proving the superiority of one's religion over other's, it is fit only to be discarded. *19*   *Indian Home Rule, 1909*

After long study and experience, I have come to the conclusion that (1) all religions are true; (2) all religions have some error in them; (3) all religions are almost as dear to me as my own Hinduism, in as much as all human beings should be as dear to one as one's own close relatives. My own veneration for other faiths is the same as that for my own faith; therefore no thought of conversion is possible.
20   *Report of the First Annual Meeting*
of International Fellowships, Sbarmati, 1928

God has created different faiths just as He has the votaries thereof. How can I even secretly harbour the thought that my neighbour's faith is inferior to mine and wish that he should give up his faith and embrace mine? As a true and loyal friend, I can only wish and pray that he may live and grow perfect in his own faith. In God's house there are many mansions and they are equally holy. *21*

Harijan, April 20, 1934

Let no one even for a moment entertain the fear that a reverent study of other religions is likely to weaken or shake one's faith in one's own. The Hindu system of philosophy regards all religions as containing the elements of truth in them and enjoins an attitude of respect and reverence towards them all. This of course presupposes regard for one's own religion. Study and appreciation of other religions need not cause a weakening of that regard; it should mean extension of that regard to other religions. *22*

Young India, December 6, 1928

It is better to allow our lives to speak for us than our words. God did not bear the Cross only 1,900 years ago, but He bears it today, and He dies and is resurrected from day to day. It would be poor comfort to the world if it had to depend upon a historical God who died 2,000 years ago. Do not then preach the God of history, but show Him as He lives today through you. *23*

Young India, August 11, 1927

I do not believe in people telling others of their faith, especially with a view to conversion. Faith does not admit of telling. It has to be lived and then it becomes self-propagating. *24*

Young India, October 20, 1927

Divine knowledge is not borrowed from books. It has to be realized in oneself. Books are at best an aid, often even a hindrance. *25*

Young India, July 17, 1924

I believe in the fundamental truth of all great religions of the world. I believe that they are all God-given, and I believe that they were necessary for the people to whom these religions were revealed. And I believe that, if only we could all of us read the scriptures of the different faiths from the standpoint of the followers of those faiths, we should find that they were at the bottom all one and were helpful to one another. *26*   *Harijan, February 16, 1934*

Belief in one God is the corner-stone of all religions. But I do not foresee a time when there would be only one religion on earth in practice. In theory, since there is one God, there can be only one religion. But in practice, no two persons I have known have had the same identical conception of God. Therefore, there will, perhaps, always be different religions answering to different temperaments and climatic conditions. *27*   *Harijan, February 2, 1934*

I believe that all the great religions of the world are true more or less. I say 'more or less' because I believe that everything that the human hand touches, by reason of the very fact that human beings are imperfect, becomes imperfect. Perfection is the exclusive attribute of God and it is indescribable, untranslatable. I do believe that it is possible for every human being to become perfect even as God is perfect. It is necessary for us all to aspire after perfection, but when that blessed state is attained, it becomes indescribable, indefinable. And, I, therefore, admit, in all humility, that even the Vedas, the Koran and the Bible are imperfect word of God and, imperfect beings that we are, swayed to and fro by a multitude of passions, it is impossible for us even to understand this word of God in its fullness. *28*   *Young India, September 22, 1927*

I do not believe in the exclusive divinity of the Vedas. I believe the Bible, the Koran and the Zend Avesta, to be as much divinely inspired as the Vedas. My belief in the Hindu scriptures does not require me to accept every word and every verse as divinely inspired. . . . I decline to be bound by any interpretation, however learned it may be, if it is repugnant to reason or moral sense. *29*   *Young India, October 6, 1921*

Temples or mosques or churches . . . I make no distinction between these different abodes of God. They are what faith has made them. They are an answer to man's craving somehow to reach the Unseen. *30*   *Harijan, March 18, 1933*

The prayer has saved my life. Without it, I should have been a lunatic long ago. I had my share of the bitterest public and private experiences. They threw me in temporary despair. If I was able to get rid of that despair, it was because of prayer. It has not been a part of my life as truth has been. It came out of sheer necessity, as I found myself in a plight where I could not possibly be happy without it. And as time went on, my faith in God increased, and more irresistible became the yearning for prayer. Life seemed to be dull and vacant without it. I had attended the Christian service in South Africa, but it had failed to grip me. I could not join them in it. They supplicated God, I could not; I failed egregiously. I started with disbelief in God and prayer, and until at a late stage in life I did not feel anything like a void in life. But at that stage, I felt that as food is indispensable for the body, so was prayer indispensable for the soul. In fact food for the body is not so necessary as prayer for the soul. For starvation is often necessary to keep the body in health, but there is no such thing as prayer starvation. You cannot possibly have a surfeit of prayer. Three of the greatest teachers of the world— Buddha, Jesus and Muhammad—have left unimpeachable testimony, that they found illumination through prayer and could not possibly live without it. Millions of Hindus, Mussulmans and Christians find their only solace in life in prayer. Either you call them liars or self-deluded people. I will say that this 'lying' has a charm for me, a truth-seeker, if it is 'lying' that has given me that mainstay or staff of life without which I could not live for a moment. In spite of despair staring me in the face on the political horizon, I have never lost my peace. In fact, I have found people who envy my peace. That peace comes from prayer. I am indifferent as to the form. Everyone is a law unto himself in that respect. But there are some well marked roads, and it is safe to walk along the beaten tracks, trodden by the ancient teachers. I have given my personal testimony. Let every one try and find that as a result of daily prayer he adds something new to his life. *31*   *Mahatma, Vol. III, 1931*

Man's ultimate aim is the realization of God, and all his activities, political, social and religious, have to be guided by the ultimate aim of the vision of God. The immediate service of all human beings becomes a necessary part of the endeavour simply because the only way to find God is to see Him in His creation and be one with it. This can only be done by service of all. And this cannot be done except through one's country. I am a part and parcel of the whole, and I cannot find Him apart from the rest of the humanity. My countrymen are my nearest neighbours. They have become so help-less, so resourceless, so inert that I must concentrate on serving them. If I could persuade myself that I should find Him in a Himalayan cave I would proceed there immediately. But I know that I cannot find Him apart from humanity. *32*   *Mahatma, Vol. IV., 1936*

It is a tragedy that religion for us means today nothing more than restrictions on food and drink, nothing more than adherence to a sense of superiority and inferiority. Let me tell you that there cannot be any grosser ignorance than this. Birth and observance of forms cannot determine one's superiority and inferiority. Character is the only determining factor. God did not create men with the badge of superiority or inferiority; no scripture which labels a human being as inferior or untouchable because of his or her birth can command our allegiance, it is a denial of God and Truth which is God. *33*

Mahatma, III, 1934

It is my conviction that all the great faiths of the world are true, are God-ordained and that they serve the purpose of God and of those who have been brought up in those surroundings and those faiths. I do not believe that the time will ever come when we shall be able to say there is only one religion in the world. In a sense, even today there is one fundamental religion in the world. But there is no such thing as a straight line in nature. Religion is one tree with many branches. As branches, you may say religions are many, but as tree, religion is only one. *34*　　　　　　　　　　　　*Mahatma, III, 1934*

Supposing a Christian came to me and said he was captivated by the reading of *Bhāgavat* and so wanted to declare himself a Hindu, I should say to him: 'No. What *Bhāgavat* offers, the Bible also offers. You have not made the attempt to find it out. Make the attempt and be a good Christian.' *35*　　　　　　　　*Mahatma, III, 1936*

I do not conceive religion as one of the many activities of mankind. The same activity may be governed by the spirit either of religion or of irreligion. There is no such thing for me therefore as leaving politics for religion. For me every, the tiniest, activity is governed by what I consider to be my religion. *36*　　　*The Diary of Mahadev Desai*

There can be no manner of doubt that this universe of sentient beings is governed by a Law. If you can think of Law without its Giver, I would say that the Law is the Law-giver, that is God. When we pray to the Law we simply yearn after knowing the Law and obeying it. We become what we yearn after. Hence the necessity for prayer. Though our present life is governed by our past, our future must by that very law of cause and effect be affected by what we do now. To the extent therefore that we feel the choice between two or more courses we must make that choice.

Why evil exists and what it is are questions which appear to be beyond our limited reason. It should be enough to know that both good and evil exist. And as often we can distinguish between good and evil, we must choose the one and shun the other. *37*
The Diary of Mahadev Desai

Those who believe in God's guidance just do the best they can and never worry. The sun has never been known to suffer from overstrain and yet who slaves with such unexampled regularity as he! And why should we think that the sun is inanimate? The difference between him and us may be that he has no choice, we have a margin, no matter how precarious it may be. But no more speculation of this sort. Suffice it for us that we have his brilliant example in the matter of tireless energy. If we completely surrender to His will and really become *ciphers,* we too voluntarily give up the right of choice and then we need no wear and tear. *38*   *Bapu's Letters to Mira*

Yes, there are subjects where reason cannot take us far and we have to accept things on faith. Faith then does not contradict reason but transcends it. Faith is a kind of sixth sense which works in cases which are without the purview of reason. Well then, given these three criteria, I can have no difficulty in examining all claims made on behalf of religion. Thus to believe that Jesus is the only begotten son of God is to me against reason, for God can't marry and beget children. The word 'son' can only be used in a figurative sense. In that sense everyone who stands in the position of Jesus is a begotten son of God. If a man is spiritually miles ahead of us, we may say that he is in a special sense the son of God, though we are all children of God. We repudiate the relationship in our lives, whereas his life is a witness to that relationship. *39*   *Mahatma, IV, 1937*

God is not a person . . . God is the force. He is the essence of life. He is pure and undefiled consciousness. He is eternal. And yet, strangely enough, all are not able to derive either benefit from or shelter in the all-pervading living presence.
    Electricity is a powerful force. Not all can benefit from it. It can only be produced by following certain laws. It is a lifeless force. Man can utilize it if he labours hard enough to acquire the knowledge of its laws.
    The living force which we call God can similarly be found if we know and follow His law leading to the discovery of Him in us. *40*
Harijan, June 22, 1947

To seek God one need not go on a pilgrimage or light lamps and burn incense before or anoint the image of the deity or paint it with red vermilion. For He resides in our hearts. If we could completely obliterate in us the consciousness of our physical body, we would see Him face to face. *41*   *Mahatma Gandhi, Pyarelal, 1946 or 1947*

No search is possible without some workable assumptions. If we grant nothing, we find nothing. Ever since its commencement, the world, the wise and the foolish included, has proceeded upon the assumption that if we are, God is, and that, if God is not, we are not. And since belief in God is co-existent with the humankind, existence of God is treated as a fact more definite than the fact that the sun is. This living faith has solved a large number of puzzles of life. It has alleviated our misery. It sustains us in life, it is our one solace in death. The very search for Truth becomes interesting and worthwhile, because of this belief. But search for Truth is search for God. Truth is God. God is, because Truth is. We embark upon the search, because we believe that there is Truth and that it can be found by diligent search and meticulous observance of the well-known and well-tried rules of search. There is no record in history of the failure of such search. Even the atheists who have pretended to disbelieve in God have believed in Truth. The trick they have performed is that of giving God another, not a new, name. His names are legion. Truth is the crown of them all.

What is true of God is true, though in a less degree, of the assumption of the truth of some fundamental moralities. As a matter of fact, they are implied in the belief in God or Truth. Departure from these has landed the truants in endless misery. Difficulty of practice should not be confused with disbelief. A Himalayan expedition has also its prescribed conditions of success. Difficulty of fulfilling the conditions does not make the expedition impossible. It only adds interest and zest to the search. Well, this expedition in search of God or Truth is infinitely more than numberless Himalayan expeditions and, therefore, much more interesting. If we have no zest for it, it is because of the weakness of our faith. What we see with our physical eyes is more real to us than the only Reality. We know that the appearances are deceptive. And yet we treat trivialities as realities. To see the trivialities as such is half the battle won. It constitutes more than half the search after Truth or God. Unless we disengage ourselves from these trivialities, we have not even the leisure for the great search, or is it to be reserved for our leisure hours?   *42*

Mahatma, III, Private conversation, 1934

There are innumerable definitions of God, because His manifestations are innumerable. They overwhelm me with wonder and awe and for a moment stun me. But I worship God as Truth only. I have not yet found Him, but I am seeking after Him. I am prepared to sacrifice the things dearest to me in pursuit of this quest. Even if the sacrifice demanded be my very life, I hope I may be prepared to give it. But as long as I have not realized this Absolute Truth, so long must I hold by the relative truth as I have conceived it.   *43*

An Autobiography

Often in my progress I have had faint glimpses of the Absolute Truth, God, and daily the conviction is growing upon me that He alone is real and all else is unreal. Let those, who wish, realize how the conviction has grown upon me; let them share my experiments and share also my conviction if they can. The further conviction has been growing upon me that whatever is possible for me is possible even for a child, and I have sound reasons for saying so. The instruments for the quest of Truth are as simple as they are difficult. They may appear quite impossible to an arrogant person, and quite possible to an innocent child. The seeker after truth should be humbler than the dust. *44*   *An Autobiography*

If we had attained the full vision of Truth, we would no longer be mere seekers, but have become one with God, for Truth is God. But being only seekers, we prosecute our quest, and are conscious of our imperfection. And if we are imperfect ourselves, religion as conceived by us must also be imperfect. We have not realized religion in its perfection, even as we have not realized God. Religion of our conception, being thus imperfect, is always subject to a process of evolution. And if all faiths outlined by men are imperfect, the question of comparative merit does not arise. All faiths constitute a revelation of Truth, but all are imperfect, and liable to error. Reverence for other faiths need not blind us to their faults. We must be keenly alive to the defects of our own faith also, yet not leave it on that account, but try to overcome those defects. Looking at all religions with an equal eye, we would not only not hesitate, but would think it our duty, to blend into our faith every acceptable feature of other faiths.

Even as a tree has a single trunk, but many branches and leaves, so there is one true and perfect Religion, but it becomes many, as it passes through the human medium. The one Religion is beyond all speech. Imperfect men put it into such language as they can command, and their words are interpreted by other men equally imperfect. Whose interpretation is to be held to be the right one? Everybody is right from his own standpoint, but it is not possible that everybody is wrong. Hence the necessity of tolerance, which does not mean indifference to one's own faith, but a more intelligent and purer love for it. Tolerance gives us spiritual insight, which is as far from fanaticism as the North Pole from the South. True knowledge of religion breaks down the barriers between faith and faith. *45*
                                        Yeranda Mandir, 1935

I believe that we can all become messengers of God, if we cease to fear man and seek only God's Truth. I do believe I am seeking only God's Truth and have lost all fear of man. *46*
                                        Young India, May 25, 1921

I have no special revelation of God's will. My firm belief is that He reveals Himself daily to every human being, but we shut our ears to the 'still small voice.' We shut our eyes to the 'pillar of fire' in front of us. *47*   *Young India, May 25, 1921*

I must go . . . with God as my only guide. He is a jealous Lord. He will allow no one to share His authority. One has, therefore, to appear before Him in all one's weakness, empty-handed and in a spirit of full surrender, and then He enables you to stand before a whole world and protects you from all harm. *48*

Young India, September 3, 1931

If I did not feel the presence of God within me, I see so much of misery and disappointment every day that I would be a raving maniac and my destination would be the *Hooghli. 49*

Young India, August 6, 1925

In a strictly scientific sense God is at the bottom of both good and evil. He directs the assassin's dagger no less than the surgeon's knife. But for all that good and evil are, for human purposes, from each other distinct and incompatible, being symbolical of light and darkness, God and Satan. *50*   *Harijan, February 20, 1937*

I am surer of His existence than of the fact that you and I are sitting in this room. Then I can also testify that I may live without air and water but not without Him. You may pluck out my eyes, but that cannot kill me. But blast my belief in God, and I am dead. You may call this a superstition, but I confess it is a superstition that I hug, even as I used to do the name of Rama in my childhood when there was any cause of danger or alarm. That was what an old nurse had taught me. *51*   *An Autobiography*

Not until we have reduced ourselves to nothingness can we conquer the evil in us. God demands nothing less than complete self-surrender as the price for the only real freedom that is worth having. And when a man thus loses himself he immediately finds himself in the service of all that lives. It becomes his delight and his recreation. He is a new man, never weary of spending himself in the service of God's creation. *52*   *Young India, December 20, 1928*

There are moments in your life when you must act, even though you cannot carry your best friends with you. The 'still small voice' within you must always be the final arbiter when there is a conflict of duty. *53*   *The Monthly Review, Calcutta, October, 1941*

I could not live for a single second without religion. Many of my political friends despair of me because they say that even my politics are derived from religion. And they are right. My politics and all other activities of mine are derived from my religion. I go further and say that every activity of a man of religion must be derived from his religion, because religion means being bound to God, that is to say God rules your every breath. *54*   *Harijan, March 21, 1934*

Religion and Truth

For me, politics bereft of religion are absolute dirt, ever to be shunned. Politics concern nations and that which concerns the welfare of nations must be one of the concerns of a man who is religiously inclined, in other words, a seeker after God and Truth. For me God and Truth are convertible terms, and if anyone told me that God was a God of untruth or a God of torture, I would decline to worship Him. Therefore, in politics also we have to establish the Kingdom of Heaven. *55*

Young India, June 18, 1925

I could not be leading a religious life unless I identified myself with the whole of mankind, and that I could not do unless I took part in politics. The whole gamut of man's activities today constitutes an indivisible whole. You cannot divide social, economic, political and purely religious work into watertight compartments. I do not know any religion apart from human activity. It provides a moral basis to all other activities which they would otherwise lack, reducing life to a maze of 'sound and fury signifying nothing.' *56*

Harijan, December 24, 1935

It is faith that steers us through stormy seas, faith that moves mountains and faith that jumps across the ocean. That faith is nothing but a living, wide-awake consciousness of God within. He who has achieved that faith wants nothing. Bodily diseased, he is spiritually healthy; physically poor, he rolls in spiritual riches. *57*

Young India, September 24, 1921

The forms are many, but the informing spirit is one. How can there be room for distinctions of high and low where there is this all-embracing fundamental unity underlying the outward diversity? For that is a fact meeting you at every step in daily life. The final goal of all religions is to realize this essential oneness. *58*

Harijan, December 15, 1933

In my early youth I was taught to repeat what in Hindu scriptures are known as the one thousand names of God. But these one thousand names of God were by no means exhaustive. We believe, and I think it is the truth, that God has as many names as there are creatures. Therefore, we also say that God is nameless, and since God has many forms, we consider Him formless, and since He speaks through many tongues, we consider Him to be speechless and so on. And, so, when I came to study Islam, I found Islam too had many names of God.

I would say with those who say 'God is Love,' God is Love. But deep down in me I used to say that though God may be Love, God is Truth above all. If it is possible for the human tongue to give the

fullest description of God, I have come to the conclusion that God is Truth. Two years ago I went a step further and said that Truth is God. You will see the fine distinction between the two statements, 'God is Truth' and 'Truth is God.' I came to that conclusion after a continuous and relentless search after truth which began fifty years ago. I then found that the nearest approach to truth was through love. But I also found that love has many meanings in the English language, and that human love in the sense of passion could become a degrading thing. I found too that love in the sense of *ahiṃsā* had only a limited number of votaries in the world. But I never found a double meaning in connexion with truth and even atheists had not demurred to the necessity of power of truth. But in their passion for discovering truth, atheists have not hesitated to deny the very exist-ence of God—from their own point of view rightly. It was because of this reasoning that I saw that rather than say that God is Truth, I should say that Truth is God. Add to this the great difficulty, that millions have taken the name of God and in His name committed nameless atrocities. Not that the scientists very often do not commit atrocities in the name of Truth. Then there is another thing in Hindu philosophy, namely, God alone is and nothing else exists, and the same truth you see emphasized and exemplified in the *kalma* of Islam. And there you find it clearly stated that God alone is, and nothing else exists. In fact, the Sanskrit word for truth is a word which literally means that which exists, *sat*. For these and many other reasons, I have come to the conclusion that the definition—Truth is God—gives me the greatest satisfaction. And when you want to find Truth as God, the only inevitable means is love, that is, nonviolence, and since I believe that ultimately the means and ends are convertible terms, I should not hesitate to say that God is Love.
59   *Mahatma, III, Speech, 1931*

From the standpoint of pure Truth, the body too is a possession. It has been truly said that desire for enjoyment creates bodies for the soul. When this desire vanishes, there remains no further need for the body, and man is free from the vicious cycle of births and deaths. The soul is omnipresent; why should she care to be confined within the cage-like body, or do evil and even kill for the sake of that cage? We thus arrive at the ideal of total renunciation, and learn to use the body for the purposes of service so long as it exists, so much so that service, and not bread, becomes with us the staff of life. We eat and drink, sleep and wake, for service alone. Such an attitude of mind brings us real happiness, and the beatific vision in the fullness of time. *60*   *Yeranda Mandir, 1935*

What . . . is Truth? A difficult question; but I have solved it for myself by saying that it is what the voice within tells you. How then, you ask, different people think of different and contrary truths? Well, seeing that the human mind works through innumerable media and that the evolution of the human mind is not the same for all, it follows that what may be truth for one may be untruth for another, and hence those who have made these experiments have come to the conclusion that there are certain conditions to be observed in making those experiments ... It is because we have at the present moment everybody claiming the right of conscience without going through any discipline whatsoever that there is so much untruth being delivered to a bewildered world. All that I can in true humility present to you is that Truth is not to be found by anybody who has not got an abundant sense of humility. If you would swim on the bosom of the ocean of Truth you must reduce yourself to a zero. *61*

Young India, October 27, 1921

Truth resides in every human heart, and one has to search for it there, and to be guided by truth as one sees it. But no one has a right to coerce others to act according to his own view of truth. *62*

Harijan, November 24, 1933

Life is an aspiration. Its mission is to strive after perfection, which is self-realization. The ideal must not be lowered because of our weaknesses or imperfections. I am painfully conscious of both in me. The silent cry daily goes out to Truth to help me to remove these weaknesses and imperfections of mine. *63*   *Harijan, June 22, 1935*

There can be no room for untruth in my writings, because it is my unshakable belief that there is no religion other than truth and because I am capable of rejecting aught obtained at the cost of truth. My writings cannot but be free from hatred towards any individual because it is my firm belief that it is love that sustains the earth. There only is life where there is love. Life without love is death. Love is the reverse of the coin of which the obverse is truth. It is my firm faith ... that we can conquer the whole world by truth and love. *64*   *The Mind of Mahatma Gandhi*

I am devoted to none but Truth and I owe no discipline to anybody but Truth. *65*   *Harijan, May 25, 1935*

Truth is the first thing to be sought for, and Beauty and Goodness will then be added unto you. That is what Christ really taught in the Sermon on the Mount. Jesus was, to my mind, a supreme artist because he saw and expressed Truth; and so was Muhammad, the Koran being the most perfect composition in all Arabic literature—at any rate, that is what scholars say. It is because both of them strove first for Truth that the grace of expression naturally came in and yet neither Jesus nor Muhammad wrote on Art. That is the Truth and Beauty I crave for, live for, and would die for. *66*

Young India, November 20, 1924

As regards God it is difficult to define Him; but the definition of truth is deposited in every human heart. Truth is that which you believe to be true at this moment, and that is your God. If a man worships this relative truth, he is sure to attain the Absolute Truth, i.e., God, in course of time. *67* *The Diary of Mahadev Desai*

I know the path. It is straight and narrow. It is like the edge of a sword. I rejoice to walk on it. I weep when I slip. God's word is: 'He who strives never perishes.' I have implicit faith in that promise. Though, therefore, from my weakness I fail a thousand times, I will not lose faith but hope that I shall see the Light when the flesh has been brought under perfect subjection, as some day it must. *68*

Young India, June 17, 1926

I am but a seeker after Truth. I claim to have found a way to it. I claim to be making a ceaseless effort to find it. But I admit that I have not yet found it. To find Truth completely is to realize oneself and one's destiny, i.e., to become perfect. I am painfully conscious of my imperfections, and therein lies all the strength I possess, because it is a rare thing for a man to know his own limitations. *69*

Young India, November 17, 1921

I am in the world feeling my way to light 'amid the encircling gloom.' I often err and miscalculate. . . . My trust is solely in God. And I trust men only because I trust God. If I had no God to rely upon, I should be, like Timon, a hater of my species. *70*

Young India, December 4, 1924

I am not a 'statesman in the garb of a saint.' But since Truth is the highest wisdom, sometimes my acts appear to be consistent with the highest statesmanship. But, I hope I have no policy in me save the policy of Truth and *ahiṃsā*. I will not sacrifice Truth and *ahiṃsā* even for the deliverance of my country or religion. That is as much as to say that neither can be so delivered. *71*

Young India, January 20, 1927

It seems to me that I understand the ideal of truth better than that of *ahiṃsā*, and my experience tells me that if I let go my hold of truth, I shall never be able to solve the riddle of *ahiṃsā*. . . . In other words, perhaps, I have not the courage to follow the straight course. Both at bottom mean one and the same thing, for doubt is invariably the result of want or weakness of faith. 'Lord, give me faith' is, therefore, my prayer day and night. *72*　　　　　　*An Autobiography*

In the midst of humiliation and so-called defeat and a tempestuous life, I am able to retain my peace, because of an underlying faith in God, translated as Truth. We can describe God as millions of things, but I have for myself adopted the formula—*Truth is God*. *73*
The Mind of Mahatma Gandhi

I claim to have no infallible guidance or inspiration. So far as my experience goes, the claim to infallibility on the part of a human being would be untenable, seeing that inspiration too can come only to one who is free from the action of opposites, and it will be difficult to judge on a given occasion whether the claim to freedom from pairs of opposites is justified. The claim to infallibility would thus always be a most dangerous claim to make. This, however, does not leave us without any guidance whatsoever. The sum-total of the experience of the sages of the world is available to us and would be for all time to come. Moreover, there are not many fundamental truths, but there is only one fundamental truth which is Truth itself, otherwise known as Nonviolence. Finite human beings shall never know in its fullness Truth and Love which is in itself infinite. But we do know enough for our guidance. We shall err, and sometimes grievously, in our application. But man is a self-governing being, and self-government necessarily includes the power as much to commit errors as to set them right as often as they are made. *74*
Young India, April 21, 1927

I may be a despicable person, but when Truth speaks through me I am invincible. *75*　　　　　　*The Epic Fast, published in 1932*

I have in my life never been guilty of saying things I did not mean— my nature is to go straight to the heart and if often I fail in doing so for the time being, I know that Truth will ultimately make itself heard and felt, as it has often done in my experience. *76*
Young India, August 20, 1925

I am a humble but very earnest seeker after Truth. And in my search, I take all fellow-seekers in uttermost confidence so that I may know my mistakes and correct them. I confess that I have often erred in my estimates and judgements. . . . And inasmuch as in every case I retraced my steps, no permanent harm was done. On the contrary, the fundamental truth of nonviolence has been made infinitely more manifest than it ever has been, and the country has in no way been permanently injured. *77*   *Young India, April 21, 1927*

I see and find beauty in Truth or through Truth. All Truth, not merely true ideas, but truthful faces, truthful pictures or songs are highly beautiful. People generally fail to see beauty in Truth, the ordinary man runs away from and becomes blind to the beauty in it. Whenever men begin to see beauty in Truth, then true art will arise. *78*   *Young India, November 13, 1925*

To a true artist only that face is beautiful which, quite apart from its exterior, shines with the truth within the soul. There is . . . no beauty apart from Truth. On the other hand, Truth may manifest itself in forms which may not be outwardly beautiful at all. Socrates, we are told, was the most truthful man of his time, and yet his features are said to have been the ugliest in Greece. To my mind he was beautiful because all his life was a striving after Truth, and you may remember that this outward form did not prevent Phidias from appreciating the beauty of Truth in him, though as an artist he was accustomed to see beauty in outward forms also. *79*   *Young India, November 13, 1925*

But it is impossible for us to realize perfect Truth so long as we are imprisoned in this mortal frame. We can only visualize it in our imagination. We cannot, through the instrumentality of this ephemeral body, see face to face Truth which is eternal. That is why in the last resort one must depend on faith. *80*   *Yeravda Mandir, 1935*

I lay claim to nothing exclusively divine in me. I do not claim prophetship. I am but a humble seeker after Truth and bent upon finding it. I count no sacrifice too great for the sake of seeing God face to face. The whole of my activity whether it may be called social, political, humanitarian or ethical is directed to that end. And as I know that God is found more often in the lowliest of His creatures than in the high and mighty, I am struggling to reach the status of these. I cannot do so without their service. Hence my passion for the service of the suppressed classes. And as I cannot render this service without entering politics, I find myself in them. Thus I am no master, I am but a struggling, erring, humble servant of India and, therethrough, of humanity. *81*   *Young India, September 11, 1924*

There is no religion higher than Truth and Righteousness. *82*
Ethical Religion, 1930

True religion and true morality are inseparably bound up with each

other. Religion is to morality what water is to the seed that is sown in the soil. *83*
Ethical Religion, 1930

I reject any religious doctrine that does not appeal to reason and is in conflict with morality. I tolerate unreasonable religious sentiment when it is not immoral. *84*
Young India, July 12, 1920

As soon as we lose the moral basis, we cease to be religious. There is no such thing as religion overriding morality. Man for instance cannot be untruthful, cruel and incontinent and claim to have God on his side. *85*
Young India, November 24, 1921

Our desires and motives may be divided into two classes—selfish and unselfish. All selfish desires are immoral, while the desire to improve ourselves for the sake of doing good to others is truly moral. The highest moral law is that we should unremittingly work for the good of mankind. *86*
Ethical Religion, 1930

If any action of mine claimed to be spiritual is proved to be unpracticable it must be pronounced to be a failure. I do believe that the most spiritual act is the most practical in the true sense of the term. *87*
Harijan, July 1, 1939

Scriptures cannot transcend reason and truth. They are intended to purify reason and illuminate truth. *88*   *Young India, January 19, 1921*

Error can claim no exemption even if it can be supported by the scriptures of the world. *89*
Young India, February 26, 1925

An error does not become truth by reason of multiplied propagation, nor does truth become error because nobody sees it. *90*
Young India, February 26, 1925

I do not hold that everything ancient is good because it is ancient. I do not advocate surrender of God-given reasoning faculty in the face of ancient tradition. Any tradition, however, ancient, if inconsistent with morality, is fit to be banished from the land. Untouchability may be considered to be an ancient tradition, the institution of child widowhood and child marriage may be considered to be an ancient tradition, and even so many an ancient horrible belief and superstitious practice. I would sweep them out of existence if I had the power. *91*
Young India, September 22, 1927

I do not disbelieve in idol worship. An idol does not excite any feeling of veneration in me. But I think that idol worship is part of human nature. We hanker after symbolism. *92*

Young India, October 6, 1921

I do not forbid the use of images in prayer. I only prefer the worship of the Formless. This preference is perhaps improper. One thing suits one man; another thing will suit another man, and no comparison can fairly be made between the two. *93*   *The Diary of Mahadev Desai*

I have come to feel that like human beings words have their evolution from stage to stage in the contents they hold. For instance the contents of the richest word—God—are not the same to every one of us. They will vary with the experience of each. *94*

Young India, August 11, 1927

I see neither contradiction nor insanity in my life. It is true that as a man cannot see his back, so can he not see his errors or insanity. But the sages have often likened a man of religion to a lunatic. I therefore hug the belief that I may not be insane and may be truly religious. Which of the two I am in truth can only be decided after my death. *95*   *Young India, August 14, 1924*

Whenever I see an erring man, I say to myself I have also erred; when I see a lustful man I say to myself, so was I once; and in this way I feel kinship with every one in the world and feel that I cannot be happy without the humblest of us being happy. *96*

Young India, February 10, 1927

I shall have to answer my God and my Maker if I give anyone less than his due, but I am sure that He will bless me if He knows that I gave one more than his due. *97*   *Young India, March 10, 1927*

Mine is a life full of joy in the midst of incessant work. In not wanting to think of what tomorrow will bring for me I feel as free as a bird. . . . The thought that I am ceaselessly and honestly struggling against the requirements of the flesh sustains me. *98*

Young India, October 1, 1925

I am too conscious of the imperfections of the species to which I belong to be irritated against any member thereof. My remedy is to deal with the wrong wherever I see it, not to hurt the wrong-doer, even as I would not like to be hurt for the wrongs I continually do. *99*   *Young India, March 12, 1931*

I remain an optimist, not that there is any evidence that I can give that right is going to prosper, but because of my unflinching faith that right must prosper in the end. . . . Our inspiration can come only from our faith that right must ultimately prevail. *100*

Harijan, December 10, 1938

There are limits to the capacity of an individual, and the moment he flatters himself that he can undertake all tasks, God is there to humble his pride. For myself, I am gifted with enough humility to look even to babes and sucklings for help. *101*

Young India, March 12, 1931

A drop in the ocean partakes of the greatness of its parent although it is unconscious of it. But it is dried up as soon as it enters upon an existence independent of the ocean. We do not exaggerate when we say that life is a mere bubble. *102*   *Young India, October 16, 1930*

I am an irrepressible optimist, because I believe in myself. That sounds very arrogant, doesn't it? But I say it from the depths of my humility. I believe in the supreme power of God. I believe in Truth and, therefore, I have no doubt in the future of this country or the future of humanity. *103*   *Young India, August 13, 1925*

Mine is not a religion of the prison-house. It has room for the least among God's creation. But it is proof against insolence, pride of race, religion or colour. *104*   *Young India, June 1, 1921*

I do not share the belief that there can or will be on earth one religion. I am striving, therefore, to find a common factor and to induce mutual tolerance. *105*   *Young India, July 31, 1924*

I hold that a life of perfect continence in thought, speech and action is necessary for reaching spiritual perfection. And a nation that does not possess such men is poorer for the want. *106*

Young India, October 13, 1920

A sinner is equal to the saint in the eye of God. Both will have equal justice, and both an equal opportunity either to go forward or to go backward. Both are His children, His creation. A saint who considers himself superior to a sinner forfeits his sainthood and becomes worse than the sinner, who, unlike the proud saint, knows not what he is doing. *107*   *Harijan, October 14, 1923*

We often confuse spiritual knowledge with spiritual attainment. Spirituality is not a matter of knowing scriptures and engaging in philosophical discussions. It is a matter of heart culture, of unmeasurable strength. Fearlessness is the first requisite of spirituality. Cowards can never be moral. *108*   *Young India, October 13, 1921*

Man should earnestly desire the well-being of all God's creation and pray that he might have the strength to do so. In desiring the well-being of all lies his own welfare; he who desires only his own or his community's welfare is selfish and it can never be well with him. . . . It is essential for man to discriminate between what he may consider to be good and what is really good for him. *109*

Harijan, October 20, 1946

I believe in the absolute oneness of God and, therefore, of humanity. What though we have many bodies? We have but one soul. The rays of the sun are many through refraction. But they have the same source. I cannot, therefore, detach myself from the wickedest soul nor may I be denied identity with the most virtuous. *110*

Young India, September 25, 1924

If I were a dictator, religion and State would be separate. I swear by my religion. I will die for it. But it is my personal affair. The State has nothing to do with it. The State would look after secular welfare, health, communications, foreign relations, currency and so on, but not your or my religion. That is everybody's personal concern. *111*

Mahatma, VII, October 1946

I am surrounded by exaggeration and untruth. In spite of my best efforts to find it, I do not know where Truth lies. But it seems to me that I have come nearer to God and Truth. It has cost me old friendships but I am not sorry for it. To me it is a sign of my having come nearer to God that I can write and speak to everybody plainly and fearlessly about the delicate issue in the teeth of the fiercest opposition, practise in full the eleven vows which I have professed, without the slightest feeling of perturbation or unrest. Sixty years of striving have at last enabled me to realize the ideal of truth and purity which I have ever set before myself. *112*

Mahatma Gandhi, The Last Phase,
Conversation, circa April 1947

All that we know is that one should do one's duty and leave the results in the hands of God. Man is supposed to be master of his own destiny, but it is only partly true. He can make his own destiny only in so far as he is allowed by the Great Power which overrides all our intentions, all our plans and carries out His own plans. I call that Power not by the name of Allah, Khuda or God but Truth. The

whole truth is embodied only within the heart of that Great Power—
Truth. *113* *Mahatma Gandhi, The Last Phase, 1947*

I know of no greater sin than to oppress the innocent in the name of
God. *114* *Mahatma Gandhi, The Last Phase, April, 1947*

When I think of my littleness and my limitations on the one hand
and of the expectations raised about me on the other, I become
dazed for the moment, but I come to find myself as soon as I realize
that these expectations are a tribute not to me, a curious mixture of
Jekyll and Hyde, but to the incarnation, however imperfect but comparatively great in me, of the two priceless qualities of truth and
nonviolence. *115* *Young India, October 3, 1925*

There is nothing on earth that I would not give up for the sake of
the country excepting of course two things and two only, namely,
truth and nonviolence. I would not sacrifice these two for all the
world. For to me Truth is God and there is no way to find Truth
except the way of nonviolence. I do not seek to serve India at the
sacrifice of Truth or God. For I know that a man who forsakes Truth
can forsake his country, and his nearest and dearest ones. *116*
Mahatma, II, Speech, December 20, 1926

III MEANS AND ENDS

Means and end are convertible terms in my philosophy of life. *1*
Young India, December 26, 1924

They say 'means are after all means.' I would say 'means are after all everything.' As the means so the end. There is no wall of separation between means and end. Indeed the Creator has given us control (and that too very limited) over means, none over the end. Realization of the goal is in exact proportion to that of the means. This is a proposition that admits of no exception. *2*   *Young India, July 17, 1924*

Ahiṃsā and Truth are so intertwined that it is practically impossible to disentangle and separate them. They are like the two sides of a coin, or rather a smooth unstamped metallic disc. Who can say, which is the obverse, and which the reverse? Nevertheless, *ahiṃsā* is the means; Truth is the end. Means to be means must always be within our reach, and so *ahiṃsā* is our supreme duty. If we take care of the means, we are bound to reach the end sooner or later. When once we have grasped this point final victory is beyond question. Whatever difficulties we encounter, whatever apparent reverses we sustain, we may not give up the quest for Truth which alone is, being God Himself. *3*   *Yeranda Mandir, 1935*

I do not believe in short-violent-cuts to success. . . . However much I may sympathize with and admire worthy motives, I am an uncompromising opponent of violent methods even to serve the noblest of causes. There is, therefore, really no meeting-ground between the school of violence and myself. But my creed of nonviolence not only does not preclude me but compels me even to associate with anarchists and all those who believe in violence. But that association is always with the sole object of weaning them from what appears to me their error. For experience convinces me that permanent good can never be the outcome of untruth and violence. Even if my belief is a fond delusion, it will be admitted that it is a fascinating delusion.   *4*

Young India, December 11, 1924

Your belief that there is no connexion between the means and the end is a great mistake. Through that mistake even men who have been considered religious have committed grevious crimes. Your reasoning is the same as saying that we can get a rose through planting a noxious weed. If I want to cross the ocean, I can do so only by means of a vessel; if I were to use a cart for that purpose, both the cart and I would soon find the bottom. 'As is the God, so is the votary' is a maxim worth considering. Its meaning has been distorted and men have gone astray. The means may be likened to a seed, the end to a tree; and there is just the same inviolable connexion between the means and the end as there is between the seed and the tree. I am not likely to obtain the result flowing from the worship of God by laying myself prostrate before Satan. If, therefore, anyone were to say: 'I want to worship God; it does not matter that I do so by means of Satan,' it would be set down as ignorant folly. We reap exactly as we sow.   *5*   *Hind Swaraj or India Home Rule, 1909*

Socialism is a beautiful word and, so far as I am aware, in socialism all the members of society are equal—none low, none high. In the individual body, the head is not high because it is the top of the body, nor are the soles of the feet low because they touch the earth. Even as members of the individual body are equal, so are the members of society. This is socialism.

In it the prince and the peasant, the wealthy and the poor, the employer and the employee are all on the same level. In terms of religion, there is no duality in socialism. It is all unity. Looking at society all the world over, there is nothing but duality or plurality. Unity is conspicuous by its absence. . . . In the unity of my conception there is perfect unity in the plurality of designs.

In order to reach this state, we may not look on things philosophically and say that we need not make a move until all are converted to socialism. Without changing our life we may go on giving addresses, forming parties and hawk-like seize the game when it comes our way. This is no socialism. The more we treat it as game to be seized, the farther it must recede from us.

Socialism begins with the first convert. If there is one such you can add zeros to the one and the first zero will account for ten and every addition will account for ten times the previous number. If, however, the beginner is a zero, in other words, no one makes the beginning, multiplicity of zeros will also produce zero value. Time and paper occupied in writing zeros will be so much waste.

This socialism is as pure as crystal. It, therefore, requires crystal-like means to achieve it. Impure means result in an impure end. Hence the prince and the peasant will not be equalled by cutting off the prince's head, nor can the process of cutting off equalize the employer and the employed. One cannot reach truth by untruthfulness. Truthful conduct alone can reach truth. Are not nonviolence and truth twins? The answer is an emphatic 'No.' Nonviolence is embedded in truth and vice versa. Hence has it been said that they are faces of the same coin. Either is inseparable from the other. Read the coin either way—the spelling of words will be different; the value is the same. This blessed state is unattainable without perfect purity. Harbour impurity of mind or body and you have untruth and violence in you.

Therefore only truthful, nonviolent and pure-hearted socialists will be able to establish a socialistic society in India and the world.   6
Harijan, July 1947

The spiritual weapon of self-purification, intangible as it seems, is the most potent means of revolutionizing one's environment and loosening external shackles. It works subtly and invisibly; it is an intense process though it might often seem a weary and long-drawn process, it is the straightest way to liberation, the surest and quickest and no effort can be too great for it. What it requires is faith—an unshakable mountain-like faith that flinches from nothing.   7   *Young India, April 30, 1925*

I am more concerned in preventing the brutalization of human nature than in the prevention of the sufferings of my own people. I know that people who voluntarily undergo a course of suffering raise themselves and the whole of humanity; but I also know that people who become brutalized in their desperate efforts to get victory over their opponents or to exploit weaker nations or weaker men, not only drag down themselves but mankind also. And it cannot be a matter of pleasure to me or anyone else to see human nature dragged to the mire. If we are all sons of the same God and partake of the same divine essence, we must partake of the sin of every person whether he belongs to us or to another race. You can understand how repugnant it must be to invoke the beast in any human being, how much more so in Englishmen, among whom I count numerous friends.   8
Young India, October 29, 1931

The method of passive resistance is the clearest and safest, because, if the cause is not true, it is the resisters, and they alone, who suffer.
9   *Young India, October 29, 1931*

IV AHIMSĀ OR THE WAY
OF NONVIOLENCE

Nonviolence is the greatest force at the disposal of mankind. It is mightier than the mightiest weapon of destruction devised by the ingenuity of man. Destruction is not the law of the humans. Man lives freely by his readiness to die, if need be, at the hands of his brother, never by killing him. Every murder or other injury, no matter for what cause, committed or inflicted on another is a crime against humanity. *1*   *Harijan, July 20, 1931*

The first condition of nonviolence is justice all round in every department of life. Perhaps, it is too much to expect of human nature. I do not, however, think so. No one should dogmatize about the capacity of human nature for degradation or exaltation. *2*
Mahatma, V., April, 1940

Just as one must learn the art of killing in the training for violence, so one must learn the art of dying in the training for nonviolence. Violence does not mean emancipation from fear, but discovering the means of combating the cause of fear. Nonviolence, on the other hand, has no cause for fear. The votary of nonviolence has to cultivate the capacity for sacrifice of the highest type in order to be free from fear. He recks not if he should lose his land, his wealth, his life. He who has not overcome all fear cannot practise *ahimsā* to perfection. The votary of *ahimsā* has only one fear, that is of God. He who seeks refuge in God ought to have a glimpse of the *Atma* that transcends the body; and the moment one has a glimpse of the imperishable *Atma* one sheds the love of the perishable body. Training in nonviolence is thus diametrically opposed to training in violence. Violence is needed for the protection of things external, nonviolence is needed for the protection of the *Atma*, for the protection of one's honour. *3* *Harijan, September 1, 1940*

It is no nonviolence if we merely love those that love us. It is nonviolence only when we love those that hate us. I know how difficult it is to follow this grand law of love. But are not all great and good things difficult to do? Love of the hater is the most difficult of all. But by the grace of God even this most difficult thing becomes easy to accomplish if we want to do it. *4* *Letter of December 31, 1934*

I have found that life persists in the midst of destruction and therefore there must be a higher law than that of destruction. Only under that law would a well-ordered society be intelligible and life worth living. And if that is the law of life, we have to work it out in daily life. Whenever there are jars, wherever you are confronted with an opponent conquer him with love. In this crude manner I have worked it out in my life. That does not mean that all my difficulties are solved. Only I have found that this law of love has answered as the law of destruction has never done.

It is not that I am incapable of anger, for instance, but I succeed on almost all occasions to keep my feelings under control. Whatever may be the result, there is always in me conscious struggle for following the law of nonviolence deliberately and ceaselessly. Such a struggle leaves one stronger for it. The more I work at this law, the more I feel the delight in my life, the delight in the scheme of the universe. It gives me a peace and a meaning of the mysteries of nature that I have no power to describe. *5* *Young India, October 1, 1931*

I saw that nations like individuals could only be made through the agony of the Cross and in no other way. Joy comes not out of infliction of pain on others but out of pain voluntarily borne by oneself. *6* *Young India, December 31, 1931*

If we turn our eyes to the time of which history has any record down to our own time, we shall find that man has been steadily progressing towards *ahiṃsā*. Our remote ancestors were cannibals. Then came a time when they were fed up with cannibalism and they began to live on chase. Next came a stage when man was ashamed of leading the life of a wandering hunter. He therefore took to agriculture and depended principally on mother earth for his food. Thus from being a nomad he settled down to civilized stable life, founded villages and towns, and from member of a family he became member of a community and a nation. All these are signs of progressive *ahiṃsā* and diminishing *hiṃsā*. Had it been otherwise, the human species should have been extinct by now, even as many of the lower species have disappeared.

Prophets and *avatārs* have also taught the lesson of *ahiṃsā* more or less. Not one of them has professed to teach *hiṃsā*. And how should it be otherwise? *Hiṃsā* does not need to be taught. Man as animal is violent, but as Spirit is nonviolent. The moment he awakes to the Spirit within, he cannot remain violent. Either he progresses towards *ahiṃsā* or rushes to his doom. That is why the prophets and *avatārs* have taught the lesson of truth, harmony, brotherhood, justice, etc.— all attributes of *ahiṃsā*. 7   *Harijan, August 11, 1940*

I claim that even now, though the social structure is not based on a conscious acceptance of nonviolence, all the world over mankind lives and men retain their possessions on the sufferance of one another. If they had not done so, only the fewest and the most ferocious would have survived. But such is not the case. Families are bound together by ties of love, and so are groups in the so-called civilized society called nations. Only they do not recognize the supremacy of the law of nonviolence. It follows, therefore, that they have not investigated its vast possibilities. Hitherto, out of sheer inertia, shall I say, we have taken it for granted that complete nonviolence is possible only for the few who take the vow of non-possession and the allied abstinences. Whilst it is true that the votaries alone can carry on research work and declare from time to time the new possibilities of the great eternal law governing man, if it is a law, it must hold good for all. The many failures we see are not of the law but of the followers, many of whom do not even know that they are under that law willy-nilly. When a mother dies for her child she unknowingly obeys the law. I have been pleading for the past fifty years for a conscious acceptance of the law and its zealous practice even in the face of failures. Fifty years' work has shown marvellous results and strengthened my faith. I do claim that by constant practice we shall come to a state of things when lawful possession will commend universal and voluntary respect. No doubt such possession will not be tainted. It will not be an insolent demonstration of the inequalities that surround us everywhere. Nor need the problem of unjust and unlawful possession appal the votary of nonviolence. He has at his disposal the nonviolent weapon of *Satyāgraha* and non-cooperation which hitherto has been found to be a complete substitute of violence whenever it has been applied honestly in sufficient measure. I have never claimed to present the complete science of nonviolence. It does not lend itself to such treatment. So far as I know, no single physical science does, not even the very exact science of mathematics. I am but a seeker. 8   *Harijan, February 22, 1942*

In the application of *Satyāgraha*, I discovered in the earliest stages that pursuit of truth did not admit of violence being inflicted on one's opponent but that he must be weaned from error by patience and sympathy. For, what appears to be truth to the one may appear to be error to another. And patience means self-suffering. So the doctrine came to mean vindication of truth, not by infliction of suffering on the opponent, but on one's self. *9*

Young India, November, 1919

In this age of wonders no one will say that a thing or idea is worthless because it is new. To say it is impossible because it is difficult, is again not in consonance with the spirit of the age. Things undreamt of are daily being seen, the impossible is ever becoming possible. We are constantly being astonished these days at the amazing discoveries in the field of violence. But I maintain that far more undreamt of and seemingly impossible discoveries will be made in the field of nonviolence. *10*   *Harijan, August 25, 1940*

Man and his deed are two distinct things. It is quite proper to resist and attack a system, but to resist and attack its author is tantamount to resisting and attacking oneself. For we are all tarred with the same brush, and are children of one and the same Creator, and as such the divine powers within us are infinite. To slight a single human being is to slight those divine powers, and thus to harm not only that being but with him the whole world. *11*   *An Autobiography*

Nonviolence is a universal principle and its operation is not limited by a hostile environment. Indeed, its efficacy can be tested only when it acts in the midst of and in spite of opposition. Our nonviolence would be a hollow thing and worth nothing, if it depended for its success on the goodwill of the authorities. *12*

Harijan, November 12, 1938

The only condition of a successful use of this force is a recognition of the existence of the soul as apart from the body and its permanent nature. And this recognition must amount to a living faith and not mere intellectual grasp. *13*   *Harijan, November 12, 1938*

Some friends have told me that truth and nonviolence have no place in politics and worldly affairs. I do not agree. I have no use for them as a means of individual salvation. Their introduction and application in everyday life has been my experiment all along. *14*

Harijan, November 12, 1938

Ahiṃsā or The Way of Nonviolence

No man could be actively nonviolent and not rise against social injustice no matter where it occurred. *15*   *Harijan, April 20, 1940*

Passive resistance is a method of securing rights by personal suffering; it is the reverse of resistance by arms. When I refuse to do a thing that is repugnant to my conscience, I use soul-force. For instance, the government of the day has passed a law which is applicable to me. I do not like it. If by using violence I force the government to repeal the law, I am employing what may be termed body-force. If I do not obey the law and accept the penalty for its breach, I use soul-force. It involves sacrifice of self.

Everybody admits that sacrifice of self is infinitely superior to sacrifice of others. Moreover, if this kind of force is used in a cause that is unjust, only the person using it suffers. He does not make others suffer for his mistakes. Men have before now done many things which were subsequently found to have been wrong. No man can claim that he is absolutely in the right or that a particular thing is wrong because he thinks so, but it is wrong for him so long as that is his deliberate judgement. It is therefore meet[1] that he should not do that which he knows to be wrong, and suffer the consequence whatever it may be. This is the key to the use of soul-force. *16*

Indian Home Rule, 1909

A·votary of *ahiṃsā* cannot subscribe to the utilitarian formula (of the greatest good of the greatest number). He will strive for the greatest good of all and die in the attempt to realize the ideal. He will therefore be willing to die, so that the others may live. He will serve himself with the rest, by himself dying. The greatest good of all inevitably includes the good of the greatest number, and, therefore, he and the utilitarian will converge in many points in their career but there does come a time when they must part company, and even work in opposite directions. The utilitarian to be logical will never sacrifice himself. The absolutist will even sacrifice himself. *17*

Young India, December 9, 1926

You might of course say that there can be no nonviolent rebellion and there has been none known to history. Well, it is my ambition to provide an instance, and it is my dream that my country may win its freedom through nonviolence. And, I would like to repeat to the world times without number, that I will not purchase my country's freedom at the cost of nonviolence. My marriage to nonviolence is such an absolute thing that I would rather commit suicide than be deflected from my position. I have not mentioned truth in this connexion, simply because truth cannot be expressed except by nonviolence. *18*   *Young India, November 12, 1931*

1. Archaic English, meaning in this context, "fit" or "suitable."

The accumulated experience of the past thirty years, the first eight of which were in South Africa, fills me with the greatest hope that in the adoption of nonviolence lies the future of India and the world. It is the most harmless and yet equally effective way of dealing with the political and economic wrongs of the down-trodden portion of humanity. I have known from early youth that nonviolence is not a cloistered virtue to be practised by the individual for the peace and final salvation, but it is a rule of conduct for society if it is to live consistently with human dignity and make progress towards the attainment of peace for which it has been yearning for ages past.   *19*
Gandhiji's Correspondence with the Government, 1942-44

Up to the year 1906, I simply relied on appeal to reason. I was a very industrious reformer. I was a good draftsman, as I always had a close grip of facts which in its turn was the necessary result of my meticulous regard for truth. But I found that reason failed to produce an impression when the critical moment arrived in South Africa. My people were excited; even a worm will and does sometimes turn — and there was talk of wreaking vengeance. I had then to choose between allying myself to violence or finding out some other method of meeting the crisis and stopping the rot and it came to me that we should refuse to obey legislation that was degrading and let them put us in jail if they liked. Thus came into being the moral equivalent of war. I was then a loyalist, because I implicitly believed that the sum total of the activities of the British Empire was good for India and for humanity. Arriving in England soon after the outbreak of the war I plunged into it and later when I was forced to go to India as a result of the pleurisy that I had developed, I led a recruiting campaign at the risk of my life, and to the horror of some of my friends. The disillusionment came in 1919 after the passage of the Black Rowlatt Act and the refusal of the government to give the simple elementary redress of proved wrongs that we had asked for. And so, in 1920, I became a rebel. Since then the conviction has been growing upon me, that things of fundamental importance to the people are not secured by reason alone but have to be purchased with their suffering. Suffering is the law of human beings; war is the law of the jungle. But suffering is infinitely more powerful than the law of the jungle for converting the opponent and opening his ears, which are otherwise shut, to the voice of reason. Nobody has probably drawn up more petitions or espoused more forlorn causes than I and I have come to this fundamental conclusion that if you want something really important to be done you must not merely satisfy the reason, you must move the heart also. The appeal of reason is more to the

1. Act depriving Indians of some fundamental civil liberties.

head but the penetration of the heart comes from suffering. It opens up the inner understanding in man. Suffering is the badge of the human race, not the sword.   *20*   *Young India, November 4, 1931*

Nonviolence is a power which can be wielded equally by all—children, young men and women or grown up people—provided they have a living faith in the God of Love and have therefore equal love for all mankind. When nonviolence is accepted as the law of life it must pervade the whole being and not be applied to isolated acts.   *21*

Harijan, September 5, 1936

If we are to be nonviolent, we must then not wish for anything on this earth which the meanest or the lowest of human beings cannot have.   *22*   *With Gandhiji in Ceylon, published in 1928*

The principle of nonviolence necessitates complete abstention from exploitation in any form.   *23*   *Harijan, November 11, 1939*

My resistance to war does not carry me to the point of thwarting those who wish to take part in it. I reason with them. I put before them the better way and leave them to make the choice.   *24*

Harijan, January 18, 1942

I would say to my critics to enter with me into the sufferings, not only of the people of India but of those, whether engaged in the war or not, of the whole world. I cannot look at this butchery going on in the world with indifference. I have an unchangeable faith that it is beneath the dignity of man to resort to mutual slaughter. I have no doubt that there is a way out.   *25*   *Hindustan Standard, July 20, 1944*

Perfect nonviolence is impossible so long as we exist physically, for we would want some space at least to occupy. Perfect nonviolence whilst you are inhabiting the body is only a theory like Euclid's point or straight line, but we have to endeavour every moment of our lives.   *26*   *Harijan, July 21, 1940*

Taking life may be a duty. We do destroy as much life as we think necessary for sustaining our body. Thus for food we take life, vegetable and other, and for health we destroy mosquitoes and the like by the use of disinfectants, etc., and we do not think that we are guilty of irreligion in doing so ... for the benefit of the species, we kill carnivorous beasts.... Even man-slaughter may be necessary in certain cases. Suppose a man runs amuck and goes furiously about, sword in hand, and killing anyone that comes in his way, and no one dares to capture him alive. Anyone who despatches this lunatic will

earn the gratitude of the community and be regarded as a benevolent
man. *27* *Young India, November 4, 1926*

I see that there is an instinctive horror of killing living beings under
any circumstances whatever. For instance, an alternative has been
suggested in the shape of confining even rabid dogs in a certain place
and allowing them to die a slow death. Now my idea of compassion
makes this thing impossible for me. I cannot for a moment bear to
see a dog, or for that matter any other living being, helplessly suffering the torture of a slow death. I do not kill a human being thus
circumstanced because I have more hopeful remedies. I should kill a
dog similarly situated because in its case I am without a remedy.
Should my child be attacked with rabies and there was no helpful
remedy to relieve his agony, I should consider it my duty to take his
life. Fatalism has its limits. We leave things to fate after exhausting
all the remedies. One of the remedies and the final one to relieve the
agony of a tortured child is to take his life. *28*
Young India, November 18, 1926

In its positive form, *ahiṃsā* means the largest love, greatest charity. If
I am a follower of *ahiṃsā*, I *must love* my enemy. I must apply the
same rules to the wrong-doer who is my enemy or a stranger to me,
as I would to my wrong-doing father or son. This active *ahiṃsā*
necessarily includes truth and fearlessness. As man cannot deceive the
loved one, he does not fear or frighten him or her. Gift of life is the
greatest of all gifts; a man who gives it in reality, disarms all hostility.
He has paved the way for an honourable understanding. And none
who is himself subject to fear can bestow that gift. He must therefore
be fearless. A man cannot practise *ahiṃsā* and be a coward at the
same time. The practice of *ahiṃsā* calls forth the greatest courage.
29 *Speeches and Writings of Mahatma Gandhi, no date given.*

Having flung aside the sword, there is nothing except the cup of love
which I can offer to those who oppose me. It is by offering that cup
that I expect to draw them close to me. I cannot think of permanent
enmity between man and man, and believing as I do in the theory of
rebirth, I live in the hope that if not in this birth, in some other
birth, I shall be able to hug all humanity in friendly embrace. *30*
Young India, April 2, 1931

Love is the strongest force the world possesses and yet it is the
humblest imaginable. *31* *Young India, August 6, 1925*

The hardest heart and the grossest ignorance must disappear before

Informal talk between Gandhi and some of his friends
(Henri Cartier-Bresson, Magnum)

the rising sun of suffering without anger and without malice. *32*

Nonviolence is 'not a resignation from all real fighting against wickedness.' On the contrary, the nonviolence of my conception is a more active and real fight against wickedness than retaliation whose very nature is to increase wickedness. I contemplate a mental and therefore a moral opposition to immoralities. I seek entirely to blunt the edge of the tyrant's sword, not by putting up against it a sharper-edged weapon, but by disappointing his expectation that I would be offering physical resistance. The resistance of the soul that I should offer would elude him. It would at first dazzle him and at last compel recognition from him, which recognition would not humiliate but would uplift him. It may be urged that this is an ideal state. And so it is. *33* *Young India, October 8, 1925*

Ahiṃsā is a comprehensive principle. We are helpless mortals caught in the conflagration of *hiṃsā*. The saying that life lives on life has a deep meaning in it. Man cannot for a moment live without consciously or unconsciously committing outward *hiṃsā*. The very fact of his living—eating, drinking and moving about—necessarily involves some *hiṃsā*, destruction of life, be it ever so minute. A votary of *ahiṃsā* therefore remains true to his faith if the spring of all his actions is compassion, if he shuns to the best of his ability the destruction of the tiniest creature, tries to save it, and thus incessantly strives to be free from the deadly coil of *hiṃsā*. He will be constantly growing in self-restraint and compassion, but he can never become entirely free from outward *hiṃsā*.

Then again, because underlying *ahiṃsā* is the unity of all life, the error of one cannot but affect all, and hence man cannot be wholly free from *hiṃsā*. So long as he continues to be a social being, he cannot but participate in the *hiṃsā* that the very existence involves. When two nations are fighting, the duty of a votary of *ahiṃsā* is to stop the war. He who is not equal to that duty, he who has no power of resisting war, he who is not qualified to resist war, may take part in war, and yet wholeheartedly try to free himself, his nation and the world from war. *34* *An Autobiography*

I make no distinction, from the point of view of *ahiṃsā* between combatants and non-combatants. He who volunteers to serve a band of dacoits [murderous robbers], by working as their carrier, or their watchman while they are about their business, or their nurse when they are wounded, is as much guilty of dacoity as the dacoits themselves. In the same way those who confine themselves to attending to the wounded in battle cannot be absolved from the guilt of war. *35* *An Autobiography*

The question is subtle. It admits of differences of opinion, and therefore I have submitted my argument as clearly as possible to those who believe in *ahiṃsā* and who are making serious efforts to practise it in every walk of life. A devotee of Truth may not do anything in deference to convention. He must always hold himself open to correction, and whenever he discovers himself to be wrong he must confess it at all costs and atone for it. *36*   *An Autobiography*

Nonviolence to be a potent force must begin with the mind. Nonviolence of the mere body without the cooperation of the mind is nonviolence of the weak or the cowardly, and has therefore no potency. If we bear malice and hatred in our bosoms and pretend not to retaliate, it must recoil upon us and lead to our destruction. For abstention from mere bodily violence not to be injurious, it is at least necessary not to entertain hatred if we cannot generate active love.
37   *Young India, April 2, 1931*

He is no follower of *ahiṃsā* who does not care a straw if he kills a man by inches by deceiving him in a trade or who would protect by force of arms a few cows and make away with the butcher or who, in order to do a supposed good to his country, does not mind killing off a few officials. All these are actuated by hatred, cowardice and fear. *38*   *Modern Review, pre-1921*

I object to violence because when it appears to do good, the good is only temporary; the evil it does is permanent. I do not believe that the killing of even every Englishman can do the slightest good to India. The millions will be just as badly off as they are today, if someone made it possible to kill off every Englishman tomorrow. The responsibility is more ours than that of the English for the present state of things. The English will be powerless to do evil if we will but be good. Hence my incessant emphasis on reform from within. *39*
Young India, May 21, 1925

History teaches one that those who have, no doubt with honest motives, ousted the greedy by using brute force against them, have in their turn become a prey to the disease of the conquered. *40*
Young India, May 6, 1926

From violence done to the foreign ruler, violence to our own people whom we may consider to be obstructing the country's progress is an easy natural step. Whatever may have been the result of violent activities in other countries and without reference to the philosophy of nonviolence, it does not require much intellectual effort to see that if we resort to violence for ridding society of many abuses which impede our progress, we shall add to our difficulties and postpone the day of freedom. The people unprepared for reforms because unconvinced of their necessity will be maddened with rage over their coercion, and will seek the assistance of the foreigner in order to retaliate. Has not this been happening before our eyes for the past many years of which we have still painfully vivid recollections? *41*

Young India, January 2, 1930

If I can have nothing to do with the organized violence of the government, I can have less to do with the unorganized violence of the people. I would prefer to be crushed between the two. *42*

Young India, November 24, 1921

I have been practising with scientific precision nonviolence and its possibilities for an unbroken period of over fifty years. I have applied it in every walk of life—domestic, institutional, economic and political. I know of no single case in which it has failed. Where it has seemed sometimes to have failed, I have ascribed it to my imperfections. I claim no perfection for myself. But I do claim to be a passionate seeker after Truth, which is but another name for God. In the course of that search the discovery of nonviolence came to me. Its spread is my life mission. I have no interest in living except for the prosecution of that mission. *43*   *Harijan, July 6, 1940*

It is to me a matter of perennial satisfaction that I retain generally the affection and trust of those whose principles and policies I oppose. The South Africans gave me personally their confidence and extended their friendship. In spite of my denunciation of British policy and system I enjoy the affection of thousands of Englishmen and women, and in spite of unqualified condemnation of modern materialistic civilization, the circle of European and American friends is ever widening. It is again a triumph of nonviolence. *44*

Young India, March 17, 1927

My experience, daily growing stronger and richer, tells me that there is no peace for individuals or for nations without practising truth and nonviolence to the uttermost extent possible for man. The policy of retaliation has never succeeded. *45*   *Young India, December 15, 1927*

My love for nonviolence is superior to every other thing mundane or supramundane. It is equalled only by my love for truth which is to me synonymous with nonviolence through which and which alone I can see and reach Truth. My scheme of life, if it draws no distinction between different religionists in India, also draws none between

different races. For me 'A man's a man for a' that.' *46*
Young India, February 20, 1930

I am but a weak aspirant, ever failing, ever trying. My failures make me more vigilant than before and intensify my faith. I can see with the eye of faith that the observance of the twin doctrine of truth and nonviolence has possibilities of which we have but very inadequate conception. *47*   *The Mind of Mahatma Gandhi*

I am an irrepressible optimist. My optimism rests on my belief in the infinite possibilities of the individual to develop nonviolence. The more you develop it in your own being, the more infectious it becomes till it overwhelms your surroundings and by and by might oversweep the world. *48*   *Harijan, January 28, 1939*

In my opinion nonviolence is not passivity in any shape or form. Nonviolence, as I understand it, is the most active force in the world. . . . Nonviolence is the supreme law. During my half a century of experience I have not yet come across a situation when I had to say that I was helpless, that I had no remedy in terms of nonviolence. *49*   *Harijan, December 24, 1935*

It is the acid test of nonviolence that in a nonviolent conflict there is no rancour left behind, and in the end the enemies are converted into friends. That was my experience in South Africa with General Smuts. He started with being my bitterest opponent and critic. Today he is my warmest friend. *50*   *Harijan, November 12, 1938*

The strength to kill is not essential for self-defence; one ought to have the strength to die. When a man is fully ready to die, he will not even desire to offer violence. Indeed, I may put it down as a self-evident proposition that the desire to kill is in inverse proportion to the desire to die. And history is replete with instances of men who by dying with courage and compassion on their lips converted the hearts of their violent opponents. *51*   *Young India, January 21, 1930*

I am but a humble explorer of the science of nonviolence. Its hidden depths sometimes stagger me just as much as they stagger fellow-workers. *52*   *Young India, November 20, 1924*

It has become the fashion these days to say that society cannot be organized or run on nonviolent lines. I join issue on that point. In a family, when a father slaps his delinquent child, the latter does not think of retaliating. He obeys his father not because of the deterrent effect of the slap but because of the offended love which he senses behind it. That, in my opinion, is an epitome of the way in which society is or should be governed. What is true of the family must be true of society which is but a larger family. *53*

Harijan, December 3, 1938

I do not want to live at the cost of the life even of a snake. I should let him bite me to death rather than kill him. But it is likely that if God puts me to that cruel test and permits a snake to assault me, I may not have the courage to die, but that the beast in me may assert itself and I may seek to kill the snake in defending this perishable body. I admit that my belief has not become so incarnate in me as to warrant my stating emphatically that I have shed all fear of snakes so as to befriend them as I would like to be able to. *54*

An Autobiography

I am not opposed to the progress of science as such. On the contrary, the scientific spirit of the West commands my admiration and if that admiration is qualified, it is because the scientist of the West takes no note of God's lower creation. I abhor vivisection with my whole soul. I detest the unpardonable slaughter of innocent life in the name of science and humanity so-called, and all the scientific discoveries stained with innocent blood I count as of no consequence. If the circulation of blood theory could not have been discovered without vivisection, the human kind could well have done without it. And I see the day clearly dawning when the honest scientist of the West will put limitations upon the present methods of pursuing knowledge. *55*

Young India, December 17, 1925

Nonviolence is not an easy thing to understand, still less to practise, weak as we are. We must all act prayerfully and humbly and continually asking God to open the eyes of our understanding being ever ready to act according to the light as we daily receive it. My task as a lover and promoter of peace, therefore, today consists in unflinching devotion to nonviolence in the prosecution of the campaign for regaining our liberty. And if India succeeds in so regaining it, it will be the greatest contribution to the world peace. *56*

Young India, February 7, 1929

Passive resistance is an all-sided sword; it can be used anyhow; it blesses him who uses it and him against whom it is used. Without drawing a drop of blood it produces far-reaching results. It never rusts and cannot be stolen. *57 Hind Swaraj or Indian Home Rule, 1909*

Disobedience to be civil must be sincere, respectful, restrained, never defiant, must be based upon some well-understood principle, must

not be capricious and above all, must have no ill-will or hatred behind it. *58*   *Young India, March 24, 1920*

Jesus Christ, Daniel and Socrates represented the purest form of passive resistance or soul-force. All these teachers counted their bodies as
nothing in comparison to their soul. Tolstoy was the best and bright-
est (modern) exponent of the doctrine. He not only expounded it,
but lived according to it. In India, the doctrine was understood and
commonly practised long before it came into vogue in Europe. It is
easy to see that soul-force is infinitely superior to body-force. If
people in order to secure redress of wrongs resort to soul-force, much
of the present suffering will be avoided. *59*

Speeches and Writings of Mahatma Gandhi, 1933

Buddha fearlessly carried the war into the enemy's camp and brought
down on its knees an arrogant priesthood. Christ drove out the mon-
eychangers from the temple of Jerusalem and drew down curses from
Heaven upon the hypocrites and the Pharisees. Both were for intensely direct action. But even as Buddha and Christ chastised, they
showed unmistakable gentleness and love behind every act of theirs.
They would not raise a finger against their enemies, but would gladly
surrender themselves rather than the truth for which they lived.
Buddha would have died resisting the priesthood, if the majesty of
his love had not proved to be equal to the task of bending the
priesthood. Christ died on the cross with a crown of thorns on his
head defying the might of a whole empire. And if I raise resistances
of a nonviolent character, I simply and humbly follow in the foot-
steps of the great teachers. *60*   *Young India, May 12, 1920*

It is a law of *Satyāgraha* that when a man has no weapon in his
hands and when he cannot think of a way out, he should take the
final step of giving up his body. *61*   *Bapu's Letters to Mira*

Ahimsā is soul-force and the soul is imperishable, changeless and eternal. The atom bomb is the acme of physical force and, as such,
subject to the law of dissipation, decay and death that governs the
physical universe. Our scriptures bear witness that when soul-force is
fully awakened in us, it becomes irresistible. But the test and condition of full awakening is that it must permeate every pore of our
being and emanate with every breath that we breathe.

But no institution can be made nonviolent by compulsion. Nonviolence and truth cannot be written into a constitution. They have to
be adopted of one's own free will. They must sit naturally upon us
like next-to-skin garments or else they become a contradiction in
terms. *62*   *Mahatma Gandhi, The Last Phase, II, circa, 1947*

Ahiṃsā or The Way of Nonviolence

Life is an aspiration. Its mission is to strive after perfection, which is self-realization. The ideal must not be lowered because of our weaknesses and imperfections. . . . One who hooks his fortunes to *ahiṃsā*, the law of love, daily lessens the circle of destruction, and to that extent promotes life and love; he who swears by *hiṃsā*, the law of hate, daily widens the circle of destruction, and to that extent promotes death and hate. *63*   *Harijan, June 22, 1935*

In life, it is impossible to eschew violence completely. Now the question arises, where is one to draw the line? The line cannot be the same for every one. For, although, essentially the principle is the same, yet everyone applies it in his or her own way. What is one man's food can be another's poison. Meat-eating is a sin for me. Yet, for another person, who has always lived on meat and never seen anything wrong in it, to give it up, simply in order to copy me, will be a sin.

If I wish to be an agriculturist and stay in a jungle, I will have to use the minimum unavoidable violence, in order to protect my fields. I will have to kill monkeys, birds and insects, which eat up my crops. If I do not wish to do so myself, I will have to engage someone to do it for me. There is not much difference between the two. To allow crops to be eaten up by animals, in the name of *ahiṃsā*, while there is a famine in the land, is certainly a sin. Evil and good are relative terms. What is good under certain conditions can become an evil or a sin, under a different set of conditions.

Man is not to drown himself in the well of the *shāstras*, but he is to dive in their broad ocean and bring out pearls. At every step he has to use his discrimination as to what is *ahiṃsā* and what is *hiṃsā*. In this, there is no room for shame or cowardice. The poet had said that the road leading up to God is for the brave, never for the cowardly. *64*   *Mahatma, VII, 1946*

To say or write a distasteful word is surely not violent especially when the speaker or writer believes it to be true. The essence of violence is that there must be a violent intention behind a thought, word, or act, i.e., an intention to do harm to the opponent so-called.

False notions of propriety or fear of wounding susceptibilities often deter people from saying what they mean and ultimately land them on the shores of hypocrisy. But if nonviolence of thought is to be evolved in individuals or societies or nations, truth has to be told, however harsh or unpopular it may appear to be for the moment. *65*   *Harijan, December 19, 1936*

Never has anything been done on this earth without direct action. I reject the word 'passive resistance' because of its insufficiency and its being interpreted as a weapon of the weak. *66*

Young India, May 12, 1920

Nonviolence presupposes ability to strike. It is a conscious, deliberate restraint put upon one's desire for vengeance. But vengeance is any day superior to passive, effeminate and helpless submission. Forgiveness is higher still. Vengeance too is weakness. The desire for vengeance comes out of fear of harm, imaginary or real. A man who fears no one on earth would consider it troublesome even to summon up anger against one who is vainly trying to injure him. *67*

Young India, August 12, 1926

Nonviolence and cowardice go ill together. I can imagine a fully armed man to be at heart a coward. Possession of arms implies an element of fear, if not cowardice. But true nonviolence is an impossibility without the possession of unadulterated fearlessness. *68*

Harijan, July 15, 1939

My creed of nonviolence is an extremely active force. It has no room for cowardice or even weakness. There is hope for a violent man to be some day nonviolent, but there is none for a coward. I have therefore said more than once in these pages that if we do not know how to defend ourselves, our women and our places of worship by the force of suffering, i.e., nonviolence, we must, if we are men, be at least able to defend all these by fighting. *69*

Young India, June 16, 1927

The people of a village near Bettia told me that they had run away whilst the police were looting their houses and molesting their womenfolk. When they said that they had run away because I had told them to be nonviolent, I hung my head in shame. I assured them that such was not the meaning of my nonviolence. I expected them to intercept the mightiest power that might be in the act of harming those who were under their protection, and draw without retaliation all harm upon their own heads even to the point of death, but never to run away from the storm centre. It was manly enough to defend one's property, honour, or religion at the point of the sword. It was manlier and nobler to defend them without seeking to injure the wrong-doer. But it was unmanly, unnatural and dishonourable to forsake the post of duty and, in order to save one's skin, to leave property, honour or religion to the mercy of the wrong-doer. I could see my way of delivering *ahiṃsā* to those who knew how to die, not to those who were afraid of death. *70*

Gandhiji in Indian Villages, published in 1927

Ahiṃsā or The Way of Nonviolence

I would risk violence a thousand times than the emasculation of a whole race. *71*   *Young India, August 4, 1920*

My nonviolence does not admit of running away from danger and leaving dear ones unprotected. Between violence and cowardly flight, I can only prefer violence to cowardice. I can no more preach nonviolence to a coward than I can tempt a blind man to enjoy healthy scenes. Nonviolence is the summit of bravery. And in my own experience, I have had no difficulty in demonstrating to men trained in the school of violence the superiority of nonviolence. As a coward, which I was for years, I harboured violence. I began to prize nonviolence only when I began to shed cowardice. *72*   *Young India, May 28, 1924*

Nonviolence cannot be taught to a person who fears to die and has no power of resistance. A helpless mouse is not nonviolent because he is always eaten by pussy. He would gladly eat the murderess if he could, but he ever tries to flee from her. We do not call him a coward, because he is made by nature to behave no better than he does. But a man who, when faced by danger, behaves like a mouse, is rightly called a coward. He harbours violence and hatred in his heart and would kill his enemy if he could without hurting himself. He is a stranger to nonviolence. All sermonizing on it will be lost on him. Bravery is foreign to his nature. Before he can understand nonviolence he has to be taught to stand his ground and even suffer death, in the attempt to defend himself against the aggressor who bids fair to overwhelm him. To do otherwise would be to confirm his cowardice and take him farther away from nonviolence. Whilst I may not actually help anyone to retaliate, I must not let a coward seek shelter behind nonviolence so-called. Not knowing the stuff of which nonviolence is made, many have honestly believed that running away from danger every time was a virtue compared to offering resistance, especially when it was fraught with danger to one's life. As a teacher of nonviolence I must, so far as it is possible for me, guard against such an unmanly belief. *73*   *Harijan, July 20, 1935*

No matter how weak a person is in body, if it is a shame to flee, he will stand his ground and die at his post. This would be nonviolence and bravery. No matter how weak he is, he will use what strength he has in inflicting injury on his opponent, and die in the attempt. This is bravery, but not nonviolence. If, when his duty is to face danger, he flees, it is cowardice. In the first case the man will have love or charity in him. In the second and third case, there would be a dislike or distrust and fear. *74*   *Harijan, August 17, 1935*

Supposing I was a Negro, and my sister was ravished by a white or lynched by a whole community, what would be my duty? I ask myself. And the answer comes to me: I must not wish ill to these, but neither must I co-operate with them. It may be that ordinarily I depend on the lynching community for my livelihood. I refuse to co-operate with them, refuse even to touch the food that comes from them, and I refuse to co-operate with even my brother Negroes who tolerate the wrong. That is the self-immolation I mean. I have often in my life resorted to the plan. Of course, a mechanical act of starvation will mean nothing. One's faith must remain undimmed whilst life ebbs out, minute by minute. But I am a very poor specimen of the practice of nonviolence, and my answer may not convince you. But I am striving very hard, and even if I do not succeed fully in this life, my faith will not diminish. *75*   *Mahatma, IV, 1936*

In this age of the rule of brute force, it is almost impossible for anyone to believe that anyone else could possibly reject the law of the final supremacy of brute force. And so I receive anonymous letters advising me that I must not interfere with the progress of the non-co-operation movement even though popular violence may break out. Others come to me and, assuming that secretly I must be plotting violence, inquire when the happy moment for declaring open violence is to arrive. They assure me that the English will never yield to anything but violence, secret or open. Yet others, I am informed, believe that I am the most rascally person living in India because I never give out my real intention and that they have not a shadow of a doubt that I believe in violence just as much as most people do.

Such being the hold that the doctrine of the sword has on the majority of mankind, and as success of non-cooperation depends principally on absence of violence during its pendency, and as my views in this matter affect the conduct of a large number of people, I am anxious to state them as clearly as possible.

I do believe that, where there is only a choice between cowardice and violence, I would advise violence. Thus when my eldest son asked me what he should have done, had he been present when I was almost fatally assaulted in 1908, whether he should have run away and seen me killed or whether he should have used his physical force which he could and wanted to use, and defend me, I told him that it was his duty to defend me even by using violence. Hence it was that I took part in the Boer War, the so-called Zulu Rebellion and the late war. Hence also do I advocate training in arms for those who believe in the method of violence. I would rather have India resort to arms in order to defend her honour than that she should in a cowardly manner become or remain a helpless witness to her own dishonour.

But I believe that nonviolence is infinitely superior to violence, forgiveness is more manly than punishment. Forgiveness adorns a soldier. But abstinence is forgiveness only when there is the power to punish; it is meaningless when it pretends to proceed from a helpless creature. A mouse hardly forgives a cat when it allows itself to be torn to pieces by her. I, therefore, appreciate the sentiment of those who cry out for the condign punishment of General Dyer and his ilk. They would tear him to pieces if they could. But I do not believe India to be a helpless creature. Only I want to use India's and my strength for a better purpose.

Let me not be misunderstood. Strength does not come from physical capacity. It comes from an indomitable will. An average Zulu is anyway more than a match for an average Englishman in bodily capacity. But he flees from an English boy, because he fears the boy's revolver or those who will use it for him. He fears death and is nerveless in spite of his burly figure. We in India may in a moment realize that one hundred thousand Englishmen need not frighten three hundred million human beings. A definite forgiveness would, therefore, mean a definite recognition of our strength. With enlightened forgiveness must come a mighty wave of strength in us, which would make it impossible for a Dyer and a Frank Johnson to heap affront on India's devoted head. It matters little to me that for the moment I do not drive my point home. We feel too downtrodden not to be angry and revengeful. But I must not refrain from saying that India can gain more by waiving the right of punishment. We have better work to do, a better mission to deliver to the world.

I am not a visionary. I claim to be a practical idealist. Religion of nonviolence is not meant merely for the *rishis* and saints. It is meant for the common people as well. Nonviolence is the law of our species as violence is the law of the brute. The spirit lies dormant in the brute, and he knows no law but that of physical might. The dignity of man requires obedience to a higher law, to the strength of the spirit.

I have ventured to place before India the ancient law of self-sacrifice. For *Satyāgraha* and its offshoots, non-co-operation and civil resistance, are nothing but new names for the law of suffering. The *rishis*, who discovered the law of nonviolence in the midst of violence, were greater geniuses than Newton. They were themselves greater warriors than Wellington. Having themselves known the use of arms, they realized their uselessness and taught a weary world that its salvation lay not through violence but through nonviolence.

Nonviolence in its dynamic condition means conscious suffering. It does not mean meek submission to the will of the evil-doer, but it means putting of one's whole soul against the will of the tyrant. Working under this law of our being, it is possible for a single individual to defy the whole might of an unjust empire to save his honour, his religion, his soul, and lay the foundation for that empire's fall or its regeneration.

And so I am not pleading for India to practise nonviolence because it is weak. I want her to practise nonviolence being conscious of her strength and power. No training in arms is required for realization of her strength. We seem to need it, because we seem to think that we are but a lump of flesh. I want to recognize that she has a soul that cannot perish and that can rise triumphant above every physical weakness and defy the physical combination of a whole world. . . . If India takes up the doctrine of the sword, she may gain momentary victory. Then India will cease to be the pride of my heart. I am wedded to India because I owe my all to her. I believe absolutely that she has a mission for the world. She is not to copy Europe blindly. India's acceptance of the doctrine of the sword will be the hour of my trial. I hope I shall not be found wanting. My religion has no geographical limits. If I have a living faith in it, it will transcend my love for India herself. My life is dedicated to the service of India through the religion of nonviolence which I believe to be the root of Hinduism. *76*

Mahatma, II, Young India, August 11, 1920

I must continue to argue till I convert opponents or I own defeat. For my mission is to convert every Indian, even Englishmen and finally the world, to nonviolence for regulating mutual relations whether political, economic, social or religious. If I am accused of being too ambitious, I should plead guilty. If I am told that my dream can never materialize, I would answer 'that is possible,' and go my way. I am a seasoned soldier of nonviolence, and I have evidence enough to sustain my faith. Whether, therefore, I have one comrade or more or none, I must continue my experiment. *77*

Mahatma, V, Harijan, January 13, 1940

It has been suggested by American friends that the atom bomb will bring in *ahiṃsā*, as nothing else can. It will, if it is meant that its destructive power will so disgust the world, that it will turn it away from violence for the time being. And this is very like a man glutting himself with the dainties to the point of nausea, and turning away from them only to return with redoubled zeal after the effect of nausea is well over. Precisely in the same manner will the world return to violence with renewed zeal, after the effect of disgust is worn out.

Often does good come out of evil. But that is God's, not man's plan. Man knows that only evil can come out of evil, as good out of good. . . . The moral to be legitimately drawn from the supreme tragedy of the atom bomb is that it will not be destroyed by counter bombs, even as violence cannot be by counter violence. Mankind has to go out of violence only through nonviolence. Hatred can be overcome only by love. Counter hatred only increases the surface, as well as the depth of hatred.

I am aware that I am repeating what I have many times stated before and practised to the best of my ability and capacity. What I first stated was itself nothing new. It was as old as the hills. Only I recited no copy-book maxim but definitely announced what I believed in every fibre of my being. Sixty years of practice in various walks of life has only enriched the belief which the experience of friends fortified. It is, however, the central truth by which one can stand alone without flinching. I believe in what Max Muller said years ago, namely, that truth needed to be repeated, as long as there were men who disbelieved it. *78*   *Mahatma, VII, Harijan, July 1946*

If India makes violence her creed, and I have survived, I would not care to live in India. She will cease to evoke any pride in me. My patriotism is subservient to my religion. I cling to India like a child to its mother's breast, because I feel that she gives me the spiritual nourishment I need. She has the environment that responds to my highest aspiration. When that faith is gone, I shall feel like an orphan without hope of ever finding a guardian. *79*

Young India, April 6, 1921

V SELF-DISCIPLINE

Civilization, in the real sense of the term, consists not in the multiplication but in the deliberate and voluntary restriction of wants. This alone promotes real happiness and contentment, and increases the capacity for service. *1*   *Yerarda Maudir, 1935*

A certain degree of physical harmony and comfort is necessary, but above that level, it becomes a hindrance instead of a help. Therefore the ideal of creating an unlimited number of wants and satisfying them seems to be a delusion and a snare. The satisfaction of one's physical needs, even the intellectual needs of one's narrow self, must meet at a point a dead stop before it degenerates into physical and intellectual voluptuousness. A man must arrange his physical and cultural circumstances so that they may not hinder him in his service of humanity, on which all his energies should be concentrated. *2*
Harijan, August 29, 1936

The relation between the body and the mind is so intimate that, if either of them got out of order, the whole system would suffer. Hence it follows that a pure character is the foundation of health in the real sense of the term; and we may say that all evil thoughts and evil passions are but different forms of disease. *3*
Guide to Health, 1930

Perfect health can be attained only by living in obedience to the laws of God, and defying the power of Satan. True happiness is impossible without true health and true health is impossible without a rigid control of the palate. All the other senses will automatically come under control when the palate has been brought under control. And he who has conquered his senses has really conquered the whole world, and he becomes a part of God. *4*   *Guide to Health, 1930*

I have taken up journalism not for its sake but merely as an aid to what I have conceived to be my mission in life. My mission is to teach by example and precept under severe restraint the use of the matchless weapon of *Satyāgraha* which is a direct corollary of nonviolence and truth. I am anxious, indeed I am impatient, to demonstrate that there is no remedy for the many ills of life save that of nonviolence. It is a solvent strong enough to melt the stoniest heart. To be true to my faith, therefore, I may not write in anger or malice. I may not write idly. I may not write merely to excite passion. The reader can have no idea of the restraint I have to exercise from week to week in the choice of topics and my vocabulary. It is a training for me. It enables me to peep into myself and to make discoveries of my weaknesses. Often my vanity dictates a smart expression or my anger a harsh adjective. It is a terrible ordeal but a fine exercise to remove these weeds. The reader sees the pages of the *Young India* fairly well-dressed-up and sometimes, with Romain Rolland, he is inclined to say 'what a fine old man this must be!' Well, let the world understand that the fineness is carefully and prayerfully cultivated. And, if it has proved acceptable to some whose opinion I cherish, let the reader understand that when that fineness has become perfectly natural, i.e., when I have become incapable of evil and when nothing harsh or haughty occupies, be it momentarily, my thought-world, then and not till then, my nonviolence will move all the hearts of all the world. I have placed before me and the reader no impossible ideal or ordeal. It is man's prerogative and birth-right. We have lost the paradise only to regain it. *5*   *Young India, July 2, 1925*

I have learnt through bitter experience the one supreme lesson to conserve my anger, and as heat conserved is transmuted into energy, even so our anger controlled can be transmuted into a power which can move the world. *6*   *Young India, September 15, 1920*

It is not that I do not get angry. I don't give vent to my anger. I cultivate the quality of patience as angerlessness, and generally speaking, I succeed. But I only control my anger when it comes. How I find it possible to control it would be a useless question, for it is a habit that everyone must cultivate and must succeed in forming by constant practice. *7*   *Harijan, May 11, 1935*

It is wrong and immoral to seek to escape the consequences of one's acts. It is good for a person who over-eats to have an ache and a fast. It is bad for him to indulge his appetite and then escape the consequences by taking tonics or other medicine. It is still worse for a person to indulge in his animal passions and escape the consequences of his acts. Nature is relentless and will have full revenge for any such violation of her laws. Moral results can only be produced by moral restraints. All other restraints defeat the very purpose for which they are intended. *8*   *The Diary of Mahadev Desai*

It is not for us to find fault with anyone else and sit in judgement over him. We should be exhausted judging ourselves only, and so long as we notice a single fault in ourselves and wish our relations and friends not to forsake us in spite of such fault, we have no right to poke our nose into other people's conduct. If in spite of ourselves we notice another's fault, we should ask him himself if we have the power and think it proper to do so, but we have no right to ask anybody else. *9*   *The Diary of Mahadev Desai*

Do not brood over the passions. When you have once come to a decision, do not be reconsidering it. Taking a vow implies that the mind ceases to think on the subject of that vow any longer. When a merchant has sold some goods, he thinks no more about them, but only about other things. The same is the case with the subject-matter of a vow. *10*   *The Diary of Mahadev Desai*

You will wish to know what the marks of a man are who wants to realize Truth which is God. He must be completely free from anger and lust, greed and attachment, pride and fear. He must reduce himself to zero and have perfect control over all his senses—beginning with the palate or tongue. Tongue is the organ of speech as well as of taste. It is with the tongue that we indulge in exaggeration, untruth and speech that hurts. The craving for taste makes us slaves to the palate so that like animals we live to eat. But with proper discipline, we can make ourselves into beings only a 'little below the angels.' He who has mastered his senses is first and foremost among men. All virtues reside in him. God manifests Himself through him. Such is the power of self-discipline. *11*   *In conversation, June, 1947*

All universal rules of conduct known as God's commandments are simple and easy to understand and to carry out, if the will is there. They only appear to be difficult because of the inertia which governs mankind. There is nothing at a standstill in nature. Only God is motionless for He was, is and will be the same yesterday, today and tomorrow, and yet is ever moving. . . . Hence I hold that if mankind is to live, it has to come increasingly under sway of truth and nonviolence. *12*   *Speech, October 30, 1947*

Self-discipline

Just as for conducting scientific experiments there is an indispensable scientific course of instruction, in the same way, strict preliminary discipline is necessary to qualify a person to make experiments in the spiritual realm. *13* *Young India, December 31, 1931*

Abstemiousness from intoxicating drinks and drugs, and from all kinds of foods, especially meat, is undoubtedly a great aid to the evolution of the spirit, but it is by no means an end in itself. Many a man eating meat and living in the fear of God is nearer his freedom than a man religiously abstaining from meat and many other things, but blaspheming God in every one of his acts. *14*
Young India, October 6, 1921

Experience teaches that animal food is unsuited to those who would curb their passions. But it is wrong to over-estimate the importance of food in the formation of character or in subjugating the flesh. Diet is a powerful factor not to be neglected. But to sum up all religion in terms of diet, as is often done in India, is as wrong as it is to disregard all restraint in regard to diet and to give full reins to one's appetite. *15* *Young India, October 7, 1926*

Experience has taught me that silence is a part of the spiritual discipline of a votary of truth. Proneness to exaggerate, to suppress or modify the truth, wittingly or unwittingly, is a natural weakness of man, and silence is necessary in order to surmount it. A man of few words will rarely be thoughtless in his speech; he will measure every word. *16* *An Autobiography*

It [silence] has now become both a physical and spiritual necessity for me. Originally it was taken to relieve the sense of pressure. Then I wanted time for writing. After, however, I had practised it for some time, I saw the spiritual value of it. It suddenly flashed across my mind that that was the time when I could best hold communion with God. And now I feel as though I was naturally built for silence. *17* *Harijan, December 10, 1938*

Silence of the sewn-up lips is no silence. One may achieve the same result by chopping off one's tongue, but that too would not be silence. He is silent who, having the capacity to speak, utters no idle word. *18* *Harijan, June 24, 1933*

All power comes from the preservation of and sublimation of the vitality that is responsible for the creation of life. This vitality is continuously and even unconsciously dissipated by evil or even rambling, disorderly, unwanted thoughts. And since thought is the root of all speech and action, the quality of the latter corresponds to that of the former. Hence perfectly controlled thought is itself power of the highest potency and becomes self-acting. . . . If man is after the image of God, he has but to will a thing in the limited sphere allotted to him and it becomes. Such power is impossible in one who dissipates his energy in any way whatsoever. *19   Harijan, July 23, 1938*

It is better to enjoy through the body than to be enjoying the thought of it. It is good to disapprove of sensual desires as soon as they arise in the mind and try to keep them down; but if, for want of physical enjoyment, the mind wallows in thoughts of enjoyment, then it is legitimate to satisfy the hunger of the body. About this I have no doubt. *20   Hindi Navajivan, May 9, 1929*

Sex urge is a fine and noble thing. There is nothing to be ashamed of in it. But it is meant only for the act of creation. Any other use of it is a sin against God and humanity. *21   Harijan, March 28, 1936*

The world seems to be running after things of transitory value. It has no time for the other. And yet, when one thinks a little deeper, it becomes clear that it is the things eternal that count in the end. . . . One such is *brahmacharya.*

What is *brahmacharya?* It is the way of life which leads us to Brahma—God. It includes full control over the process of reproduction. The control must be in thought, word and deed. If the thought is not under control, the other two have no value. . . . For one whose thought is under control, the other is mere child's play. *22*
Harijan, June 8, 1947

It is true that he who has attained perfect *brahmacharya* does not stand in need of protecting walls. But the aspirant undoubtedly needs them, even as a young mango plant has need of a strong fence round it. A child goes from its mother's lap to the cradle and from cradle to the push-cart—till he becomes a man who has learnt to walk without aid. To cling to the aid when it is needless is surely harmful.

It appears to me that even the true aspirant does not need the above-mentioned restraints. *Brahmacharya* is not a virtue that can be cultivated by outward restraints. He who runs away from a necessary contact with a woman does not understand the full meaning of *brahmacharya.* However attractive a woman may be, her attraction will produce no effect on the man without the urge. . . .

The true *brahmachari* will shun false restraints. He must create his own fences according to his limitations, breaking them down when he feels that they are unnecessary. The first thing is to know what true *brahmacharya* is, then to realize its value, and lastly to try to cultivate this priceless virtue. I hold that true service of the country demands this observance. *23*   *Harijan, June 15, 1947*

I know from my own experience, that as long as I looked upon my wife carnally, we had no real understanding. Our love did not reach a high plane. There was affection between us always, but we came closer and closer, the more we, or rather I, became restrained. There never was any want of restraint on the part of my wife. Very often she would show restraint, but she rarely resisted me although she showed disinclination very often. All the time I wanted carnal pleasure I could not serve her. The moment I bade goodbye to a life of carnal pleasure, our whole relationship became spiritual. Lust died and love reigned instead. *24*   *Mahatma, IV, 1936*

As an external aid to *brahmacharya*, fasting is as necessary as selection and restriction in diet. So overpowering are the senses that they can be kept under control only when they are completely hedged in on all sides, from above and from beneath. It is common knowledge that they are powerless without food, and so fasting undertaken with a view to control of the senses is, I have no doubt, very helpful. With some, fasting is of no avail, because assuming that mechanical fasting alone will make them immune, they keep their bodies without food, but feast their minds upon all sorts of delicacies, thinking all the while what they will eat and what they will drink after the fast terminates. Such fasting helps them in controlling neither palate nor lust. Fasting is useful when mind co-operates with starving body, that is to say, when it cultivates a distaste for the objects that are denied to the body. Mind is at the root of all sensuality. Fasting, therefore, has a limited use, for a fasting man may continue to be swayed by passion. *25*   *An Autobiography*

Brahmacharya is such only if it persists under all conditions and in the face of every possible temptation. If a beautiful woman approaches the marble statue of a man, it will not be affected in the least. A *brahmachari* is one who reacts in a similar case in the same way as marble does. But just as the marble statue refrains from using its eyes or ears, even so a man should avoid every occasion of sin.

You argue that the sight and the company of woman have been found to be inimical to self-restraint and are therefore to be avoided. This argument is fallacious. *Brahmacharya* hardly deserves the name if it can be observed only by avoiding the company of women even when such company is kept with a view to serve. It amounts to physical renunciation unbacked by the essential mental detachment, and lets us down in critical times. *26*   *The Diary of Mahadev Desai*

For 20 years I was in the closest touch with the West in South
Africa. I have known the writings on sex by eminent writers like
Havelock Ellis, Bertrand Russell, and their theories. They are all
thinkers of eminence, integrity and experience. They have suffered
for their convictions and for giving expression to the same. While
totally repudiating institutions like marriage, etc., and the current
code of morals—and there I disagree with them—they are firm be-
lievers in the possibility and desirability of purity in life independently of those institutions and usages. I have come across men and
women in the West who lead a pure life although they do not accept
or observe the current usages and social conventions. My research
runs somewhat in that direction. If you admit the necessity and
desirability of reform, of discarding the old, wherever necessary, and
building a new system of ethics and morals suited to the present age,
then the question of seeking the permission of others or convincing
them does not arise. A reformer cannot afford to wait till others are
converted; he must take the lead and venture forth alone even in the
teeth of universal opposition. I want to test, enlarge and revise the
current definition of *brahmacharya* ... in the light of my observation,
study and experience. Therefore, whenever an opportunity presents
itself I do not evade it or run away from it. On the contrary, I deem
it my duty, *dharma*, to meet it squarely in the face and find out
where it leads to and where I stand. To avoid the contact of a
woman, or to run away from it out of fear, I regard as unbecoming
of an aspirant after true *brahmacharya*. I have never tried to cultivate
or seek sex contact for carnal satisfaction. I do not claim to have
completely eradicated the sex feeling in me. But it is my claim that I
can keep it under control.   *27*

Mahatma Gandhi, The Last Phase, circa 1947

The whole train of thought which underlies birth control is erroneous
and dangerous. Its supporters claim that a man has not only the
right, but it is his duty to satisfy the animal instinct, and that his
development would be arrested if he did not discharge this duty. I
think this claim is false. It is idle to expect self-restraint from one
who takes to artificial methods. In fact birth control is advocated on
the ground that restraint of animal passion is an impossibility. To say
that such restraint is impossible or unnecessary or harmful is the
negation of all religion. For the whole superstructure of religion rests
on the foundations of self-control.   *28*   *The Diary of Mahadev Desai*

I want to revert to the subject of birth control by contraceptives. It
is dinned into one's ears that the gratification of the sex urge is a
solemn obligation like the obligation of discharging debts lawfully
incurred, and that not to do so would involve the penalty of

intellectual decay. This sex urge has been isolated from the desire for progeny, and it is said by the protagonists of the use of contraceptives that the conception is an accident to be prevented except when the parties desire to have children. I venture to suggest that this is a most dangerous doctrine to preach anywhere; much more so in a country like India, where the middle-class male population has become imbecile through abuse of the creative function. If satisfaction of the sex urge is a duty, the unnatural vice and several other ways of gratification would be commendable. The reader should know that even persons of note have been known to approve of what is commonly known as sexual perversion. He may be shocked at the statement. But if it somehow or other gains the stamp of respectability, it will be the rage amongst boys and girls to satisfy their urge among the members of their own sex. For me, the use of contraceptives is not far removed from the means to which persons have hitherto resorted for the gratification of their sexual desire with the results that very few know. I know what havoc secret vice has played among schoolboys and schoolgirls. The introduction of contraceptives under the name of science and the imprimatur of known leaders of society has intensified the complication and made the task of the reformers who work for purity of social life wellnigh impossible for the moment. I betray no confidence when I inform the reader, that there are unmarried girls of impressionable age, studying in schools and colleges, who study birth control literature and magazines with avidity, and even possess contraceptives. It is impossible to confine their use to married women. Marriage loses its sanctity when its purpose and highest use is conceived to be the satisfaction of the animal passion without contemplating the natural result of such satisfaction.
29
March 28, 1936

It is wrong to call me an ascetic. The ideals that regulate my life are presented for acceptance by mankind in general. I have arrived at them by gradual evolution. Every step was thought out, well-considered, and taken with the greatest deliberation. Both my continence and nonviolence were derived from personal experience and became necessary in response to the calls of public duty. The isolated life I had to lead in South Africa whether as a householder, legal practitioner, social reformer or politician, required, for the due fulfillment of these duties, the strictest regulation of sexual life and a rigid practice of nonviolence and truth in human relations, whether with my own countrymen or with the Europeans. I claim to be no more than an average man with less than average ability. Nor can I claim any special merit for such nonviolence or continence as I have been able to reach with laborious research. *30* *Harijan, October 3, 1936*

My mind is made up. On the lonesome way of God on which I have set out, I need no earthly companions. Let those who will, therefore, denounce me, if I am the impostor they imagine me to be, though they may not say so in so many words. It might disillusion millions who persist in regarding me as a Mahatma. I must confess, the prospect of being so debunked greatly pleases me. *31*

In conversation, February 25, 1947

VI INTERNATIONAL PEACE

I do not believe that an individual may gain spiritually and those that surround him suffer. I believe in *advaita*. I believe in the essential unity of man and for that matter of all that lives. Therefore I believe that if one man gains spiritually, the whole word gains with him and, if one man falls, the whole world falls to that extent. *1*

Young India, December 4, 1924

There is not a single virtue which aims at, or is content with, the welfare of the individual alone. Conversely, there is not a single moral offence which does not, directly or indirectly, affect many others besides the actual offender. Hence, whether an individual is good or bad is not merely his own concern, but really the concern of the whole community, nay, of the whole world. *2*   *Ethical Religion, 1930*

Though there is repulsion enough in Nature, she *lives* by attraction. Mutual love enables Nature to persist. Man does not live by destruction. Self-love compels regard for others. Nations cohere because there is mutual regard among individuals composing them. Some day we must extend the national law to the universe, even as we have extended the family law to form nations—a larger family. *3*

Young India, March 2, 1922

Mankind is one, seeing that all are equally subject to the moral law. All men are equal in God's eyes. There are, of course, differences of race and status and the like, but the higher the status of a man, the greater is his responsibility. *4*   *Ethical Religion, 1930*

My mission is not merely brotherhood of Indian humanity. My mission is not merely freedom of India, though today it undoubtedly engrosses practically the whole of my life and the whole of my time. But through realization of freedom of India I hope to realize and carry on the mission of the brotherhood of man. My patriotism is not an exclusive thing. It is all-embracing and I should reject that patriotism which sought to mount upon the distress or the exploitation of other nationalities. The conception of my patriotism is nothing if it is not always, in every case without exception, consistent with the broadest good of humanity at large. Not only that, but my religion and my patriotism derived from my religion embrace all life. I want to realize brotherhood or identity not merely with the beings called human, but I want to realize identity with all life, even with such things as crawl upon earth. I want, if I don't give you a shock, to realize identity with even the crawling things upon earth, because we claim descent from the same God, and that being so, all life in whatever form it appears must be essentially one.   5

Young India, April 4, 1929

It is impossible for one to be an internationalist without being a nationalist. Internationalism is possible only when nationalism becomes a fact, i.e., when peoples belonging to different countries have organized themselves and are able to act as one man. It is not nationalism that is evil, it is the narrowness, selfishness, exclusiveness which is the bane of modern nations which is evil. Each wants to profit at the expense of, and rise on the ruin of, the other.   6

Young India, June 18, 1925

I am a humble servant of India and in trying to serve India, I serve humanity at large. . . . After nearly fifty years of public life, I am able to say today that my faith in the doctrine that the service of one's nation is not inconsistent with the service of the world has grown. It is a good doctrine. Its acceptance alone will ease the situation in the world and stop the mutual jealousies between nations inhabiting this globe of ours.   7   *Harijan, November 17, 1933*

Interdependence is and ought to be as much the ideal of man as self-sufficiency. Man is a social being. Without inter-relation with society he cannot realize his oneness with the universe or suppress his egotism. His social interdependence enables him to test his faith and to prove himself on the touchstone of reality. If man were so placed or could so place himself as to be absolutely above all dependence on his fellow-beings he would become so proud and arrogant as to be a veritable burden and nuisance to the world. Dependence on society teaches him the lesson of humanity. That a man ought to be able to satisfy most of his essential needs himself is obvious; but it is no less obvious to me that when self-sufficiency is carried to the length of

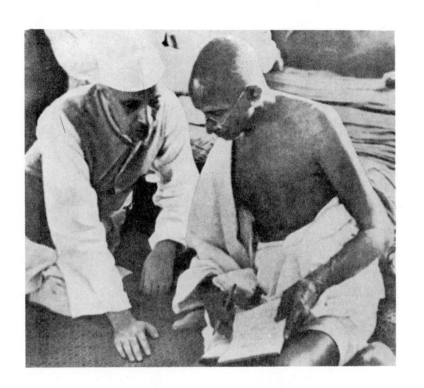

Gandhi and Jawaharlal Nehru, 1945
(By courtesy of the Information Service of India, Paris)

isolating oneself from society it almost amounts to sin. A man cannot become self-sufficient even in respect of all the various operations from the growing of cotton to the spinning of the yarn. He has at some stage or other to take the aid of the members of his family. And if one may take help from one's own family, why not from one's neighbours? Or otherwise what is the significance of the great saying, 'The world is my family'? *8*   *Young India, March 21, 1929*

Duties to self, to the family, to the country and to the world are not independent of one another. One cannot do good to the country by injuring himself or his family. Similarly one cannot serve the country injuring the world at large. In the final analysis we must die that the family may live, the family must die that the country may live and the country must die that the world may live. But only pure things can be offered in sacrifice. Therefore, self-purification is the first step. When the heart is pure, we at once realize what is our duty at every moment. *9*   *The Diary of Mahadev Desai*

The golden way is to be friends with the world and to regard the whole human family as one. He who distinguishes between the votaries of one's own religion and those of another mis-educates the members of his own and opens the way for discard and irreligion. *10*   *In conversation, May 6, 1946*

I live for India's freedom and would die for it, because it is part of Truth. Only a free India can worship the true God. I work for India's freedom because my *swadeshi* teaches me that being born in it and having inherited her culture, I am fittest to serve *her* and *she* has a prior claim to my service. But my patriotism is not exclusive; it is calculated not only not to hurt another nation but to benefit all in the true sense of the word. India's freedom as conceived by me can never be a menace to the world. *11*   *April 3, 1924*

We want freedom for our country, but not at the expense or exploitation of others, not so as to degrade other countries. I do not want the freedom of India if it means the extinction of England or the disappearance of Englishmen. I want the freedom of my country so that other countries may learn something from my free country, so that the resources of my country might be utilized for the benefit of mankind. Just as the cult of patriotism teaches us today that the individual has to die for the family, the family has to die for the village, the village for the district, the district for the province, and the province for the country, even so, a country has to be free in order that it may die, if necessary, for the benefit of the world. My love therefore of nationalism or my idea of nationalism is that my country may become free, that if need be, the whole country may die, so that the human race may live. There is no room for race-hatred there. Let that be our nationalism. *12*

From Yeravda Mandir, published 1935

There is no limit to extending our services to our neighbours across State-made frontiers. God never made those frontiers. *13*

Young India, December 31, 1931

My goal is friendship with the whole world and I can combine the greatest love with the greatest opposition to wrong. *14*

Young India, March 10, 1920

For me patriotism is the same as humanity. I am patriotic because I am human and humane. It is not exclusive, I will not hurt England or Germany to serve India. Imperialism has no place in my scheme of life. The law of a patriot is not different from that of the patriarch. And a patriot is so much the less a patriot if he is a lukewarm humanitarian. There is no conflict between private and political law. *15*

Young India, March 16, 1921

Our non-co-operation is neither with the English nor with the West. Our non-co-operation is with the system the English have established, with the material civilization and its attendant greed and exploitation of the weak. Our non-co-operation is a retirement within ourselves. Our non-co-operation is a refusal to co-operate with the English administrators on their own terms. We say to them: 'Come and co-operate with us on our terms and it will be well for us, for you and the world.' We must refuse to be lifted off our feet. A drowning man cannot save others. In order to be fit to save others, we must try to save ourselves. Indian nationalism is not exclusive, nor aggressive, nor destructive. It is health-giving, religious and therefore humanitarian. India must learn to live before she can aspire to die for humanity. *16*

Young India, October 13, 1921

I do not want England to be defeated or humiliated. It hurts me to find St. Paul's Cathedral damaged. It hurts me as much as I would be hurt if I heard that Kashi Vishvanath temple or the Juma Masjid was damaged. I would like to defend both the Kashi Vishvanath temple and the Juma Masjid and even St. Paul's Cathedral with my life, but would not take a single life for their defence. That is my fundamental difference with the British people. My sympathy is there with them nevertheless. Let there be no mistake on the part of the Englishmen, Congressmen, or others whom my voice reaches, as to where my sympathy lies. It is not because I love the British nation and hate the German. I do not think that the Germans as a nation are any worse than the English, or the Italians are any worse. We are all tarred with the same brush; we are all members of the vast human family. I decline to draw any distinctions. I cannot claim any superiority for Indians. We have the same virtues and the same vices. Humanity is not divided into watertight compartments so that we cannot go from one to another. They may occupy one thousand rooms, but they are all related to one another. I would not say: 'India should be all in all, let the whole world perish.' That is not my message. India should be all in all, consistently with the well-being of other nations of the world. I can keep India intact and its freedom also intact only if I have goodwill towards the whole of the human family and not merely for the human family which inhabits this little spot of the earth called India. It is big enough compared to other smaller nations, but what is India in the wide world or in the universe? *17*

Harijan, September 29, 1940

Not to believe in the possibility of permanent peace is to disbelieve in the godliness of human nature. Methods hitherto adopted have failed because rock-bottom sincerity on the part of those who have striven has been lacking. Not that they have realized this lack. Peace is unattained by part performance of conditions, even as a chemical combination is impossible without complete fulfilment of the conditions of attainment thereof. If the recognized leaders of mankind who have control over the engines of destructions were wholly to renounce their use, with full knowledge of its implications, permanent peace can be obtained. This is clearly impossible without the Great Powers of the earth renouncing their imperialistic design. This again seems impossible without great nations ceasing to believe in soul-destroying competition and to desire to multiply wants and, therefore, increase their material possessions. *18 Harijan, May 16, 1936*

I do suggest that the doctrine [of nonviolence] holds good also as between States and States. I know that I am treading on delicate ground if I refer to the late war. But I fear I must in order to make the position clear. It was a war of aggrandizement, as I have understood, on either part. It was a war for dividing the spoils of the exploitation of weaker races—otherwise euphemistically called the world commerce. . . . It would be found that before general disarmament in Europe commences, as it must some day, unlesss Europe is to commit suicide, some nation will have to dare to disarm herself and take large risks. The level of nonviolence in that nation, if that event happily comes to pass, will naturally have risen so high as to command universal respect. Her judgements will be unerring, her decisions firm, her capacity for heroic self-sacrifice will be great, and

she will want to live as much for other nations as for herself.   *19*
Young India, October 8, 1925

One thing is certain. If the mad race for armaments continues, it is bound to result in a slaughter such as has never occurred in history. If there is a victor left the very victory will be a living death for the nation that emerges victorious. There is no escape from the impending doom save through a bold and unconditional acceptance of the nonviolent method with all its glorious implications.   *20*
Harijan, November 12, 1938

If there were no greed, there would be no occasion for armaments. The principle of nonviolence necessitates complete abstention from exploitation in any form.   *21*   *The Mind of Mahatma Gandhi*

Immediately the spirit of exploitation is gone, armaments will be felt as a positive unbearable burden. Real disarmament cannot come unless the nations of the world cease to exploit one another.   *22*
The Mind of Mahatma Gandhi

I would not like to live in this world if it is not to be one world.   *23*
Speech, March, 1947

VII MAN AND MACHINE

I must confess that I do not draw a sharp line or any distinction between economics and ethics. Economics that hurt the moral well-being of an individual or a nation are immoral and, therefore, sinful. Thus, the economics that permit one country to prey upon another are immoral. *1*

Young India, October 13, 1921

The end to be sought is human happiness combined with full mental and moral growth. I use the adjective moral as synonymous with spiritual. This end can be achieved under decentralization. Centralization as a system is inconsistent with a nonviolent structure of society. *2*

Harijan, January 18, 1942

I would categorically state my conviction that the mania for mass production is responsible for the world crisis. Granting for the moment that the machinery may supply all the needs of humanity, still, it would concentrate production in particular areas, so that you would have to go about in a roundabout way to regulate distribution, whereas, if there is production and distribution both in the respective areas where things are required, it is automatically regulated, and there is less chance for fraud, none for speculation. *3*

Harijan, November 2, 1934

Mass production takes no note of the real requirement of the consumer. If mass production were in itself a virtue, it should be capable of indefinite multiplication. But it can be definitely shown that mass production carries within it its own limitations. If all countries adopted the system of mass production there would not be a big enough market for their products. Mass production must then come to a stop. *4*

Harijan, November 1, 1934

All Men Are Brothers

I don't believe that industrialization is necessary in any case for any country. It is much less so for India. Indeed I believe that independent India can only discharge her duty towards a groaning world by adopting a simple but ennobled life by developing her thousands of cottages and living at peace with the world. High thinking is inconsistent with a complicated material life, based on high speed imposed on us by Mammon worship. All the graces of life are possible, only when we learn the art of living nobly.

There may be sensation in living dangerously. We must draw the distinction between living in the face of danger and living dangerously. A man who dares to live alone in a forest infested by wild beasts and wilder men without a gun and with God as his only help, lives in the face of danger. A man who lives perpetually in mid-air and dives to the earth below to the admiration of a gaping world lives dangerously. One is a purposeful, the other a purposeless life.   *5*

Mahatma, Vol. VII, Correspondence, 1946

What is the cause of the present chaos? It is exploitation, I will not say, of the weaker nations by the stronger, but of sister nations by sister nations. And my fundamental objection to machinery rests on the fact that it is machinery that has enabled these nations to exploit others.   *6*   *Young India, October 22, 1931*

I would destroy that system today, if I had the power. I would use the most deadly weapons, if I believed that they would destroy it. I refrain only because the use of such weapons would only perpetuate the system, though it may destroy its present administrators. Those who seek to destroy men rather than manners, adopt the latter and become worse than those whom they destroy under the mistaken belief that the manners will die with the men. They do not know the root of the evil.   *7*   *Young India, March 17, 1927*

Machinery has its place; it has come to stay. But it must not be allowed to displace necessary human labour. An improved plough is a good thing. But if by some chance one man could plough up, by some mechanical invention of his, the whole of the land of India and control all the agricultural produce and if the millions had no other occupation, they would starve, and being idle, they would become dunces, as many have already become. There is hourly danger of many more being reduced to that unenviable state.

I would welcome every improvement in the cottage machine, but I know that it is criminal to displace hand-labour by the introduction of power-driven spindles unless one is at the same time ready to give millions of farmers some other occupation in their homes.   *8*

Young India, November 5, 1925

Man and Machine

What I object to, is the 'craze' for machinery, not machinery as such. The craze is for what they call labour-saving machinery. Men go on 'saving labour' till thousands are without work and thrown on the open streets to die of starvation. I want to save time and labour, not for a fraction of mankind, but for all; I want the concentration of wealth, not in the hands of a few, but in the hands of all. Today machinery merely helps a few to ride on the back of millions. The impetus behind it all is not the philanthropy to save labour, but greed. It is against this constitution of things that I am fighting with all my might.

The supreme consideration is man. The machine should not tend to make atrophied the limbs of man. For instance, I would make intelligent exceptions. Take the case of the Singer Sewing Machine. It is one of the few useful things ever invented, and there is a romance about the device itself. Singer saw his wife labouring over the tedious process of sewing and seaming with her own hands, and simply out of his love for her he devised the sewing machine in order to save her from unnecessary labour. He, however, saved not only her labour but also the labour of everyone who could purchase a sewing machine.

It is an alteration in the condition of labour that I want. This mad rush for wealth must cease, and the labourer must be assured, not only of a living wage, but a daily task that is not a mere drudgery. The machine will, under these conditions, be as much a help to the man working it as to the State, or the man who owns it. The present mad rush will cease, and the labourer will work (as I have said) under attractive and ideal conditions. This is but one of the exceptions I have in mind. The sewing machine had love at its back. The individual is the one supreme consideration. The saving of labour of the individual should be the object, and the honest humanitarian. consideration, and not greed, the motive. Replace greed by love and everything will come right. *9*   *Young India, November 13, 1924*

Hand-spinning does not, it is not intended that it should, compete with, in order to displace, any existing type of industry; it does not aim at withdrawing a single able-bodied person, who can otherwise find a remunerative occupation from his work. The sole claim advanced on its behalf is that it alone offers an immediate, practicable, and permanent solution of that problem of problems that confronts India, viz., the enforced idleness for nearly six months in the year of an overwhelming majority of India's population, owing to lack of a suitable supplementary occupation to agriculture and the chronic starvation of the masses that results therefrom. *10*

Young India, October 21, 1926

I have not contemplated, much less advised, the abandonment of a

single healthy, life-giving industrial activity for the sake of hand-spinning. The entire foundation of the spinning wheel rests on the fact that
there are crores [one crore is ten million] of semi-employed people in
India. And I should admit that if there were none such, there would be no
room for the spinning wheel. *11*   *Young India, May 27, 1926*

A starving man thinks first of satisfying his hunger before anything
else. He will sell his liberty and all for the sake of getting a morsel of
food. Such is the position of millions of the people of India. For
them, liberty, God and all such words are merely letters put together
without the slightest meaning. They jar upon them. If we want to
give these people a sense of freedom we shall have to provide them
with work which they can easily do in their desolate home and which
would give them at least the barest living. This can only be done by
the spinning wheel. And when they have become self-reliant and are
able to support themselves, we are in a position to talk to them
about freedom, about Congress, etc. Those, therefore, who bring
them work and means of getting a crust of bread will be their de-
liverers and will be also the people who will make them hunger for
liberty. *12*   *Young India, March 18, 1926*

Little do town-dwellers know how the semi-starved masses of India
are slowly sinking to lifelessness. Little do they know that their
miserable comfort represents the brokerage they get for the work
they do for the foreign exploiter, that the profits and the brokerage
are sucked from the masses. Little do they realize that the government established by law in British India is carried on for this exploitation of the masses. No sophistry, no jugglery in figures can explain
away the evidence that the skeletons in many villages present to the
naked eye. I have no doubt whatsoever that both England and the
town-dwellers of India will have to answer, if there is a God above,
for this crime against humanity which is perhaps unequalled in history. *13*   *Young India, March 23, 1922*

I would favour the use of the most elaborate machinery if thereby
India's pauperism and resulting idleness be avoided. I have suggested
hand-spinning as 'the only ready means of driving away penury and
making famine of work and wealth impossible. The spinning wheel
itself is a piece of valuable machinery, and in my own humble way I
have tried to secure improvements in it in keeping with the special
conditions of India. *14*   *Young India, November 3, 1921*

I would say that if the village perishes, India will perish too. India
will be no more India. Her own mission in the world will get lost.
The revival of the village is possible only when it is no more

exploited. Industrialization on a mass scale will necessarily lead to passive or active exploitation of the villagers as the problems of competition and marketing come in. Therefore we have to concentrate on the village being self-contained, manufacturing mainly for use. Provided this character of the village industry is maintained, there would be no objection to villagers using even the modern machines and tools that they can make and can afford to use. Only they should not be used as a means of exploitation of others. *15*

Harijan, August 29, 1936

VIII POVERTY IN THE MIDST OF PLENTY

That economics is untrue which ignores or disregards moral values. The extension of the law of nonviolence in the domain of economics means nothing less than the introduction of moral values as a factor to be considered in regulating international commerce. *1*

Young India, December 26, 1924

According to me the economic constitution of India and for that matter of the world, should be such that no one under it should suffer from want of food and clothing. In other words everybody should be able to get sufficient work to enable him to make the two ends meet. And this ideal can be universally realized only if the means of production of the elementary necessaries of life remain in the control of the masses. These should be freely available to all as God's air and water are or ought to be; they should not be made a vehicle of traffic for the exploitation of others. Their monopolization by any country, nation or group of persons would be unjust. The neglect of this simple principle is the cause of the destitution that we witness today not only in this unhappy land but in other parts of the world too. *2*

Young India, November 15, 1928

My ideal is equal distribution, but so far as I can see, it is not to be realized. I therefore work for equitable distribution. *3*

Young India, March 17, 1927

Love and exlusive possession can never go together. Theoretically when there is perfect love, there must be perfect non-possession. The body is our last possession. So a man can only exercise perfect love and be completely dispossessed, if he is prepared to embrace death and renounce his body for the sake of human service.

Poverty in the midst of Plenty

But that is true in theory only. In actual life, we can hardly exercise perfect love, for the body as a possession will always remain with us. Man will ever remain imperfect and it will always be his part to try to be perfect. So that perfection in love or non-possession will remain an unattainable ideal as long as we are alive, but towards which we must ceaselessly strive. *4   Modern Review, October, 1935*

I suggest that we are thieves in a way. If I take anything that I do not need for my own immediate use, and keep it, I thieve it from somebody else. I venture to suggest that it is the fundamental law of Nature, without exception, that Nature produces enough for our wants from day to day, and if only everybody took enough for himself and nothing more, there would be no pauperism in this world, there would be no man dying of starvation in this world. But so long as we have got this inequality, so long we are thieving. I am no socialist and I do not want to dispossess those who have got possessions; but I do say that, personally, those of us who want to see light out of darkness have to follow this rule. I do not want to dispossess anybody. I should then be departing from the rule of *ahiṃsā*. If somebody else possesses more than I do, let him. But so far as my own life has to be regulated, I do say that I dare not possess anything which I do not want. In India we have got three millions of people having to be satisfied with one meal a day, and that meal consisting of a *chapāti* containing no fat in it, and a pinch of salt. You and I have no right to anything that we really have until these three millions are clothed and fed better. You and I, who ought to know better, must adjust our wants, and even undergo voluntary starvation in order that they may be nursed, fed and clothed. *5*
   Address to Students, Y.M.C.A. Auditorium, Madras, 1916, text uncertain

Non-possession is allied to non-stealing. A thing not originally stolen must nevertheless be classified stolen property, if one possesses it without needing it. Possession implies provision for the future. A seeker after Truth, a follower of the Law of Love cannot hold any-thing against tomorrow. God never stores for the morrow; He never creates more than what is strictly needed for the moment. If, there-fore, we repose faith in His providence, we should rest assured, that He will give us everything that we require. Saints and devotees, who have lived in such faith, have always derived a justification for it from their experience. Our ignorance or negligence of the Divine Law, which gives to man from day to day his daily bread and no more, has given rise to inequalities with all the miseries attendant upon them. The rich have a superfluous store of things which they do not need, and which are therefore neglected and wasted, while millions are starved to death for want of sustenance. If each retained possession only of what he needed, no one would be in want, and all would live in contentment. As it is, the rich are discontented no less than the poor. The poor man would fain become a millionaire, and the millionaire a multimillionaire. The rich should take the initiative in dispossession with a view to a universal diffusion of the spirit of contentment. If only they keep their own property within moderate limits, the starving will be easily fed, and will learn the lesson of contentment along with the rich. *6* *Yeravda Mandir, 1935*

Economic equality is the master key to nonviolent independence. Working for economic equality means abolishing the eternal conflict between capital and labour. It means the levelling down of the few rich in whose hands is concentrated the bulk of the nation's wealth on the one hand, and a levelling up of the semi-starved naked millions on the other. A nonviolent system of government is clearly an impossibility so long as the wide gulf between the rich and the hungry millions persists. The contrast between the palaces of New Delhi and the miserable hovels of the poor, labouring class cannot last one day in a free India in which the poor will enjoy the same power as the richest in the land. A violent and bloody revolution is a certainty one day unless there is a voluntary abdication of riches and the power that riches give and sharing them for the common good. I adhere to my doctrine of trusteeship in spite of the ridicule that has been poured upon it. It is true that it is difficult to reach. So is nonviolence difficult to attain. *7* *Constructive Programme, 1944*

The real implication of equal distribution is that each man shall have the wherewithal to supply all his natural wants and more. For example, if one man has a weak digestion and requires only a quarter of a pound of flour for his bread and another needs a pound, both should be in a position to satisfy their wants. To bring this ideal into being the entire social order has got to be reconstructed. A society based on nonviolence cannot nurture any other ideal. We may not perhaps be able to realize the goal but we must bear it in mind and work unceasingly to near it. To the same extent as we progress towards our goal we shall find contentment and happiness, and to that extent too, shall we have contributed towards the bringing into being of a nonviolent society.

Now let us consider how equal distribution can be brought about through nonviolence. The first step towards it is for him who has made this ideal part of his being to bring about the necessary changes in his personal life. He would reduce his wants to a minimum, bearing in mind the poverty of India. His earnings would be free of dishonesty. The desire for speculation would be renounced. His habitation would be in keeping with his new mode of life. There would be self-restraint exercised in every sphere of life. When he has done all that is possible in his own life, then only will he be in a position to preach this ideal among his associates and neighbours.

Indeed at the root of this doctrine of equal distribution must lie that of the trusteeship of the wealthy for superfluous wealth possessed by them. For according to the doctrine they may not possess a rupee more than their neighbours. How is this to be brought about? Nonviolently? Or should the wealthy be dispossessed of their possessions? To do this we would naturally have to resort to violence. This violent action cannot benefit the society. Society will be the poorer, for it will lose the gifts of a man who knows how to accumulate wealth. Therefore the nonviolent way is evidently superior. The rich man will be left in possession of his wealth, of which he will use what he reasonably requires for his personal needs and will act as a trustee for the remainder to be used for the society. In this argument honesty on the part of the trustee is assumed.

If however, in spite of the utmost effort, the rich do not become guardians of the poor in the true sense of the term and the latter are more and more crushed and die of hunger, what is to be done? In trying to find out the solution of this riddle I have lighted on nonviolent non-co-operation and civil disobedience as the right and infallible means. The rich cannot accumulate wealth without the co-operation of the poor in society. If this knowledge were to penetrate to and spread amongst the poor, they would become strong and would learn how to free themselves by means of nonviolence from the crushing inequalities which have brought them to the verge of starvation. *8*

Harijan, August 25, 1940

I cannot imagine anything nobler or more national than that for, say, one hour in the day, we should all do the labour that the poor must do, and thus identify ourselves with them and through them with all mankind. I cannot imagine better worship of God than that in His name I should labour for the poor even as they do. *9*

Young India, October 20, 1921

'Earn thy bread by the sweat of thy brow' says the Bible. Sacrifices may be of many kinds. One of them may well be bread labour. If all laboured for their bread and no more, then there would be enough food and enough leisure for all. Then there would be no cry of over-population, no disease and no such misery as we see around. Such labour will be the highest form of sacrifice. Men will no doubt do many other things either through their bodies or through their minds, but all this will be labour of love for the common good. There will then be no rich and no poor, none high and none low, no touchable and no untouchable. *10*   *Harijan, June 29, 1935*

'Why should I, who have no need to work for food, spin?' may be the question asked. Because I am eating what does not belong to me. I am living on the spoliation of my countrymen. Trace the course of every pice [bronze Indian coin] that finds its way into your pocket, and you will realize the truth of what I write. . . .

I must refuse to insult the naked by giving them clothes they do not need, instead of giving them work which they sorely need. I will not commit the sin of becoming their patron, but on learning that I had assisted in impoverishing them, I would give them neither crumbs nor cast-off clothing, but the best of my food and clothes and associate myself with them in work. . . .

God created man to work for his food and said that those who ate without work were thieves. *11*   *Young India, October 13, 1921*

We should be ashamed of resting or having a square meal so long as there is one able-bodied man or woman without work or food. *12*
                    Young India, October 13, 1921

I hate privilege and monopoly. Whatever cannot be shared with the masses is taboo to me. *13*   *Harijan, November 2, 1934*

It is open to the world . . . to laugh at my dispossessing myself of all property. For me the dispossession has been a positive gain. I would like people to compete with me in my contentment. It is the richest treasure I own. Hence it is perhaps right to say that though I preach poverty, I am a rich man! *14*   *Young India, April 30, 1925*

No one has ever suggested that grinding pauperism can lead to anything else than moral degradation. Every human being has a right to live and therefore to find the wherewithal to feed himself and where necessary to clothe and house himself. But for this very simple performance we need no assistance from economists or their laws.

'Take no thought for the morrow' is an injunction which finds an echo in almost all the religious scriptures of the world. In a well-ordered society the securing of one's livelihood should be and is found to be the easiest thing in the world. Indeed the test of orderliness in a country is not the number of millionaires it owns, but the absence of starvation among its masses. *15*
                    Speech at Muir Central College, circa 1916

My *ahiṃsā* would not tolerate the idea of giving a free meal to a healthy person who has not worked for it in some honest way and if I had the power, I would stop every *sadāvrata* where free meals are given. It has degraded the nation and it has encouraged laziness, idleness, hypocrisy and even crime. *16*   *Young India, May 13, 1925*

Poverty in the midst of Plenty

True to his poetical instinct, the poet lives for the morrow and would have us do likewise. He presents to our admiring gaze the beautiful picture of the birds early in the morning singing hymns of praise as they soar into the sky. These birds have had their day's food and soared with rested wings, in whose veins new blood had flown during the previous night. But I have had the pain of watching birds who for want of strength could not be coaxed even into a flutter of their wings. The human bird under the Indian sky gets up weaker than when he pretended to retire. For millions it is an eternal vigil or an eternal trance. It is an indescribably painful state which has got to be experienced to be realized. I have found it impossible to soothe suffering patients with a song from Kabir. The hungry millions ask for one poem—invigorating food. They cannot be given it. They must earn it. And they can earn only by the sweat of their brow. *17*

Young India, October 13, 1921

Imagine, therefore, what a calamity it must be to have 300 millions unemployed, several millions becoming degraded every day for want of employment, devoid of self-respect, devoid of faith in God. I may as well place before the dog over there the message of God as before those hungry millions who have no lustre in their eyes and whose only God is their bread. I can take before them a message of God only by taking the message of sacred work before them. It is good enough to talk of God whilst we are sitting here after a nice breakfast and looking forward to a nicer luncheon, but how am I to talk of God to the millions who have to go without two meals a day? To them God can only appear as bread and butter. *18*

Young India, October 13, 1921

To a people famishing and idle, the only acceptable form in which God can dare appear is work and promise of food as wages. *19*

Young India, October 13, 1921

For the poor the economic is the spiritual. You cannot make any other appeal to those starving millions. It will fall flat on them. But you take food to them and they will regard you as their God. They are incapable of any other thought. *20*   *Young India, March 5, 1927*

By the nonviolent method, we seek not to destroy the capitalist, we seek to destroy capitalism. We invite the capitalist to regard himself as a trustee for those on whom he depends for the making, the retention and the increase of his capital. Nor need the worker wait for his conversion. If capital is power, so is work. Either power can be used destructively or creatively. Either is dependent on the other. Immediately the worker realizes his strength, he is in a position to become a co-sharer with the capitalist instead of remaining his slave. If he aims at becoming the sole owner, he will most likely be killing the hen that lays the golden eggs.   *21*   *Young India, March 26, 1931*

Every man has an equal right to the necessaries of life even as birds and beasts have. And since every right carries with it a corresponding duty and the corresponding remedy for resisting any attack upon it, it is merely a matter of finding out the corresponding duties and remedies to vindicate the elementary fundamental equality. The corresponding duty is to labour with my limbs and the corresponding remedy is to non-co-operate with him who deprives me of the fruit of my labour. And if I would recognize the fundamental equality, as I must, of the capitalist and the labourer, I must not aim at his destruction. I must strive for his conversion. My non-co-operation with him will open his eyes to the wrong he may be doing.   *22*
Young India, March 26, 1931

I cannot picture to myself a time when no man shall be richer than another. But I do picture to myself a time when the rich will spurn to enrich themselves at the expense of the poor and the poor will cease to envy the rich. Even in a most perfect world, we shall fail to avoid inequalities, but we can and must avoid strife and bitterness. There are numerous examples extant of the rich and the poor living in perfect friendliness. We have but to multiply such instances.   *23*
Young India, October 7, 1926

I do not believe that the capitalists and the landlords are all exploiters by an inherent necessity, or that there is a basic or irreconcilable antagonism between their interests and those of the masses. All exploitation is based on co-operation, willing or forced, of the exploited. However much we may detest admitting it, the fact remains that there would be no exploitation if people refused to obey the exploiter. But self comes in and we hug the chains that bind us. This must cease. What is needed is not the extinction of landlords and capitalists, but a transformation of the existing relationship between them and the masses into something healthier and purer.   *24*
Amrita Bazar Patrika, August 3, 1934

The idea of class war does not appeal to me. In India a class war is not only not inevitable, but it is avoidable if we have understood the message of nonviolence. Those who talk about class war as being inevitable have not understood the implications of nonviolence or have understood them only skin-deep.   *25*
Amrita Bazar Patrika, August 3, 1934

Poverty in the midst of Plenty

Exploitation of the poor can be extinguished not by effecting the destruction of a few millionaires, but by removing the ignorance of the poor and teaching them to non-co-operate with their exploiters. That will convert the exploiters also. I have even suggested that ultimately it will lead to both being equal partners. Capital as such is not evil; it is its wrong use that is evil. Capital in some form or other will always be needed. *26*   *Harijan, July 28, 1940*

Those who own money now are asked to behave like the trustees holding their riches on behalf of the poor. You may say that trusteeship is a legal fiction. But, if people meditate over it constantly and try to act up to it, then life on earth would be governed far more by love than it is at present. Absolute trusteeship is an abstraction like Euclid's definition of a point, and is equally unattainable. But if we strive for it, we shall be able to go further in realizing a state of equality on earth than by any other method. *27*

Mahatma, Vol. IV., 1934

Complete renunciation of one's possessions is a thing which very few even among ordinary folk are capable of. All that can legitimately be expected of the wealthy class is that they should hold their riches and talents in trust and use them for the service of the society. To insist on more would be to kill the goose that laid the golden eggs. *28*   *Speech, April 11, 1945*

IX DEMOCRACY AND THE PEOPLE

My notion of democracy is that under it the weakest should have the same opportunity as the strongest. That can never happen except through nonviolence. *1*   *Interview, April, 1940*

I have always held that social justice, even unto the least and the lowliest, is impossible of attainment by force. I have believed that it is possible by proper training of the lowliest by nonviolent means to secure the redress of the wrongs suffered by them. That means is nonviolent non-co-operation. At times, non-co-operation becomes as much a duty as co-operation. No one is bound to co-operate in one's own undoing or slavery. Freedom received through the effort of others, however benevolent, cannot be retained when such effort is withdrawn. In other words, such freedom is not real freedom. But the lowliest can feel its glow, as soon as they learn the art of attaining it through nonviolent non-co-operation. *2*   *Interview, April, 1940*

Civil disobedience is the inherent right of a citizen. He dare not give it up without ceasing to be a man. Civil disobedience is never followed by anarchy. Criminal disobedience can lead to it. Every State puts down criminal disobedience by force. It perishes if it does not. But to put down civil disobedience is to attempt to imprison conscience. *3*   *Young India, January 5, 1922*

True democracy or the *swarāj* of the masses can never come through untruthful and violent means, for the simple reason that the natural corollary to their use would be to remove all opposition through the suppression or extermination of the antagonists. That does not make for individual freedom. Individual freedom can have the fullest play only under a regime of unadulterated *ahiṃsā*. *4*   *Harijan, May 27, 1939*

126

Democracy and the People

The fact that there are so many men still alive in the world shows that it is based not on the force of arms but on the force of truth or love. Therefore, the greatest and most unimpeachable evidence of the success of this force is to be found in the fact that, in spite of the wars of the world, it still lives on.

Thousands, indeed tens of thousands, depend for their existence on a very active working of this force. Little quarrels of millions of families in their daily lives disappear before the exercise of this force. Hundreds of nations live in peace. History does not and cannot take note of this fact. History is really a record of every interruption of the even working of the force of love or of the soul. Two brothers quarrel; one of them repents and re-awakens the love that was lying dormant in him; the two again begin to live in peace; nobody takes note of this. But if the two brothers, through the intervention of solicitors or some other reason take up arms or go to law—which is another form of the exhibition of brute force—their doings would be immediately noticed in the press, they would be the talk of their neighbours and would probably go down in history. And what is true of families and communities is true of nations. There is no reason to believe that there is one law for families and another for nations. History, then, is a record of an interruption of the course of nature. Soul-force, being natural, is not noted in history. *5*

India Home Rule, 1909

Self-government depends entirely upon our own internal strength, upon our ability to fight against the heaviest odds. Indeed, self-government which does not require that continuous striving to attain it and to sustain it, is not worth the name. I have therefore endeavoured to show both in word and deed that political self-government—that is self-government for a large number of men and women—is no better than individual self-government, and therefore, it is to be attained by precisely the same means that are required for individual self-government or self-rule. *6*

With Gandhiji in Ceylon, published in 1928

The true source of rights is duty. If we all discharge our duties, rights will not be far to seek. If leaving duties unperformed we run after rights, they will escape us like a will-o'-the-wisp. The more we pursue them, the farther will they fly. *7*   *Young India, January 8, 1925*

To me political power is not an end but one of the means of enabling people to better their condition in every department of life. Political power means capacity to regulate national life through national representatives. If national life becomes so perfect as to become self-regulated, no representation becomes necessary. There is then a state of enlightened anarchy. In such a state very one is his own ruler. He rules himself in such a manner that he is never a hindrance to his neighbour. In the ideal State, therefore, there is no political power because there is no State. But the ideal is never fully realized in life. Hence the classical statement of Thoreau that that government is best which governs the least. *8*

Young India, July 2, 1931

I believe that true democracy can only be an outcome of nonviolence. The structure of a world federation can be raised only on a foundation of nonviolence, and violence will have to be totally given up in world affairs. *9*

Gandhiji's Correspondence with the Government, 1942-44

My idea of society is that while we are born equal, meaning that we have a right to equal opportunity, all have not the same capacity. It is, in the nature of things, impossible. For instance, all cannot have the same height, or colour or degree of intelligence, etc.; therefore in the nature of things, some will have ability to earn more and others less. People with talents will have more, and they will utilize their talents for this purpose. If they utilize kindly, they will be performing the work of the State. Such people exist as trustees, on no other terms. I would allow a man of intellect to earn more, I would not cramp his talent. But the bulk of his greater earnings must be used for the good of the State, just as the income of all earning sons of the father go to the common family fund. They would have their earnings only as trustees. It may be that I would fail miserably in this. But that is what I am sailing for. *10*

Young India, November 26, 1931

I hope to demonstrate that real *swarāj* will come not by the acquisition of authority by a few but by the acquisition of the capacity by all to resist authority when abused. In other words, *swarāj* is to be attained by educating the masses to a sense of their capacity to regulate and control authority. *11*   *Young India, January 29, 1925*

Mere withdrawal of the English is not independence. It means the consciousness in the average villager that he is the maker of his own destiny, he is his own legislator through his chosen representative. *12*   *Young India, February 13, 1930*

We have long been accustomed to think that power comes only through legislative assemblies. I have regarded this belief as a grave error brought about by inertia or hypnotism. A superficial study of the British history has made us think that all power percolates to the people from parliaments. The truth is that power resides in the people and it is entrusted for the time being to those whom they may choose as their representatives. The parliaments have no power or even existence independently of the people. It has been my effort for the last twenty-one years to convince the people of this simple truth. Civil disobedience is the storehouse of power. Imagine a whole people unwilling to conform to the laws of the legislature and prepared to suffer the consequences of non-compliance! They will bring the whole legislative and the executive machinery to a standstill. The police and the military are of use to coerce minorities however powerful they may be. But no police or military coercion can bend the resolute will of a people, out for suffering to the uttermost.

And parliamentary procedure is good only when its members are willing to conform to the will of the majority. In other words, it is fairly effective only among compatibles. *13*   *Mahatma, Vol. VI.,*
"Constructive Programme," December 1941

What we want, I hope, is a government not based on coercion even of a minority but on its conversion. If it is a change from white military rule to a brown, we hardly need make any fuss. At any rate the masses then do not count. They will be subject to the same spoliation as now, if not even worse. *14*
Young India, December 19, 1929

I feel that fundamentally the disease is the same in Europe as it is in India, in spite of the fact that in the former the people enjoy political self-government. . . . The same remedy is, therefore, likely to be applicable. Shorn of all camouflage, the exploitation of the masses of Europe is sustained by violence.

Violence on the part of the masses will never remove the disease. Anyway up to now experience shows that success of violence has been short-lived. It has led to greater violence. What has been tried hitherto has been a variety of violence and artificial checks dependent mainly upon the will of the violent. At the crucial moment these checks have naturally broken down. It seems to me, therefore, that sooner or later, the European masses will have to take to nonviolence if they are to find their deliverance. *15*
Young India, September 3, 1925

I am not interested in freeing India merely from the English yoke. I am bent upon freeing India from any yoke whatsoever. I have no desire to exchange 'king log for king stork.' Hence for me the movement of *swarāj* is a movement of self-purification. *16*
Young India, June 12, 1924

Our tyranny, if we impose our will on others, will be infinitely worse than that of the handful of Englishmen who form the bureaucracy. Theirs is a terrorism imposed by a minority struggling to exist in the midst of opposition. Ours will be a terrorism imposed by a majority and therefore worse and really more godless than the first. We must therefore eliminate compulsion in any shape from our struggle. If we are only a handful holding freely the doctrine of non-co-operation, we may have to die in the attempt to convert others to our view, but we shall have truly defended and represented our cause. If however we enlist under our banner men by force, we shall be denying our cause and God, and if we seem to succeed for the moment, we shall have succeeded in establishing a worse terror. *17*

Young India, October 27, 1921

A born democrat is a born disciplinarian. Democracy comes naturally to him who is habituated normally to yield willing obedience to all laws, human or divine. I claim to be a democrat both by instinct and training. Let those who are ambitious to serve democracy qualify themselves by satisfying first this acid test of democracy. Moreover, a democrat must be utterly selfless. He must think and dream not in terms of self or party but only of democracy. Only then does he acquire the right of civil disobedience. I do not want anybody to give up his convictions or to suppress himself. I do not believe that a healthy and honest difference of opinion will injure our cause. But opportunism, camouflage or patched up compromises certainly will. If you must dissent, you should take care that your opinions voice your innermost convictions and are not intended merely as a convenient party cry.

I value individual freedom but you must not forget that man is essentially a social being. He has risen to his present status by learning to adjust his individualism to the requirements of social progress. Unrestricted individualism is the law of the beast of the jungle. We have learnt to strike the mean between individual freedom and social restraint. Willing submission to social restraint for the sake of the well-being of the whole society enriches both the individual and the society of which one is a member. *18*   *Harijan, May 27, 1939*

The golden rule of conduct, therefore, is mutual toleration, seeing that we will never all think alike and we shall see Truth in fragment and from different angles of vision. Conscience is not the same thing for all. Whilst, therefore, it is a good guide for individual conduct, imposition of that conduct upon all will be an insufferable interference with everybody's freedom of conscience. *19*

Young India, September 23, 1926

Democracy and the People

Differences of opinion should never mean hostility. If they did, my wife and I should be sworn enemies of one another. I do not know two persons in the world who had no difference of opinion, and as I am a follower of the Gita, I have always attempted to regard those who differ from me with the same affection as I have for my nearest and dearest. *20*   *Young India, March 26, 1931*

I shall continue to confess blunders each time the people commit them. The only tyrant I accept in this world is the 'still small voice' within me. And even though I have to face the prospect of a minority of one, I humbly believe I have the courage to be in such a hopeless minority. *21*   *Young India, March 2, 1922*

I can truthfully say that I am slow to see the blemishes of fellow beings, being myself full of them, and therefore being in need of their charity. I have learnt not to judge any one harshly and to make allowances for defects that I may detect. *22*   *Harijan, March 11, 1939*

I have often been charged with having an unyielding nature. I have been told that I would not bow to the decisions of the majority. I have been accused of being autocratic. . . . I have never been able to subscribe to the charge of obstinacy or autocracy. On the contrary, I pride myself on my yielding nature in non-vital matters. I detest autocracy. Valuing my freedom and independence I shall equally cherish them for others. I have no desire to carry a single soul with me, if I cannot appeal to his or her reason. My unconventionality I carry to the point of rejecting the divinity of the oldest *shāstras* if they cannot convince my reason. But I have found by experience that, if I wish to live in society and still retain my independence, I must limit the points of utter independence to matters of first-rate importance. In all others which do not involve a departure from one's personal religion or moral code, one must yield to the majority. *23*
Young India, July 14, 1920

I do not believe in the doctrine of the greatest good of the greatest number. It means in its nakedness that in order to achieve the supposed good of 51 per cent the interest of 49 per cent may be, or rather, should be sacrificed. It is a heartless doctrine and has done harm to humanity. The only real, dignified, human doctrine is the greatest good of all, and this can only be achieved by uttermost self-sacrifice. *24*   *The Diary of Mahadev Desai*

Those who claim to lead the masses must resolutely refuse to be led by them, if we want to avoid mob law and desire ordered progress for the country. I believe that mere protestation of one's opinion and surrender to the mass opinion is not only not enough, but in matters of vital importance, leaders must *act* contrary to the mass of opinion if it does not commend itself to their reason.   25

Young India, no date given, probably February 23, 1922

A leader is useless when he acts against the prompting of his own conscience, surrounded as he must be by people holding all kinds of views. He will drift like an anchorless ship, if he has not the inner voice to hold him firm and guide him.   26

Young India, February 23, 1922

While admitting that man actually lives by habit, I hold that it is better for him to live by the exercise of will. I also believe that men are capable of developing their will to an extent that will reduce the exploitation to a minimum. I look upon an increase of the power of the State with the greatest fear because, although while apparently doing good by minimizing exploitation, it does the greatest harm to mankind by destroying individuality which lies at the root of all progress. We know of so many cases where men have adopted trusteeship, but none where the State has really lived for the poor.   27

Mahatma, Vol. IV, 1934

The State represents violence in a concentrated and organized form. The individual has a soul, but as the State is a soulless machine, it can never be weaned from violence to which it owes its very existence.   28   *Modern Review, October, 1935*

It is my firm conviction that if the State suppressed capitalism by violence, it will be caught in the coil of violence itself and fail to develop nonviolence at any time.   29   *Modern Review, October, 1935*

Self-government means continuous effort to be independent of government control whether it is foreign government or whether it is national. *Swarāj* government will be a sorry affair if people look up to it for the regulation of every detail of life.   30

Young India, August 6, 1925

We must be content to die, if we cannot live as free men and women. 31   *Young India, January 5, 1922*

The rule of majority has a narrow application, i.e., one should yield to the majority in matters of detail. But it is slavery to be amenable to the majority, no matter what its decisions are. Democracy is not a state in which people act like sheep. Under democracy individual

Democracy and the People

liberty of opinion and action is jealously guarded. *32*
Young India, March 2, 1922

In matters of conscience the law of majority has no place. *33*
Young India, August 4, 1920

It is my certain conviction that no man loses his freedom except through his own weakness. *34*   *Inda's Case for Swaraj, February 1932*

It is not so much British guns that are responsible for our subjection as our voluntary co-operation. *35*   *Young India, February 9, 1921*

Even the most despotic government cannot stand except for the consent of the governed which consent is often forcibly procured by the despot. Immediately the subject ceases to fear the despotic force, his power is gone. *36*   *Young India, June 30, 1920*

Most people do not understand the complicated machinery of the government. They do not realize that every citizen silently but none the less certainly sustains the government of the day in ways of which he has no knowledge. Every citizen therefore renders himself responsible for every act of his government. And it is quite proper to support it so long as the actions of the government are bearable. But when they hurt him and his nation, it becomes his duty to withdraw his support. *37*   *Young India, July 28, 1920*

It is true that in the vast majority of cases, it is the duty of a subject to submit to wrongs on failure of the usual procedure, so long as they do not affect his vital being. But every nation and every individual have the right, and it is their duty, to rise against an intolerable wrong. *38*   *Young India, June 9, 1920*

There is no bravery greater than a resolute refusal to bend the knee to an earthly power, no matter how great, and that without bitterness of spirit and in the fullness of faith that the spirit alone lives, nothing else does. *39*   *Harijan, October 15, 1939*

The outward freedom that we shall attain will only be in exact proportion to the inward freedom to which we may have grown at a given moment. And if this is the correct view of freedom, our chief energy must be concentrated upon achieving reform from within.
40   *Young India, November 1, 1928*

The true democrat is he who with purely nonviolent means defends

his liberty and, therefore, his country's and ultimately that of the
whole of mankind. *41*   *Harijan, April 15, 1939*

Democracy disciplined and enlightened is the finest thing in the
world. A democracy prejudiced, ignorant, superstitious will land itself
in chaos and may be self-destroyed. *42*   *Young India, July 30, 1931*

Democracy and violence can ill go together. The States that are today
nominally democratic have either to become frankly totalitarian or, if
they are to become truly democratic, they must become courageously
nonviolent. It is a blasphemy to say that nonviolence can only be
practised by individuals and never by nations which are composed of
individuals. *43*   *Harijan, November 12, 1938*

For me the only training in *swarāj* we need is the ability to defend
ourselves against the whole world and to live our life in perfect
freedom even though it may be full of defects. Good government is
no substitution for self-government. *44*
                                       Young India, September 22, 1920

I do not blame the British. If we were weak in numbers as the British
are, we would perhaps have resorted to the same methods as they are
employing. Terrorism and deception are weapons not of the strong
but of the weak. The British are weak in numbers, we are weak in
spite of our numbers. The result is that each is dragging the other
down. It is common experience that Englishmen lose in character
after residence in India and that Indians lose in courage and manli-
ness by contact with Englishmen. This process of weakening is good
neither for us two nations, nor for the world.

But if we Indians take care of ourselves the English and the rest of
the world would take care of themselves. Our contribution to the
progress of the world must, therefore, consist in setting our own
house in order. *45*   *Young India, September 22, 1920*

What then is the meaning of non-co-operation in terms of the law of
suffering? We must voluntarily put up with the losses and incon-
veniences that arise from having to withdraw our support from a
government that is ruling against our will. 'Possession of power and
riches is a crime under an unjust government, poverty in that case is
a virtue, says Thoreau. It may be that in the transition state we may
make mistakes; there may be avoidable suffering. These things are
preferable to national emasculation.

We must refuse to wait for the wrong to be righted till the wrong-
doer has been roused to a sense of his iniquity. We must not, for fear
of ourselves or others having to suffer, remain participators in it. But

we must combat the wrong by ceasing to assist the wrong-doer directly or indirectly.

If a father does injustice, it is the duty of his children to leave the parental roof. If the headmaster of a school conducts his institution on an immoral basis, the pupils must leave the school. If the chairman of a corporation is corrupt, the members thereof must wash their hands clean of his corruption by withdrawing from it; even so if a government does a grave injustice the subject must withdraw cooperation wholly or partially, sufficiently to wean the ruler from wickedness. In each case conceived by me there is an element of suffering whether mental or physical. Without such suffering it is not possible to attain freedom. *46* *Young India, June 16, 1920*

The moment I became a *satyāgrahi* from that moment I ceased to be a subject, but never ceased to be a citizen. A citizen obeys laws voluntarily and never under compulsion or for fear of the punishment prescribed for their breach. He breaks them when he considers it necessary and welcomes the punishment. That robs it of its edge or of the disgrace which it is supposed to imply. *47*

Mahatma, Vol. VI, May 1943

Complete civil disobedience is rebellion without the element of violence in it. An out-and-out civil resister simply ignores the authority of the State. He becomes an outlaw claiming to disregard every unmoral State law. Thus, for instance, he may refuse to pay taxes, he may refuse to recognize the authority in his daily intercourse. He may refuse to obey the law of trespass and claim to enter military barracks in order to speak to the soldiers, he may refuse to submit to limitations upon the manner of picketing and may picket within the proscribed area. In doing all this he never uses force and never resists force when it is used against him. In fact, he invites imprisonment and other uses of force against himself. This he does because and when he finds the bodily freedom he seemingly enjoys to be an intolerable burden. He argues to himself that a State allows personal freedom only in so far as the citizen submits to its regulations. Submission to the State law is the price a citizen pays for his personal liberty. Submission, therefore, to a State wholly or largely unjust is an immoral barter for liberty. A citizen who thus realizes the evil nature of a State is not satisfied to live on its sufferance, and therefore appears to the others who do not share his belief to be a nuisance to society whilst he is endeavouring to compel the State, without committing a moral breach, to arrest him. Thus considered, civil resistance is a most powerful expression of a soul's anguish and an eloquent protest against the continuance of an evil State. Is not this the history of all reform? Have not reformers, much to the disgust of their fellows, discarded even innocent symbols associated with an evil practice?

When a body of men disown the State under which they have hitherto lived, they nearly establish their own government. I say nearly, for they do not go to the point of using force when they are resisted by the State. Their 'business,' as of the individual, is to be locked up or shot by the State, unless it recognizes their separate existence, in other words bows to their will. Thus three thousand Indians in South Africa after due notice to the Government of the Transvaal crossed the Transvaal border in 1914 in defiance of the Transvaal Immigration Law and compelled the government to arrest them. When it failed to provoke them to violence or to coerce them into submission, it yielded to their demands. A body of civil resisters is, therefore, like an army subject to all the discipline of a soldier, only harder because of want of excitement of an ordinary soldier's life. And as a civil resistance army is or ought to be free from passion because free from the spirit of retaliation, it requires the fewest number of soldiers. Indeed one *perfect* civil resister is enough to win the battle of Right against Wrong. *48*   *Young India, November 10, 1921*

Discipline has a place in nonviolent strategy, but much more is required. In a *Satyāgraha* army everybody is a soldier and a servant. But at a pinch every *satyāgrahi* soldier has also to be his own general and leader. Mere discipline cannot make for leadership. The latter calls for faith and vision. *49*   *Harijan, July 28, 1940*

Where self-reliance is the order of the day, where no one has to look expectantly at another, where there are no leaders and no followers, or where all are leaders and all are followers, the death of a fighter, however eminent, makes not for slackness but on the other hand intensifies the struggle. *50*   *Sabarmati, circa, 1928*

Every good movement passes through five stages, indifference, ridicule, abuse, repression, and respect. We had indifference for a few months. Then the Viceroy graciously laughed at it. Abuse, including misrepresentation, has been the order of the day. The Provincial Governors and the anti-non-co-operation press have heaped as much abuse upon the movement as they have been able to. Now comes repression, at present yet in its fairly mild form. Every movment that survives repression, mild or severe, invariably commands respect which is another name for success. This repression, if we are true, may be treated as a sure sign of the approaching victory. But, if we are true, we shall neither be cowed down nor angrily retaliate and be violent. Violence is suicide. *51*   *Young India, March 9, 1921*

My confidence is unshaken. If a single *satyāgrahi* holds out to the end, victory is absolutely certain. *52*   *Sbarmati, 1928*

My work will be finished, if I succeed in carrying conviction to the human family that every man or woman, however weak in body, is the guardian of his or her self-respect and liberty. This defence avails, though the whole world may be against the individual resister. *53*

Mahatma, Vol. VI., August 9, 1944

X EDUCATION

Real education consists in drawing the best out of yourself. What better book can there be than the book of humanity? *1*

Harijan, March 30, 1934

I hold that true education of the intellect can only come through a proper exercise and training of the bodily organs, e.g., hands, feet, eyes, ears, nose, etc. In other words an intelligent use of the bodily organs in a child provides the best and quickest way of developing his intellect. But unless the development of the mind and body goes hand in hand with a corresponding awakening of the soul, the former alone would prove to be a poor lopsided affair. By spiritual training I mean education of the heart. A proper and all-round development of the mind, therefore, can take place only when it proceeds *pari passu* with the education of the physical and spiritual faculties of the child. They constitute an indivisible whole. According to this theory, therefore, it would be a gross fallacy to suppose that they can be developed piecemeal or independently of one another. *2*

Harijan, May 8, 1937

By education I mean an all-round drawing out of the best in child and man—body, mind and spirit. Literacy is not the end of education nor even the beginning. It is only one of the means whereby man and woman can be educated. Literacy in itself is no education. I would therefore begin the child's education by teaching it a useful handicraft and enabling it to produce from the moment it begins its training. Thus every school can be made self-supporting, the condition being that the State takes over the manufactures of these schools.

I hold that the highest development of the mind and the soul is possible under such a system of education. Only every handicraft has to be taught not merely mechanically as is done today but scientifically, i.e., the child should know the why and the wherefore of every process. I am not writing this without some confidence, because it has the backing of experience. This method is being adopted more or less completely wherever spinning is being taught to workers. I have myself taught sandal-making and even spinning on these lines with good results. This method does not exclude a knowledge of history and geography. But I find that this is being taught by transmitting such general information by word of mouth. One imparts ten times as much in this manner as by reading and writing. The signs of the alphabet may be taught later when the pupil has learnt to distinguish wheat from the chaff and when he has somewhat developed his or her tastes. This is a revolutionary proposal, but it saves immense labour and enables a student to acquire in one year what he may take much longer to learn. This means all-round economy. Of course the pupil learns mathematics whilst he is learning his handicraft. 3

Harijan, July 31, 1937

I admit my limitations. I have no university education worth the name. My high school career was never above the average. I was thankful if I could pass my examinations. Distinction in the school was beyond my aspiration. Nevertheless I do hold very strong views on education in general, including what is called higher education. And I owe it to the country that my views should be clearly known and taken for what they may be worth. I must shed the timidity that has led almost to self-suppression. I must not fear ridicule, and even loss of popularity or prestige. If I hide my belief, I shall never correct errors of judgement. I am always eager to discover them and more than eager to correct them.

Let me now state my conclusions held for a number of years and enforced wherever I had opportunity of enforcing them:

1. I am not opposed to education even of the highest type attainable in the world.
2. The State must pay for it wherever it has definite use for it.
3. I am opposed to all higher education being paid for from the general revenue.
4. It is my firm conviction that the vast amount of the so-called education in arts, given in our colleges, is sheer waste and has resulted in unemployment among the educated classes. What is more, it has destroyed the health, both mental and physical, of the boys and girls who have the misfortune to go through the grind in our colleges.
5. The medium of a foreign language through which higher education has been imparted in India has caused incalculable intellectual and moral injury to the nation. We are too near our own times to

judge the enormity of the damage done. And we who have received such education have both to be victims and judges—an almost impossible feat.

I must give my reasons for the conclusions set forth above. This I can best do, perhaps, by giving a chapter from my own experience.

Up to the age of 12 all the knowledge I gained was through Gujarati, my mother tongue. I knew then something of arithmetic, history and geography. Then I entered a High School. For the first three years the mother tongue was still the medium. But the schoolmaster's business was to drive English into the pupil's head. Therefore more than half of our time was given to learning English and mastering its arbitrary spelling and pronunciation. It was a painful discovery to have to learn a language that was not pronounced as it was written. It was a strange experience to have to learn the spelling by heart. But that is by the way, and irrelevant to my argument. However, for the first three years, it was comparatively plain sailing.

The pillory began with the fourth year. Everything had to be learnt through English—geometry, algebra, chemistry, astronomy, history, geography. The tyranny of English was so great that even Sanskrit or Persian had to be learnt through English, not through the mother tongue. If any boy spoke in Gujarati which he understood, he was punished. It did not matter to the teacher, if a boy spoke bad English which he could neither pronounce correctly nor understand fully. Why should the teacher worry? His own English was by no means without blemish. It could not be otherwise. English was as much a foreign language to him as to his pupils. The result was chaos. We the boys had to learn many things by heart, though we could not understand them fully and often not at all. My head used to reel as the teacher was struggling to make his exposition on geometry understood by us. I could make neither head nor tail of geometry till we reached the thirteenth theorem of the first book of Euclid. And let me confess to the reader that in spite of all my love for the mother tongue, I do not to this day know the Gujarati equivalents of the technical terms of geometry, algebra and the like. I know now that what I took four years to learn of arithmetic, geometry, algebra, chemistry and astronomy, I should have learnt easily in one year, if I had not to learn them through English but Gujarati. My grasp of the subjects would have been easier and clearer. My Gujarati vocabulary would have been richer. I would have made use of such knowledge in my own home. This English medium created an impassable barrier between me and the members of my family, who had not gone through English schools. My father knew nothing of what I was doing. I could not, even if I had wished it, interest my father in what I was learning. For though he had ample intelligence, he knew not a word of English. I was fast becoming a stranger in my own home. I certainly became a superior person. Even my dress began to undergo imperceptible changes. What happened to me was not an uncommon experience. It was common to the majority.

The first three years in the High School made little addition to my stock of general knowledge. They were a preparation for fitting the boys for teaching them everything through English. High Schools were schools for cultural conquest by the English. The knowledge gained by the three hundred boys of my High School became a circumscribed possession. It was not for transmission to the masses.

A word about literature. We had to learn several books of English prose and English poetry. No doubt all this was nice. But that knowledge has been of no use to me in serving or bringing me in touch with the masses. I am unable to say that if I had not learnt what I did of English prose and poetry, I should have missed a rare treasure. If I had, instead, passed those precious seven years in mastering Gujarati and had learnt mathematics, sciences, and Sanskrit and other subjects through Gujarati, I could easily have shared the knowledge so gained with my neighbours. I would have enriched Gujarati, and who can say that I would not have with my habit of application and my inordinate love for the country and mother tongue, made a richer and greater contribution to the service of the masses?

I must not be understood to decry English or its noble literature. The columns of the *Harijan* are sufficient evidence of my love of English. But the nobility of its literature cannot avail the Indian nation any more than the temperate climate or the scenery of England can avail her. India has to flourish in her own climate and scenery and her own literature, even though all the three may be inferior to the English climate, scenery and literature. We and our children must build on our own heritage. If we borrow another, we impoverish our own. We can never grow on foreign victuals. I want the nation to have the treasures contained in that language, for that matter in other languages of the world, through its own vernaculars. I do not need to learn Bengali in order to know the beauties of Rabindranath's matchless productions. I get them through good translations. Gujarati boys and girls do not need to learn Russian to appreciate Tolstoy's short stories. They learn them through good translations. It is the boast of Englishmen that the best of the world's literary output is in the hands of that nation in simple English inside of a week of its publication. Why need I learn English to get at the best of what Shakespeare and Milton thought and wrote?

It would be good economy to set apart a class of students whose business would be to learn the best of what is to be learnt in the different languages of the world and give the translation in the vernaculars. Our masters chose the wrong way for us, and habit has made the wrong appear as right. . . .

Universities must be made self-supporting. The State should simply educate those whose services it would need. For all other branches of learning it should encourage private effort. The medium of instruction should be altered at once and at any cost, the provincial languages being given their rightful place. I would prefer temporary chaos in higher education to the criminal waste that is daily accumulating. . . .

Thus I claim that I am not an enemy of higher education. But I am an enemy of higher education as it is given in this country. Under my scheme there will be more and better libraries, more and better laboratories, more and better research institutes. Under it we should have an army of chemists, engineers and other experts who will be real servants of the nation, and answer the varied and growing requirements of a people who are becoming increasingly conscious of their rights and wants. And all these experts will speak, not a foreign tongue, but the language of the people. The knowledge gained by them will be the common property of the people. There will be truly original work instead of mere imitation. And the cost will be evenly and justly distributed. *4*   *Harijan, July 9, 1938*

The Indian culture of our times is in the making. Many of us are striving to produce a blend of all the cultures which seem today to be in clash with one another. No culture can live, if it attempts to be exclusive. There is no such thing as pure Aryan culture in existence today in India. Whether the Aryans were indigenous to India or were unwelcome intruders, does not interest me much. What does interest me is the fact that my remote ancestors blended with one another with the utmost freedom and we of the present generation are a result of that blend. Whether we are doing any good to the country of our birth and the tiny globe which sustains us or whether we are a burden, the future alone will show. *5*   *Harijan, May 9, 1936*

I do not want my house to be walled in on all sides and my windows to be stuffed. I want the cultures of all lands to be blown about my house as freely as possible. But I refuse to be blown off my feet by any. I would have our young men and women with literary tastes to learn as much of English and other world-languages as they like, and then expect them to give the benefits of their learning to India and to the world like a Bose, a Ray or the Poet himself.[1] But I would not have a single Indian to forget, neglect or be ashamed of his mother tongue, or to feel that he or she cannot think or express the

---

1. Sir Jagdish Chandra Bose and Sir P. C. Ray were eminent Indian scientists; 'the Poet' refers to Rabindranath Tagore.

best thoughts in his or her own vernacular. Mine is not a religion of the prison-house. *6*
Young India, June 1, 1921

Music means rhythm, order. Its effect is electrical. It immediately soothes. Unfortunately like our *shāstras*, music has been the prerogative of the few. It has never become nationalized in the modern sense. If I had any influence with volunteer boy scouts and *Seva Samiti* organizations, I would make compulsory a proper singing in company of national songs. And to that end I should have great musicians attending every congress or conference and teaching mass music. *7*
Young India, September 8, 1920

In Pandit Khare's opinion, based upon wide experience, music should form part of the syllabus of primary education. I heartily endorse the proposition. The modulation of the voice is as necessary as the training of the hand. Physical drill, handicrafts, drawing and music should go hand in hand in order to draw the best out of the boys and girls and create in them a real interest in their tuition. *8*
Harijan, September 11, 1937

The eyes, the ears and the tongue come before the hand. Reading comes before writing and drawing before tracing the letters of the alphabet. If this natural method is followed, the understanding of the children will have much better opportunity of development than when it is under check by beginning the children's training with the alphabet. *9*
The Mind of Mahatma Gandhi

Nothing can be farther from my thought than that we should become exclusive or erect barriers. But I do respectfully contend that an appreciation of other cultures can fitly follow, never precede, an appreciation and assimilation of our own.... An academic grasp without practice behind it is like an embalmed corpse, perhaps lovely to look at but nothing to inspire or ennoble. My religion forbids me to belittle or disregard other cultures, as it insists under pain of civil suicide upon imbibing and living my own. *10*
Young India, September 1, 1921

The utterly false idea that intelligence can be developed only through book-reading should give place to the truth that the quickest development of the mind can be achieved by artisan's work being learnt in a scientific manner. True development of the mind commences immediately the apprentice is taught at every step why a particular manipulation of the hand or a tool is required. The problem of the unemployment of students can be solved without difficulty, if they will rank themselves among the common labourers. *11*

Harijan, January 9, 1927

I am not sure that it is not better for the children to have much of the preliminary instruction imparted to them vocally. To impose on children of tender age a knowledge of the alphabet and the ability to read before they can gain general knowledge is to deprive them, whilst they are fresh, of the power of assimilating instruction by word of mouth. *12*   *Young India, September 16, 1926*

Literary training by itself adds not an inch to one's moral height and character-building is independent of literary training. *13*

Young India, June 1, 1921

I am a firm believer in the principle of free and compulsory primary education for India. I also hold that we shall realize this only by teaching the children a useful vocation and utilizing it as a means for cultivating their mental, physical and spiritual faculties. Let no one consider these economic calculations in connexion with education as sordid or out of place. There is nothing essentially sordid about economic calculations. True economics never militates against the highest ethical standard, just as true ethics to be worth its name must, at the same time, be also good economics. *14*   *Harijan, October 9, 1937*

I value education in the different sciences. Our children cannot have too much of chemistry and physics. *15*   *The Mind of Mahatma Gandhi*

I would develop in the child his hands, his brain and his soul. The hands have almost atrophied. The soul has been altogether ignored. *16*   *The Mind of Mahatma Gandhi*

As regards children's curiosity about the facts of life, we should tell them if we know, and admit our ignorance if we do not. If it is something that must not be told, we should check them and ask them not to put such questions even to anyone else. We must never put them off. They know more things than we imagine. If they do not know and if we refuse to tell them, they try to acquire the knowledge in a questionable manner. But if it has to be withheld from them, we must take such risk. *17*   *The Diary of Mahadev Desai*

A wise parent allows the children to make mistakes. It is good for them once in a while to burn their fingers. *18*

Mahatma Gandhi, The Last Phase, Vol. I, circa 1946

We cannot properly control or conquer the sexual passion by turning a blind eye to it. I am, therefore, strongly in favour of teaching young boys and young girls the significance and right use of their generative organs. In my own way I have tried to impart this knowledge to young children of both sexes, for whose training I was responsible. But the sex education that I stand for must have for its object the conquest and sublimation of the sex passion. Such education should automatically serve to bring home to children the essential distinction between man and brute, to make them realize that it is man's privilege and pride to be gifted with the faculties of head and heart both, that he is a thinking no less than a feeling animal, and to renounce the sovereignty of reason over the blind instinct is, therefore, to renounce a man's estate. In man, reason quickens and guides the feeling, in brute the soul lies ever dormant. To awaken the heart is to awaken the dormant soul, to awaken reason and to inculcate discrimination between good and evil. Today, our entire environment—our reading, our thinking, and our social behaviour—is generally calculated to subserve and cater for the sex urge. To break through its coils is no easy task. But it is a task worthy of our highest endeavour. *19*

Mahatma, Vol. IV, 1936

XI WOMEN

I am firmly of opinion that India's salvation depends on the sacrifice and enlightenment of her women. *1*   *Harijan, June 27, 1936*

Ahiṃsā means infinite love, which again means infinite capacity for suffering. Who but woman, the mother of man, shows this capacity in the largest measure? She shows it as she carries the infant and feeds it during nine months and derives joy in the suffering involved. What can beat the suffering caused by the pangs of labour? But she forgets them in the joy of creation. Who again suffers daily so that her babe may wax from day to day? Let her transfer that love to the whole of humanity, let her forget that she ever was or can be the object of man's lust. And she will occupy her proud position by the side of man as his mother, maker and silent leader. It is given to her to teach the art of peace to the warring world thirsting for that nectar. *2*   *Harijan, February 24, 1940*

My own opinion is that, just as fundamentally man and woman are one, their problem must be one in essence. The soul in both is the same. The two live the same life, have the same feelings. Each is a complement of the other. The one cannot live without the other's active help.

But somehow or other man has dominated woman from ages past, and so woman has developed an inferiority complex. She has believed in the truth of man's interested teaching that she is inferior to him. But the seers among men have recognized her equal status.

Nevertheless there is no doubt that at some point there is bifurcation. Whilst both are fundamentally one, it is also equally true that in the form there is a vital difference between the two. Hence the vocations of the two must also be different. The duty of motherhood, which the vast majority of women will always undertake, requires qualities which man need not possess. She is passive, he is active. She is essentially mistress of the house. He is the bread-winner. She is the keeper and distributor of the bread. She is the caretaker in every sense of the term. The art of bringing up the infants of the race is her special and sole prerogative. Without her care the race must become extinct.

In my opinion it is degrading both for man and woman that woman should be called upon or induced to forsake the hearth and shoulder the rifle for the protection of that hearth. It is a reversion to barbarity and the beginning of the end. In trying to ride the horse that man rides, she brings herself and him down. The sin will be on man's head for tempting or compelling his companion to desert her special calling. There is as much bravery in keeping one's home in good order and condition as there is in defending it against attack from without.   *3*   *Harijan, February 24, 1940*

If I were born a woman, I would rise in rebellion against any pretension on the part of man that woman is borne to be his plaything. I have mentally become a woman in order to steal into her heart. I could not steal into my wife's heart until I decided to treat her differently than I used to do, and so I restored to her all her rights by dispossessing myself of all my so-called rights as her husband.   *4*
Young India, December 8, 1927

Of all the evils for which man has made himself responsible, none is so degrading, so shocking or so brutal as his abuse of the better half of humanity—to me, the female sex, not the weaker sex. It is the nobler of the two, for it is even today the embodiment of sacrifice, silent suffering, humility, faith and knowledge.   *5*
Young India, September 15, 1921

Woman must cease to consider herself the object of man's lust. The remedy is more in her hands than man's.   *6*
Young India, July 21, 1921

Chastity is not a hot-house growth. It cannot be protected by the surrounding wall of the *purdah*. It must grow from within, and to be worth anything it must be capable of withstanding every unsought temptation.   *6*   *Young India, February 3, 1927*

And why is there all this morbid anxiety about female purity? Have women any say in the matter of male purity? We hear nothing of women's anxiety about men's chastity. Why should men arrogate to themselves the right to regulate female purity? It cannot be superimposed from without. It is a matter of evolution from within and therefore of individual self-effort. *8*

Young India, November 25, 1926

Woman, I hold, is the personification of self-sacrifice, but unfortunately today she does not realize what a tremendous advantage she has over man. As Tolstoy used to say, they are labouring under the hypnotic influence of man. If they would realize the strength of nonviolence they would not consent to be called the weaker sex. *9*

Young India, January 14, 1932

To call woman the weaker sex is a libel; it is man's injustice to woman. If by strength is meant brute strength, then, indeed, is woman less brute than man. If by strength is meant moral power, then woman is immeasurably man's superior. Has she not greater intuition, is she not more self-sacrificing, has she not greater powers of endurance, has she not greater courage? Without her man could not be. If nonviolence is the law of our being, the future is with woman.... Who can make a more effective appeal to the heart than woman? *10*   *Young India, April 10, 1930*

Women are special custodians of all that is pure and religious in life. Conservative by nature, if they are slow to shed superstitious habits, they are also slow to give up all that is pure and noble in life. *11*

Harijan, March 25, 1931

I believe in the proper education of women. But I do believe that woman will not make her contribution to the world by mimicking or running a race with men. She can run the race, but she will not rise to the great heights she is capable of by mimicking man. She has to be the complement of man. *12*   *Harijan, February 27, 1937*

Woman is the companion of man gifted with equal mental capacities. She has the right to participate in the minutest detail of the activities of man, and she has the same right of freedom and liberty as he. She is entitled to a supreme place in her own sphere of activity as man is in his. This ought to be the natural condition of things, and not a result only of learning to read and write. By sheer force of a vicious custom, even the most ignorant and worthless men have been enjoying a superiority over women which they do not deserve and ought not to have. *13*   *Women and Social Injustice, published in 1942*

If only women will forget that they belong to the weaker sex, I have no doubt that they can do infinitely more than men against war. Answer for yourselves what your great soldiers and generals would do, if their wives and daughters and mothers refused to countenance their participation in militarism in any shape or form.   *14*

Women and Social Injustice, published in 1942

A sister who is a good worker, and was anxious to remain celibate in order to serve better the country's cause, has recently married having met the mate of her dreams. But she imagines that in doing so she has done wrong and fallen from the high ideal which she had set before herself. I have tried to rid her mind of this delusion. It is no doubt an excellent thing for girls to remain unmarried for the sake of service, but the fact is that only one in a million is able to do so. Marriage is a natural thing in life and to consider it derogatory in any sense is wholly wrong. When one imagines any act a fall it is difficult, however hard one tries, to raise oneself. The ideal is to look upon marriage as a sacrament and therefore to lead a life of self-restraint in the married estate. Marriage in Hinduism is one of the four *āshramas*. In fact the other three are based on it.

The duty of the above-mentioned and other sisters who think like her is, therefore, not to look down upon marriage but to give it its due place and make of it the sacrament it is. If they exercise the necessary self-restraint, they will find growing within themselves a greater strength for service. She who wishes to serve will naturally choose a partner in life who is of the same mind, and their joint service will be the country's gain.   *15*   *Harijan, March 22, 1942*

Marriage confirms the right of union between two partners to the exclusion of all the others when in their joint opinion they consider such union to be desirable, but it confers no right upon one partner to demand obedience of the other to one's wish for union. What should be done when one partner on moral or other grounds cannot conform to the wishes of the other is a separate question. Personally if divorce was the only alternative, I should not hesitate to accept it, rather than interrupt my moral progress assuming that I want to restrain myself on purely moral grounds.   *16*

Young India, October 8, 1925

It is a tragedy that generally speaking our girls are not taught the duties of motherhood. But if married life is a religious duty, motherhood must be too. To be an ideal mother is no easy task. The procreation of children has to be undertaken with a full sense of responsibility. The mother should know what is her duty from the moment she conceives right up to the time the child is born. And she who gives intelligent, healthy and well brought up children to the country is surely rendering a service. When the latter grow up they too will be ready to serve. The truth of the matter is that those who are filled with a living spirit of service will always serve whatever their position in life. They will never adopt a way of life which will interfere with service. *17* *Women and Social Injustice, published in 1942*

'Some people oppose a modification of laws relating to the right of a married woman to own property on the ground that economic independence of woman would lead to the spread of immorality among women and disruption of domestic life. What is your attitude on the question?'

I would answer the question by a counter question: Has not independence of man and his holding property led to the spread of immorality among men? If you answer 'yes' then let it be so also with women. And when women have rights of ownership and the rest like men, it will be found that the enjoyment of such rights is not responsible for their vices or their virtues. Morality which depends upon the helplessness of a man or woman has not much to recommend it. Morality is rooted in the purity of our hearts. *18*
Women and Social Injustice, published in 1942

A young man has sent me a letter which can be given here only in substance. It is as under:

'I am a married man. I had gone out to a foreign country. I had a friend whom both I and my parents implicitly trusted. During my absence he seduced my wife who has now conceived of him. My father now insists that the girl should resort to abortion; otherwise, he says, the family would be disgraced. To me it seems that it would be wrong to do so. The poor woman is consumed with remorse. She cares neither to eat nor drink, but is always weeping. Will you kindly tell me as to what my duty is in the case?'

I have published this letter with great hesitation. As everybody knows such cases are by no means infrequent in society. A restrained public discussion of the question, therefore, does not seem to me to be out of place.

It seems to me clear as daylight that abortion would be a crime. Countless husbands are guilty of the same lapse as this poor woman, but nobody ever questions them. Society not only excuses them but does not even censure them. Then, again, the woman cannot conceal her shame while man can successfully hide his sin.

The woman in question deserves to be pitied. It would be the sacred duty of the husband to bring up the baby with all the love and tenderness that he is capable of and to refuse to yield to the counsels of his father. Whether he should continue to live with his wife is a ticklish question. Circumstances may warrant separation from her. In that case he would be bound to provide for her maintenance and education and to help her to live a pure life. Nor should

I see anything wrong in his accepting her repentance if it is sincere and genuine. Nay, further, I can imagine a situation when it would be the sacred duty of the husband to take back an erring wife who has completely expiated for and redeemed her error.   *19*

Woman and Social Injustice, published in 1942

Passive resistance is regarded as the weapon of the weak, but the resistance for which I had to coin a new name altogether is the weapon of the strongest. I had to coin a new word to signify what I meant. But its matchless beauty lies in the fact that, though it is the weapon of the strongest, it can be wielded by the weak in body, by the aged, and even by the children if they have stout hearts. And since resistance in *Satyāgraha* is offered through self-suffering, it is a weapon pre-eminently open to women. We found last year that women in India, in many instances, surpassed their brothers in sufferings and the two played a noble part in the campaign. For the ideal of self-suffering became contagious and they embarked upon amazing acts of self-denial. Supposing that the women and the children of Europe became fired with the love of humanity, they would take the men by storm and reduce militarism to nothingness in an incredibly short time. The underlying idea is that women, children and others have the same soul, the same potentiality. The question is one of drawing out the limitless power of truth.   *20*

Women and Social Injustice, published in 1942

When a woman is assaulted, she may not stop to think in terms of *himsā* or *ahimsā*. Her primary duty is self-protection. She is at liberty to employ every method or means that comes to her mind, in order to defend her honour. God has given her nails and teeth. She must use them with all her strength and, if need be, die in the effort. The man or woman who has shed all fear of death will be able not only to protect himself or herself but others also through laying down his or her life. In truth, we fear death most, and hence we ultimately submit to superior physical force. Some will bend the knee to the invader, some will resort to bribery, some will crawl on their bellies or submit to other forms of humiliation, and some women will even give their bodies rather than die. I have not written this in a carping spirit. I am only illustrating human nature. Whether we crawl on our bellies, or whether a woman yields to the lust of man, is symbolic of that same love of life which makes us stoop to anything. Therefore, only he who loses his life shall save it. To enjoy life one should give up the lure of life. That should be part of our nature.   *21*

Speech, December 22, 1916

For me there can be no preparation for violence. All preparation

must be for nonviolence if courage of the highest type is to be developed.... If there are women who when assailed by miscreants cannot resist themselves without arms, they do not need to be *advised* to carry arms. They *will* do so. There is something wrong in this constant inquiry as to whether to bear arms or not. People have to learn to be naturally independent. If they will remember the central teaching, namely, that the real, effective resistance lies in nonviolence, they will mould their conduct accordingly. And that is what the world has been doing, although unthinkingly. Since it has not the highest courage, namely, courage born of nonviolence, it arms itself even unto the atom bomb. Those who do not see in it the futility of violence will naturally arm themselves to the best of their ability.
22   *Harijan, February 9, 1947*

It is for American women to show what power women can be in the world. But that can only be when you cease to be the toys of men's idle hours. You have got freedom. You can become a power for peace by refusing to be carried away by the flood-tide of the pseudo-science glorifying self-indulgence that is engulfing the West today and apply your minds instead to the science of nonviolence; for forgiveness is your nature. By aping men, you neither become men nor can you function as your real selves and develop your special talent that God has given you. God has vouchsafed to women the power of nonviolence more than to man. It is all the more effective because it is mute. Women are the natural messengers of the gospel of nonviolence if only they will realize their high estate. 23
        Mahatma Gandhi, The Last Phase, Vol. II, In conversation, circa 1947

But it is my firm conviction that if the men and women of India cultivate in themselves the courage to face death bravely and nonviolently, they can laugh to scorn the power of armaments and realize the ideal of unadulterated independence in terms of the masses which would serve as an example to the world. In that women can take the lead for they are a personification of the power of self-suffering. 24
        Mahatma Gandhi, The Last Phase, Vol. II, In conversation, circa, 1947

XII MISCELLANEOUS

I do not want to foresee the future. I am concerned with taking care of the present. God has given me no control over the moment following. *1*   *Young India, May 25, 1921*

I have been known as a crank, faddist, madman. Evidently the reputation is well deserved. For wherever I go, I draw to myself cranks, faddists and madmen. *2*   *Young India, June 13, 1929*

The world knows so little of how much my so-called greatness depends upon the incessant toil and drudgery of silent, devoted, able and pure workers, men as well as women. *3*
Young India, April 26, 1928

I look upon myself as a dull person. I take more time than others in understanding some things, but I do not care. There is a limit to man's progress in intelligence; but the development of the qualities of the heart knows no bounds. *4*   *The Dairy of Mahadev Desai*

It may fairly be said that intellect has played a subordinate part in my life. I think I am a dull person. It is literally true in my case that God provides the man of faith with such intelligence as he needs. I have always honoured and reposed faith in elders and wise men. But my deepest faith is in truth so that my path though difficult to tread has seemed easy to me. *5*   *The Diary of Mahadev Desai*

In the majority of cases addresses presented to me contain adjectives which I am ill able to carry. Their use can do good neither to the writers nor to me. They unnecessarily humiliate me, for I have to confess that I do not deserve them. When they are deserved, their use is superfluous. They cannot add to the strength of the qualities possessed by me. They may, if I am not on my guard, easily turn my head. The good that a man does is more often than not better left unsaid. Imitation is the sincerest flattery. *6 Young India, May 21, 1925*

The goal ever recedes from us. The greater the progress the greater the recognition of our unworthiness. Satisfaction lies in the effort, not in the attainment. Full effort is full victory. *7*

Young India, March 9, 1922

I have not conceived my mission to be that of a knight-errant wandering everywhere to deliver people from difficult situations. My humble occupation has been to show people how they can solve their own difficulties. *8* *Harijan, June 28, 1942*

If I seem to take part in politics, it is only because politics encircle us today like the coil of a snake from which one cannot get out, no matter how much one tries. I wish therefore to wrestle with the snake. *9* *Young India, May 12, 1920*

My work of social reform was in no way less or subordinate to political work. The fact is, that when I saw that to a certain extent my social work would be impossible without the help of political work, I took to the latter and only to the extent that it helped the former. I must therefore confess that work of social reform or self-purification of this nature is a hundred times dearer to me than what is called purely political work. *10* *Young India, August 6, 1931*

I am, myself, the father of four boys whom I have brought up to the best of my lights. I have been an extremely obedient son to my parents, and an equally obedient pupil to my teachers. I know the value of filial duty. But I count duty to God above all these. *11*

Mahatma, Vol. II, Speech, October, 1920

I deny being a visionary. I do not accept the claim of saintliness. I am of the earth, earthy. . . . I am prone to as many weaknesses as you are. But I have seen the world. I have lived in the world with my eyes open. I have gone through the most fiery ordeals that have fallen to the lot of man. I have gone through this discipline. *12*

Speeches and Writings of Mahatma Gandhi, 1933

I have never made a fetish of consistency. I am a votary of Truth and I must say what I feel and think at a given moment on the question, without regard to what I may have said before on it. . . . As my vision gets clearer, my views must grow clearer with daily practice.

Where I have deliberately altered an opinion, the change should be obvious. Only a careful eye would notice a gradual and imperceptible evolution. *13*   *Harijan, September 28, 1934*

I am not at all concerned with appearing to be consistent. In my pursuit after Truth I have discarded many ideas and learnt many new things. Old as I am in age, I have no feeling that I have ceased to grow inwardly or that my growth will stop with the dissolution of the flesh. What I am concerned with is my readiness to obey the call of Truth, my God, from moment to moment. *14*

Harijan, April 29, 1933

At the time of writing I never think of what I have said before. My aim is not to be consistent with my previous statements on a given question, but to be consistent with truth, as it may present itself to me at a given moment. The result has been that I have grown from truth to truth; I have saved my memory an undue strain; and what is more, whenever I have been obliged to compare my writing even fifty years ago with the latest, I have discovered no inconsistency between the two. But friends who observe inconsistency will do well to take the meaning that my latest writings may yield unless of course they prefer the old. But before making the choice, they should try to see if there is not an underlying and abiding consistency between the two seeming inconsistencies. *15*   *Mahatma, Vol. V., September 25, 1939*

It is better in prayer to have a heart without words than words without a heart. *16*   *Young India, January 23, 1930*

Behind my non-co-operation there is always the keenest desire to co-operate on the slightest pretext even with the worst of opponents. To me, a very imperfect mortal, ever in need of God's grace, no one is beyond redemption. *17*   *Young India, June 4, 1925*

My non-co-operation has its root not in hatred, but in love. My personal religion peremptorily forbids me to hate anybody. I learnt this simple yet grand doctrine when I was twelve years old through a school book and the conviction has persisted up to now. It is daily growing on me. It is a burning passion with me. *18*

Young India, August 6, 1925

What is true of individuals is true of nations. One cannot forgive too much. The weak can never forgive. Forgiveness is the attribute of the strong. *19*   *Young India, April 2, 1931*

Suffering has its well-defined limits. Suffering can be both wise and unwise, and when the limit is reached, to prolong it would be not wise, but the height of folly. *20*   *Young India, March 12, 1931*

Ours will only then be a truly spiritual nation when we shall show more truth than gold, greater fearlessness than pomp of power and wealth, greater charity than love of self. If we will but clean our houses, our palaces and temples of the attributes of wealth and show in them the attributes of morality, one can offer battle to any combination of hostile forces, without having to carry the burden of a heavy militia. *21*   *Mahatma, Vol. I, Speech, December 22, 1916*

I would far rather that India perished than that she won freedom at the sacrifice of truth. *22*   *The Mind of Mahatma Gandhi*

If I had no sense of humour, I should long ago have committed suicide. *23*   *Young India, August 18, 1921*

My philosophy, if I can be said to have any, excludes the possibility of harm to one's cause by outside agencies. The harm comes deservedly and only when the cause itself is bad or, being good, its champions are untrue, faint-hearted or unclean. *24*
Harijan, July 25, 1936

Somehow I am able to draw the noblest in mankind, and that is what enables me to maintain my faith in God and human nature. *25*
Harijan, April 15, 1939

If I was what I want to be I would not then need to argue with anyone. My word would go straight home. Indeed I would not even need to utter the word. The mere will on my part would suffice to produce the required effect. But I am painfully aware of my limitations. *26*   *Harijan, March 2, 1932*

Rationalists are admirable beings, rationalism is a hideous monster when it claims for itself omnipotence. Attribution of omnipotence to reason is as bad a piece of idolatry as is worship of stock and stone believing it to be God. I plead not for the suppression of reason, but for a due recognition of that in us which sanctifies reason. *27*
Young India, October 14, 1926

In every branch of reform constant study giving one a mastery over one's subject is necessary. Ignorance is at the root of failures, partial or complete, of all reform movements whose merits are admitted, for every project masquerading under the name of reform is not necessarily worthy of being so designated. *28*   *Harijan, April 24, 1937*

Gandhi planting a tree in remembrance of his stay at Kingsley Hall, London, 1931 (Photo Keystone)

In dealing with living entities, the dry syllogistic method leads not only to bad logic but sometimes to fatal logic. For if you miss even a tiny factor—and you never have control over all the factors that enter into dealings with human beings—your conclusion is likely to be wrong. Therefore, you never reach the final truth, you only reach an approximation; and that too if you are extra careful in your dealings. *29*   *Harijan, August 14, 1937*

It is a bad habit to say that another man's thoughts are bad and ours only are good and that those holding different views from ours are the enemies of the country. *30*   *Indian Home Rule, 1944*

Let us honour our opponents for the same honesty of purpose and patriotic motives that we claim for ourselves. *31*
Young India, June 4, 1925

It is true that I have often been let down. Many have deceived me and many have been found wanting. But I do not repent of my association with them. For I know how to non-co-operate, as I know how to co-operate. The most practical, the most dignified way of going on in the world is to take people at their word, when you have no positive reason to the contrary. *32 Young India, December 26, 1924*

If we are to make progress, we must not repeat history but make new history. We must add to the inheritance left by our ancestors. If we may make new discoveries and inventions in the phenomenal world, must we declare our bankruptcy in the spiritual domain? Is it impossible to multiply the exceptions so as to make them the rule? Must man always be brute first and man after, if at all? *33*
Young India, May 6, 1926

In every great cause it is not the number of fighters that counts but it is the quality of which they are made that becomes the deciding factor. The greatest men of the world have always stood alone. Take the great prophets, Zoroaster, Buddha, Jesus, Muhammad—they all stood alone like many others whom I can name. But they had living faith in themselves and their God, and believing as they did that God was on their side, they never felt lonely. *34*
Young India, October 10, 1929

Meetings and group organizations are all right. They are of some help, but very little. They are like the scaffolding that an architect erects— a temporary and makeshift expedient. The thing that really matters is an invincible faith that cannot be quenched. *35*
Harijan, January 28, 1939

No matter how insignificant the thing you have to do, do it as well as you can, give it as much of your care and attention as you would give to the thing you regard as most important. For it will be by those small things that you shall be judged. *36 Harijan, July 27, 1935*

As to the habit of looking to the West for light, I can give little guidance if the whole of my life has not provided any. Light used to go out from the East. If the Eastern reservoir has become empty, naturally the East will have to borrow from the West. I wonder if light, if it is light and not a miasma, can ever be exhausted. As a boy I learnt that it grew with the giving. Anyway I have acted in that belief and have, therefore, traded on the ancestral capital. It has never failed me. This, however, does not mean that I must act like a frog in the well. There is nothing to prevent me from profiting by the light that may come from the West. Only I must take care that I am not overpowered by the glamour of the West. I must not mistake the glamour for true light. *37*   *Harijan, January 13, 1940*

I do not subscribe to the superstition that everything is good because it is ancient. I do not believe either that anything is good because it is Indian. *38*   *Young India, January 8, 1925*

I am no indiscriminate worshipper of all that goes under the name 'ancient.' I never hesitate to demolish all that is evil or immoral, no matter how ancient it may be, but with that reservation, I must confess to you, that I am an adorer of ancient institutions and it hurts me to think that people in their rush for everything modern despise all their ancient traditions and ignore them in their lives. *39*
With Gandhiji In Ceylon, published in 1928

True morality consists, not in following the beaten track, but in finding out the true path for ourselves and in fearlessly following it. *40*   *Ethical Religion, 1930*

No action which is not voluntary can be called moral. So long as we act like machines, there can be no question of morality. If we want to call an action moral, it should have been done consciously and as a matter of duty. Any action that is dictated by fear or by coercion of any kind ceases to be moral. *41*   *Ethical Religion, 1930*

One earns the right of fiercest criticism when one has convinced one's neighbours of one's affection for them and one's sound judgement, and when one is sure of not being in the slightest degree ruffled if one's judgement is not accepted or enforced. In other words, there should be love faculty for clear perception and complete toleration to enable one to criticize. *42*   *Babu's Letters to Mira,*

The word 'criminal' should be taboo from our dictionary. Or we are all criminals. 'Those of you that are without sin cast the first stone.' And no one was found to dare cast the stone at the sinning harlot. As a jailer once said, all are criminals in secret. There is profound truth in that saying, uttered half in jest. Let them be therefore good companions. I know that this is easier said than done. And that is exactly what the Gita and as a matter of fact all religions enjoin upon us to do. *43*   *Babu's Letters to Mira,*

Man is the maker of his own destiny in the sense that he has the freedom of choice as to the manner in which he uses his freedom. But he is no controller of results. *44*   *Harijan, March 23, 1940*

Goodness must be joined with knowledge. Mere goodness is not of much use. One must retain the fine discriminating quality which goes with spiritual courage and character. One must know in a crucial situation when to speak and when to be silent, when to act and when to refrain. Action and non-action in these circumstances become identical instead of being contradictory. *45*

Hindusthan Standard, December 8, 1946

Everything created by God, animate or inanimate, has its good side and bad side. The wise man, like the fabled bird which separating the cream of milk from its water helps himself to the cream leaving the water alone, will take the good from everything leaving the bad alone. *46*   *Mahatma, Vol. II, Letter, 1927*

It was forty years back, when I was passing through a severe crisis of scepticism and doubt, that I came across Tolstoy's book, *The Kingdom of God is Within You,* and was deeply impressed by it. I was at that time a believer in violence. Its reading cured me of my scepticism and made me a firm believer in *ahiṃsā*. What has appealed to me most in Tolstoy's life is that he practised what he preached and reckoned no cost too great in his pursuit of truth. Take the simplicity of his life, it was wonderful. Born and brought up in the midst of luxury and comfort of a rich aristocratic family, blessed in an abundant measure with all the stores of the earth that desire can covet, this man who had fully known all the joys and pleasures of life turned his back upon them in the prime of his youth and afterwards never once looked back.

He was the most truthful man of this age. His life was a constant endeavour, an unbroken tide of striving to seek the truth, and to practise it as he found it. He never tried to hide truth or tone it down but set it before the world in its entirety without equivocation or compromise, undeterred by the fear of any earthly power.

He was the greatest apostle of nonviolence that the present age has produced. No one in the West, before him or since, has written and spoken on nonviolence so fully or insistently and with such penetration and insight as he. I would even go further and say that his remarkable development of this doctrine puts to shame the present-day narrow and lop-sided interpretation put upon it by the votaries of *ahiṃsā* in this land of ours. In spite of India's proud claim of being the *karmabhumi*, the land of realization, and in spite of some of the greatest discoveries in the field of *ahiṃsā* that our ancient sages have made, what often goes by the name of *ahiṃsā* among us today is a travesty of it. True *ahiṃsā* should mean a complete freedom from ill will and anger and hate and an overflowing love for all. For inculcating this true and higher type of *ahiṃsā* amongst us, Tolstoy's life with its ocean-like love should serve as a beacon light and a never-failing source of inspiration. Tolstoy's critics have sometimes said that his life was a colossal failure, that he never found his ideal, the mystical green stick, in whose quest his entire life was passed. I do not hold with these critics. True, he himself said so. But that only shows his greatness. It may be that he failed to fully realize his ideal in life, but that is only human. No one can attain perfection while he is in the body for the simple reason that the ideal state is impossible so long as one has not completely overcome his ego, and ego cannot be wholly got rid of so long as one is tied down by shackles of the flesh. It was a favourite saying of Tolstoy that the moment one believes that he has reached his ideal, his further progress stops and his retrogression begins and that the very virtue of an ideal consists in that it recedes from us the nearer we go. To say, therefore, that Tolstoy on his own admission failed to reach his ideal does not detract a jot from his greatness, it only shows his humility.

Much has been often sought to be made of the so-called inconsistencies of Tolstoy's life; but they were more apparent than real. Constant development is the law of life and a man who always tries to maintain his dogmas in order to appear consistent drives himself into a false position. That is why Emerson said that foolish consistency was the hobgoblin of little minds. Tolstoy's so-called inconsistencies were a sign of his development and his passionate regard for truth. He often seemed inconsistent because he was continuously outgrowing his own doctrines. His failures were public, his struggles and triumphs private. The world saw only the former, the latter remained unseen probably by Tolstoy himself most of all. His critics tried to make capital out of his faults, but no critic could be more exacting than he was with regard to himself. Ever on the alert for his short-comings, before his critics had time to point at them, he had already proclaimed them to the world magnified a thousandfold and imposed upon himself the penance that seemed to him necessary. He welcomed criticism even when it was exaggerated and like all truly great men dreaded the world's praise. He was great even in his failures and his failures give us a measure not of the futility of his ideals but of his success.

The third great point was a doctrine of 'bread labour,' that every one was bound to labour with his body for bread and most of the grinding misery in the world was due to the fact that men failed to discharge their duties in this respect. He regarded all schemes to ameliorate the poverty of the masses by the philanthropy of the rich, while they themselves shirked body labour and continued to live in luxury and ease, as hypocrisy and a sham, and suggested that if only man got off the backs of the poor, much of the so-called philanthropy would be rendered unnecessary.

And with him to believe was to act. So in the afternoon of his life, this man who had passed all his days in the soft lap of luxury took to a life of toil and hard labour. He took to boot-making and farming at which he worked hard for full eight hours a day. But his body labour did not blunt his powerful intellect; on the contrary it rendered it all the more keen and resplendent and it was in this period of his life that his most vigorous book—*What is Art?*—which he considered to be his masterpiece, was written in the intervals saved from the practice of his self-chosen vocation.

Literature, full of the virus of self-indulgence, and served out in attractive forms, is flooding our country from the West and there is the greatest need for our youth to be on their guard. The present is for them an age of transition of ideals and ordeals; the one thing needful for the world, its youth and particularly the youth of India in this crisis, is Tolstoy's progressive self-restraint, for it alone can lead to true freedom for themselves, the country and the world. It is we ourselves, with our inertia, apathy and social abuse that more than England or anybody else block our way to freedom. And if we cleanse ourselves of our shortcomings and faults, no power on earth can even for a moment withhold *swarāj* from us. . . . The three essential qualities of Tolstoy's life mentioned by me are of the utmost use to the youth in this hour of the world's trial.   47

Mahatma, Vol. II, Message on Tolstoy Centenary, 1928

It is my settled conviction that no deserving institution ever dies for want of support. Institutions that have died have done so either because there was nothing in them to commend them to the public or because those in control lost faith, or which is perhaps the same thing, lost stamina. I would therefore urge the conductors of such institutions not to give in because of the general depression. It is a time of test for worthy institutions. *48 Young India, October 15, 1925*

I had learnt at the outset not to carry on public work with borrowed money. One could rely on people's promise in most matters except in matters of money. *49*   *An Autobiography*

I disbelieve in the conversion of one person by another. My effort should never be to undermine another's faith but to make him a better follower of his own faith. This implies the belief in the truth of all religions and respect for them. It again implies true humility, a recognition of the fact that the divine light having been vouchsafed to all religions through an imperfect medium of flesh, they must share in more or less degree the imperfection of the vehicle. *50*
Mahatma, Vol. II, January, 1929

[To X who asked if it was true that Gandhi had allowed a venomous snake to pass over his body, he wrote:]
    It is both true and not true. The snake was passing over my body. In a case like that, what could I or anyone else do except to lie motionless? This hardly calls for any praise. And who knows whether or not the snake was poisonous? The idea that death is not a fearful event has been cherished by me for many a year, so that I recover soon enough from the shock of the death even of near and dear ones. *51*   *The Diary of Mahadev Desai*

We have been taught to believe that what is beautiful need not be useful and what is useful cannot be beautiful. I want to show that what is useful can also be beautiful. *52   Mahatma, Vol. I, circa 1946*

People who claim to pursue 'art for art's sake' are unable to make good their claim. There is a place for art in life, apart from the question—What is art? But art can only be a means to the end which we must all of us achieve. If however it becomes an end in itself, it enslaves and degrades humanity. *53*   *The Diary of Mahadev Desai*

There are two aspects of things—the outward and the inward. It is purely a matter of emphasis with me. The outward has no meaning except in so far as it helps the inward. All true art is thus the expression of the soul. The outward forms have value only in so far as they are the expression of the inner spirit in man. Art of that nature has the greatest possible appeal for me. But I know that many call themselves artists, and are recognized as such, and yet in their works there is absolutely no trace of the soul's upward urge and unrest. *54*   *Young India, November 13, 1924*

All true art must help the soul to realize its inner self. In my own case, I find that I can do entirely without external forms in my soul's realization. My room may have blank walls; and I may even dispense with the roof, so that I may gaze out upon the starry heavens overhead that stretch in an unending expanse of beauty. What conscious art of man can give me the panoramic scenes that open out before me, when I look up to the sky above with all its shining stars? This, however, does not mean that I refuse to accept the value of productions of art, generally accepted as such, but only that I personally feel how inadequate these are compared with the eternal symbols of beauty in Nature. These productions of man's art have their value only so far as they help the soul onward towards self-realization. *55*
Young India, November 13, 1924

I love music and all the other arts, but I do not attach such value to them as is generally done. I cannot, for example, recognize the value of those activities which require technical knowledge for their understanding. . . . When I gaze at the star-sown heaven, and the infinite beauty it affords my eyes, that means to me more than all that human art can give me. That does not mean that I ignore the value of those works generally called artistic; but personally, in comparison with the infinite beauty of Nature, I feel their unreality too intensely. . . . Life is greater than all art. I would go even further and declare that the man whose life comes nearest to perfection is the greatest artist; for what is art without the sure foundation and framework of a noble life? *56*   *Among the Great, Dilip Kumar Roy, 1945*

Truly beautiful creations come when right perception is at work. If these moments are rare in life they are also rare in art. *57*
Young India, November 13, 1924

True art takes note not merely of form but also of what lies behind. There is an art that kills and an art that gives life. True art must be evidence of happiness, contentment and purity of its authors. *58*
Young India, August 11, 1921

We have somehow accustomed ourselves to the belief that art is independent of the purity of private life. I can say with all the experience at my command that nothing could be more untrue. As I am nearing the end of my earthly life I can say that purity of life is the highest and truest art. The art of producing good music from a cultivated voice can be achieved by many, but the art of producing that music from the harmony of a pure life is achieved very rarely.   *59*

Harijan, February 19, 1938

If I can say so without arrogance and with due humility, my message and methods are, indeed, in their essentials for the whole world and it gives me keen satisfaction to know that it has already received a wonderful response in the hearts of a large and daily growing number of men and women in the West.   *60*   *Young India, August 11, 1920*

The highest honour that my friends can do me is to enforce in their own lives the programme that I stand for or to resist me to their utmost if they do not believe in it.   *61*   *Young India, June 12, 1924*

GLOSSARY

Advaita   Non-duality. A school of philosophy associated with the Indian philosopher, Sankaráchárya (788-820), which believes that there is only one Absolute Truth; all else is appearance.

Ahimsā   Nonviolence, positively the practice of love.

Āshram (Āsrama)   Hermitage; a quiet place where people having common ideals lead a community life and follow a particular discipline. The place where Gandhi resided with his co-workers and disciples was referred to as the *āshram*.

Āshrama (Āsrama)   Hindu idealism prescribes four stages or periods of good life, called *āshramas*: the period of study and self-discipline; of life as a householder and man of the world; of contemplation and gradual withdrawal from worldly ties; of total renunciation.

Ātma   Soul, self.

Avatār   A divine incarnation.

Baniā   Member of the third caste among the Hindus, whose traditional occupation is trade and commerce.

Bhāgavat (Bhāgavata)   A sacred book of the Hindus dealing also with the life and teachings of Lord Krishna.

Brahmacharya (Brahma-carya)   Celibacy; a life of self-discipline and continence dedicated to higher pursuits.

Brāhmin (Brāhmana)   Member of the first caste among the Hindus whose traditional occupation is priesthood or devotion to learning.

Chapāti   Cake of unleavened bread.

Charkhā   Spinning wheel.

Dharma   Religion; moral law or practice; duty.

Diwān   Chief minister of a princely state.

Himsā   Violence.

Kalma   Designates the profession of faith whereby a Muslim witnesses the unity of God.

Khaddar   Hand-spun and hand-woven cloth.

Mahātmā   Lit. A great soul; a title generally given to saints. In later years Gandhi was generally referred to in India as the Mahatma.

Manu   An ancient preceptor and author of the Code of Laws, named after him.

Moksha (Mokṣa)   Emancipation from earthly attachments; liberation from the cycle of births.

Muni   Seer; sage; particularly a Jaina saint.

Nawāb   Muslim dignitary or ruler.

Purdah   Veil worn by woman in some eastern countries.

Rishi (Ṛṣi)   Sage.

Sadāvrata   Giving of alms to the poor.

Saṃskār (Saṃskāra)   Indelible impression left by past action.

Satyāgraha   Lit. Holding on to truth. Name given by Gandhi to the technique of nonviolent resistance as practised by him and under his guidance.

Sevā Samiti   A society for voluntary social service.

Shāstra (Ṡāstra)   Hindu scripture.

Swadeshī   Love of one's own country or patronage of things indigenous and native.

Swarāj   Self-rule.

Vakīl   Pleader; lawyer.

Vedas (Veda)   The earliest and most sacred writings of the Hindus.

Glossary

Upanishad (Upaniṣad) Ancient discourses on philosophy which are generally regarded as the source material of Hindu metaphysics. There are more than a hundred such *Upanishads* of which ten are considered as principal.

SOURCES

The abbreviations used below refer to the following books which were consulted:

AMG *An autobiography or the story of my experiments with Truth,* by M. K. Gandhi. Published by Navajivan Publishing House, Ahmedabad, originally in two volumes, Vol. I in 1927 and Vol. II in 1929; the edition used was published in August 1948.

MGP *Mahatma Gandhi, the last phase,* by Pyarelal. Published by Navajivan Publishing House, Ahmadebad, in two volumes, Vol. I in February 1956 and Vol. II in February 1958.

MT *Mahatma, life of Mohandas Karamchand Gandhi,* by D. G. Tendulkar. Published by Vithalbhai K. Jhaveri & D. G. Tendulkar, Bombay 6, in eight volumes, Vol. I in August 1951, Vol. II in December 1951, Vol. III in March 1952, Vol. IV in July 1952, Vol. V in October 1952, Vol. VI in March 1953, Vol. VII in August 1953, Vol. VIII in January 1954.

BM *Bapu's letters to Mira.* Published by Navajivan Publishing House, Ahmedabad, August 1949.

CWMG *The collected works of Mahatma Gandhi.* Published by The Publications Division, Ministry of Information and Broadcasting, Government of India, New Delhi; Vol. I was published in January 1958.

DM *The diary of Mahadev Desai.* Published by Navajivan Publishing House, Ahmedabad; Vol. I was published in 1953.

HS *Hind Swaraj or Indian Home Rule,* by M. K. Gandhi. Published by Navajivan Publishing House, Ahmedabad, originally in 1938; the edition used was published in 1946.

Sources

WSI *Women and social injustice,* by M. K. Gandhi. Published by Navajivan Publishing House, Ahmedabad, originally in 1942; the edition used was published in 1954.

MM *The mind of Mahatma Gandhi,* compiled by R. K. Prabhu and U. R. Rao. Published by Oxford University Press, London, in March 1945.

SB *Selections from Gandhi,* by Nirmal Kumar Bose. Published by Navajivan Publishing House, Ahmedabad, in 1948.

Reference to the journals in which the passages were originally published will be found in the above books. See the text for the source and date of each quote, when known.

Chapter I

1. AMG, 4.
2. AMG, 4.
3. AMG, 4-5.
4. AMG, 5.
5. SB, 45.
6. AMG, 11.
7. AMG, 12.
8. AMG, 12-13.
9. AMG, 14.
10. AMG, 15.
11. AMG, 15-16.
12. AMG, 18.
13. AMG, 19.
14. AMG, 21.
15. AMG, 23-24.
16. AMG, 26-27.
17. AMG, 31.
18. AMG, 31-32.
19. AMG, 32-33.
20. AMG, 33.
21. AMG, 33.
22. AMG, 33.
23. AMG, 36.
24. AMG, 37.
25. AMG, 37.
26. AMG, 38.
27. AMG, 38.
28. AMG, 47.
29. AMG, 50-51.
30. MT, II, 47-48.
31. AMG, 52.
32. AMG, 52.
33. AMG, 52-53.

34. AMG, 54.
35. CWMG, I, 3.
36. AMG, 63.
37. AMG, 64-65.
38. AMG, 66-67.
39. AMG, 79-80.
40. AMG, 81-82.
41. AMG, 84.
42. AMG, 101.
43. AMG, 101.
44. AMG, 102.
45. AMG, 105.
46. AMG, 115.
47. AMG, 118.
48. AMG, 123.
49. AMG, 128.
50. AMG, 129.
51. AMG, 130.
52. AMG, 134.
53. AMG, 135.
54. AMG, 140-41.
55. AMG, 157.
56. AMG, 157-58.
57. AMG, 162-63.
58. AMG, 163-64.
59. AMG, 165.
60. AMG, 168.
61. AMG, 190.
62. AMG, 190-91.
63. AMG, 191-92.
64. AMG, 192.
65. AMG, 197.
66. AMG, 212.
67. AMG, 205.
68. AMG, 229-30.

69. AMG, 231.
70. AMG, 232-33.
71. AMG, 235.
72. AMG, 236-37.
73. AMG, 239-40.
74. AMG, 241.
75. AMG, 249-50.
76. AMG, 250.
77. AMG, 250-51.
78. AMG, 251.
79. AMG, 256.
80. AMG, 257.
81. AMG, 334.
82. AMG, 261.
83. AMG, 262-63.
84. AMG, 264.
85. AMG, 268.
86. AMG, 337.
87. AMG, 338.
88. MT, II, 49.
89. AMG, 342.
90. AMG, 349.
91. AMG, 364-65.
92. AMG, 383.
93. AMG, 384.
94. AMG, 385.
95. AMG, 386.
96. AMG, 391.
97. AMG, 391-92.
98. AMG, 392-93.
99. AMG, 398.
100. AMG, 398.
101. AMG, 406.
102. AMG, 406.
103. AMG, 409.

104. AMG, 411-12.
105. AMG, 414.
106. AMG, 414-15.
107. AMG, 415.
108. AMG, 418.
109. AMG, 418-19.
110. AMG, 419.
111. AMG, 443-44.
112. AMG, 449.
113. AMG, 421-23.
114. AMG, 424-25.
115. AMG, 425.
116. AMG, 427.
117. SB, 167-68.
118. SB, 168-70.
119. SB, 214.
120. SB, 214.
121. MT, II, 113.
122. MT, II, 340.
123. AMG, 614; see
     also MM, 4.
124. AMG, 615.
125. AMG, 616.
126. MM, 7.
127. MM, 8.
128. MT, II, 417.
129. SB, 150.
130. MT, II, 421-23.
131. MT, II, 425-26.
132. MT, III, 142.
133. MT, III, 155-57.
134. MT, IV, 93.
135. MT, IV, 95.
136. MT, VI, 356.
137. SB, 216.
138. MGP, II, 475.
139. MT, IV, 66-67.
140. MT, VI, 177.
141. MT, V, 241-42.
142. MT, V, 378-79.
143. MT, VII, 100.
144. MGP, II, 801.
145. MGP, II, 808.
146. MT, I, 285.
147. MGP, II, 800.
148. MGP, II, 453.
149. MGP, II, 463.
150. MT, VIII, 22-23.
151. MGP, II, 246.
152. MGP, II, 246.

153. MGP, II, 324.
154. MM, 16.
155. MGP, II, 324.
156. MGP, II, 101.
157. MGP, II, 327.
158. MGP, I, 562.
159. MM, 9.
160. MM, 9.
161. MGP, II, 766.
162. MGP, II, 417.
163. MGP, II, 782.
164. SB, 238.

Chapter II

1. MM, 85.
2. SB, 223.
3. AMG, 341.
4. MM, 21.
5. MM, 22.
6. MM, 22.
7. MM, 22.
8. MM, 22-23.
9. SB, 9.
10. MGP, I, 421-22.
11. AMG, 615.
12. AMG, 615-16.
13. AMG, 616.
14. SB, 8.
15. MM, 24.
16. SB, 224.
17. SB, 224.
18. SB, 225.
19. SB, 225.
20. SB, 226-27.
21. SB, 228.
22. SB, 226.
23. SB, 227-28.
24. SB, 228.
25. SB, 228.
26. MM, 84.
27. MM, 84.
28. MM, 82.
29. MM, 86.
30. MM, 96.
31. MT, III, 139-40.
32. MT, IV, 108-09.
33. MT, III, 343.
34. MT, III, 300.

35. MT, IV, 121.
36. DM, 138.
37. DM, 227-28.
38. BM, 171.
39. MT, IV, 167-68.
40. MGP, I, 599.
41. MGP, II, 247.
42. MT, III, 359-60.
43. AMG, 6.
44. AMG, 6-7.
45. SB, 225.
46. MM, 23.
47. MM, 23.
48. MM, 24.
49. MM, 24.
50. MM, 27.
51. MM, 27.
52. MM, 30.
53. MM, 33.
54. MM, 70.
55. MM, 70.
56. MM, 71.
57. MM, 80.
58. MM, 78.
59. MT, III, 176-77.
60. SB, 17.
61. MM, 17.
62. MM, 19-20.
63. MM, 20.
64. MM, 21.
65. MM, 23.
66. MM, 38.
67. DM, 249-50.
68. MM, 12.
69. MM, 13.
70. MM, 13.
71. MM, 1.
72. MM, 5.
73. MM, 10.
74. MM, 15.
75. MM, 23.
76. MM, 20.
77. MM, 20.
78. MM, 37.
79. MM, 38.
80. SB, 9.
81. SB, 46-47.
82. SB, 223.
83. SB, 223.
84. SB, 223.

85. SB, 223.
86. SB, 223.
87. SB, 224.
88. SB, 229.
89. SB, 229.
90. SB, 229.
91. SB, 229.
92. SB, 230.
93. DM, 168.
94. SB, 238.
95. MM, 1.
96. MM, 2-3.
97. MM, 3.
98. MM, 3.
99. MM, 3.
100. MM, 5.
101. MM, 5.
102. MM, 5.
103. MM, 10.
104. MM, 81.
105. MM, 82.
106. MM, 106.
107. MM, 167.
108. SB, 210.
109. MGP, I, 348.
110. MGP, II, 784.
111. MT, VII, 264.
112. MGP, II, 143.
113. MGP, II, 91.
114. MGP, II, 143.
115. MM, 14.
116. MT, II, 312.

Chapter III

1. SB, 13.
2. SB, 37.
3. SB, 14.
4. MM, 126.
5. HS, 51-52.
6. MGP, II, 140-41.
7. SB, 160-61.
8. SB, 161.
9. SB, 162.

Chapter IV

1. MM, 49.

2. MT, V, 344.
3. SB, 16.
4. SB, 18.
5. SB, 24.
6. SB, 18.
7. SB, 23.
8. SB, 24-25.
9. SB, 17-18.
10. SB, 31-32.
11. SB, 27-28.
12. SB, 33.
13. SB, 32.
14. SB, 33.
15. SB, 33.
16. SB, 34.
17. SB, 38-39.
18. SB, 142-43.
19. SB, 145.
20. SB, 146-47.
21. SB, 147.
22. SB, 16.
23. SB, 33.
24. SB, 144.
25. SB, 145.
26. SB, 147.
27. SB, 149.
28. SB, 149.
29. SB, 151.
30. SB, 151-52.
31. SB, 152.
32. SB, 152.
33. SB, 152.
34. AMG, 427-28.
35. AMG, 428.
36. AMG, 429.
37. SB, 154.
38. SB, 155.
39. SB, 157.
40. SB, 157.
41. SB, 159-60.
42. SB, 206.
43. MM, 42.
44. MM, 3-4.
45. MM, 44.
46. MM, 44.
47. MM, 44.
48. MM, 46.
49. MM, 46.
50. MM, 46.
51. MM, 48-49.

52. MM, 48.
53. MM, 50.
54. MM, 52.
55. MM, 54.
56. MM, 58.
57. MM, 63.
58. MM, 64.
59. MM, 68.
60. MM, 68-69.
61. DM, 296.
62. MGP, II, 124-25.
63. MGP, II, 507.
64. MT, VII, 152-53.
65. SB, 150-51.
66. SB, 153.
67. SB, 153.
68. SB, 154.
69. SB, 154.
70. SB, 155-56.
71. SB, 156.
72. MM, 47.
73. MM, 49.
74. MM, 50.
75. MT, IV, 61.
76. MT, II, 5-8.
77. MT, V, 273.
78. MT, VII, 171-73.
79. MM, 133.

Chapter V

1. SB, 39.
2. SB, 39.
3. SB, 268.
4. SB, 268.
5. SB, 271-72; see also MM, 44.
6. MM, 11.
7. MM, 11.
8. MM, 108.
9. DM, 98.
10. DM, 298.
11. MGP, II, 233.
12. MGP, II, 442.
13. MGP, II, 792.
14. SB, 221.
15. SB, 221.
16. MM, 32.
17. MM, 33.

18. MM, 32-33.
19. MGP, I, 573.
20. SB, 217.
21. SB, 18.
22. MGP, I, 599.
23. MGP, I, 600.
24. MT, IV, 57-58.
25. AMG, 258.
26. DM, 80.
27. MGP, I, 588-89.
28. DM, 253.
29. MT, IV, 73.
30. SB, 215-16.
31. MGP, I, 586.

Chapter VI

1. SB, 27.
2. SB, 27.
3. SB, 22.
4. MM, 137.
5. MM, 135.
6. MM, 134.
7. MM, 135-36.
8. MM, 136.
9. DM, 287.
10. MGP, I, 359.
11. SB, 43.
12. SB, 43.
13. SB, 44.
14. SB, 152.
15. MM, 133.
16. SB, 113.
17. SB, 171-72.
18. MM, 59-60.
19. MM, 60-61.
20. MM, 63.
21. MM, 63.
22. MM, 63.
23. MGP, II, 90.

Chapter VII

1. MM, 128.
2. SB, 73.
3. SB, 71.
4. MM, 121.
5. MT, VII, 224-25.

6. SB, 64-65.
7. SB, 66.
8. SB, 66.
9. SB, 67-68.
10. SB, 58.
11. SB, 58.
12. SB, 59.
13. SB, 65.
14. SB, 66-67.
15. SB, 71.

Chapter VIII

1. SB, 41.
2. SB, 40.
3. SB, 77.
4. SB, 17.
5. SB, 75.
6. SB, 75-76.
7. SB, 77-78.
8. SB, 78-79.
9. SB, 52.
10. SB, 54.
11. SB, 50.
12. SB, 49.
13. MM, 11.
14. MM, 101.
15. SB, 76.
16. SB, 49.
17. SB, 48-49.
18. SB, 49.
19. SB, 49.
20. MM, 104.
21. MM, 116.
22. MM, 117.
23. SB, 81.
24. SB, 91.
25. SB, 92.
26. SB, 94.
27. MT, IV, 13-14.
28. MGP, I, 66.

Chapter IX

1. MT, V, 343.
2. MT, V, 342.
3. MM, 65.
4. SB, 143.

5. SB, 22.
6. SB, 37.
7. SB, 38.
8. SB, 41.
9. SB, 43.
10. SB, 82-83.
11. SB, 109.
12. SB, 109.
13. MT, VI, 23.
14. SB, 111.
15. SB, 111.
16. SB, 118.
17. SB, 193-94.
18. SB, 190.
19. SB, 20.
20. MM, 3.
21. MM, 9.
22. MM, 9.
23. MM, 11.
24. DM, 149.
25. SB, 201.
26. SB, 201-02.
27. MT, IV, 15.
28. SB, 42.
29. SB, 42.
30. SB, 109.
31. SB, 109.
32. SB, 110.
33. SB, 110.
34. SB, 116.
35. SB, 116.
36. SB, 116.
37. SB, 191.
38. SB, 191.
39. MM, 100.
40. SB, 36.
41. MM, 132.
42. MM, 130.
43. MM, 131.
44. MT, II, 24.
45. MT, II, 25-26.
46. MT, I, 357.
47. MT, VI, 269.
48. SB, 192-93.
49. SB, 203.
50. SB, 203.
51. SB, 204.
52. SB, 203.
53. MT, VI, 336.

Sources

Chapter X

1. SB, 251.
2. SB, 256.
3. SB, 256-57.
4. SB, 261-66.
5. SB, 266-67.
6. SB, 267.
7. SB, 274.
8. SB, 274.
9. MM, 162.
10. SB, 254.
11. SB, 256.
12. SB, 256.
13. SB, 255.
14. SB, 258.
15. MM, 161.
16. MM, 161.
17. DM, 188.
18. MGP, I, 44.
19. MT, IV, 76.

Chapter XI

1. SB, 239.
2. SB, 241.
3. SB, 239-40.
4. MM, 111.
5. MM, 111-12.
6. MM, 111.
7. SB, 248.
8. SB, 248.
9. MM, 112.
10. MM, 112.
11. MM, 112.
12. MM, 113.
13. WSI, 4-5.
14. WSI, 18.
15. SB, 246.
16. SB, 246-47.
17. WSI, 180.
18. WSI, 184.
19. WSI, 87.
20. WSI, 187.
21. MT, VI, 78.
22. MGP, I, 327.
23. MGP, II, 103.
24. MGP, II, 104.

Chapter XII

1. SB, 11.
2. MM, 4.
3. MM, 8.
4. DM, 315.
5. DM, 318.
6. MM, 8-9.
7. SB, 19.
8. SB, 44.
9. SB, 45.
10. SB, 45.
11. MT, II, 27-28.
12. MM, 16.
13. MM, 41.
14. MM, 41.
15. MT, V, 206.
16. MM, 31.
17. MM, 69.
18. MM, 70.
19. MM, 79.
20. MM, 66.
21. MT, I, 241-42.
22. MM, 145.
23. MM, 9.
24. MM, 12.
25. MM, 12.
26. MM, 12.
27. SB, 28-29.
28. SB, 29.
29. SB, 45.
30. SB, 193.
31. SB, 193.
32. SB, 193.
33. SB, 182.
34. SB, 209.
35. SB, 209.
36. SB, 209.
37. SB, 278.
38. SB, 275.
39. SB, 275-76.
40. SB, 300.
41. SB, 300.
42. BM, 59.
43. BM, 218.
44. MGP, I, 421.
45. MGP, I, 429-30.
46. MT, II, 384.
47. MT, II, 418-20.
48. SB, 268-69.
49. SB, 269.
50. MT, II, 450.
51. DM, 167-68.
52. MGP, I, 168.
53. DM, 160.
54. SB, 273.
55. SB, 273.
56. MM, 39.
57. SB, 274.
58. SB, 274.
59. SB, 274.
60. MM, 135.
61. MM, 8.

A SELECTED BIBLIOGRAPHY[1]

CHIEF WORKS BY GANDHI

A guide to health, Madras, S. Ganesan, 1921.
Basic education, Ahmedabad, Navajivan Publishing House, 1951.
Bapu's letters to Mira (1924-1948), Ahmedabad, Navajivan Publishing House, 1949.
Christian missions, Ahmedabad, Navajivan Press, 1941.
Communal unity, Ahmedabad, Navajivan Publishing House, 1949.
Delhi diary, Ahmedabad, Navajivan Publishing House, 1948.
Diet and diet reform, Ahmedabad, Navajivan Publishing House, 1949.
Economics of Khadi, Ahmedabad, Navajivan Press, 1941.
Ethical religion, Madras, S. Ganesan, 1922.
For pacifists, Ahmedabad, Navajivan Publishing House, 1949.
From Yeravda Mandir, Ahmedabad, Navajivan Press, 1937.
Harijan, Ahmedabad, Navajivan Press, 1933-40, 1942, 1946-48.
Hind Swaraj, Ahmedabad, Navajivan Press, 1938.
Jail experiences, Madras, Tagore & Co., 1922.
My early life (edited by Mahadev Desai), Bombay, Oxford University Press, 1932.
My soul's agony, Ahmedabad, Navajivan Press, 1932.
Nonviolence in peace and war, Ahmedabad, Navajivan Publishing House. Part I, 1945, Part II, 1949.
Rebuilding our villages, Ahmedabad, Navajivan Publishing House, 1952.
Sarvodaya, Ahmedabad, Navajivan Publishing House, 1951.
Satyagraha, Ahmedabad, Navajivan Publishing House, 1951.
Satyagraha in South Africa, Madras, S. Ganesan, 1928.
Self-restraint v. Self-indulgence, Ahmedabad, Navajivan Publishing House, 1947.
Songs from prison (adapted by John S. Hoyland), London, Allen & Unwin, 1934.

1. This bibliography has been supplied through the courtesy of Sahitya Akademi. Several recent works in English have been added.

A Selected Bibliography

Speeches and writings, Madras, G. A. Natesan & Co., 1933.
Swadeshi, true and false, Poona, 1939.
The story of my experiments with truth, Ahmedabad, Navajivan Publishing House, 1940.
Towards new education, Ahmedabad, Navajivan Publishing House, 1953.
Towards nonviolent socialism, Ahmedabad, Navajivan Publishing House, 1951.
To a Gandhian capitalist, Bombay, Hind Kitabs, 1951.
To the students, Ahmedabad, Navajivan Publishing House, 1949.
Unto this last, Ahmedabad, Navajivan Publishing House, 1951.
Women and social injustice, Ahmedabad, Navajivan Press, 1942.
Young India, Ahmedabad, Navajivan Press, 1919-32.
Young India, Madras, S. Ganesan, 1919-22, 1924-26, 1927-28 (Vols. 1, 2, 3).

WORKS ON GANDHI

English

All-India Congress Committee
Satyagraha in Gandhiji's own words, Allahabad, 1935.

Andrews, C. F.
Mahatma Gandhi's ideas, London, Allen & Unwin, 1929.
Mahatma Gandhi at work, London, Allen & Unwin, 1931.

Birla, G. D.
In the shadow of the Mahatma, India, Orient Longmans Ltd., 1953.

Bose, Nirmal Kumar
Studies in Gandhism, Calcutta, Indian Associated Publishing Co., 1947.
Selections from Gandhi, Ahmedabad, Navajivan Publishing House, 1948.
My days with Gandhi, Calcutta, Nishana, 1953.

Brailsford, H. N.
Rebel India, London, Victor Gollancz, 1931.

Brockway, Fenner A.
The Indian crisis, London, Victor Gollancz, 1930.

Cambell-Johnson, Alan
Mission with Mountbatten, London, Robert Hale Ltd., 1951.

Catlin, George
In the path of Mahatma Gandhi, London, Macdonald Co., 1948.

Chakravarty, Amiya
Mahatma Gandhi and the modern world, Calcutta, Book House, 1945.

Desai, Mahadev
The diary, Ahmedabad, Navajivan Publishing House, 1953.

All Men Are Brothers

The epic of Travancore, Ahmedabad, Navajivan Press, 1937.
Gandhiji in Indian villages, Madras, S. Ganesan, 1927.
The story of Bardoli, Ahmedabad, Navajivan Press, 1929.
With Gandhiji in Ceylon, Madras, S. Ganesan, 1928.

Diwakar, R. R.
Glimpses of Gandhiji, Bombay, Hind Kitabs, 1949.
Satyagraha—its technique and history, Bombay, Hind Kitabs, 1946.

Doke, Joseph J.
M. K. Gandhi, Madras, G. A. Natesan & Co., 1909.

Fischer, Louis
A week with Gandhi, New York, Duell, Sloan & Pearce, 1942.
The life of Mahatma Gandhi, New York, Harper & Brothers, 1950.

Gandhi, Manubehn
Bapu—my mother, Ahmedabad, Navajivan Publishing House, 1949.

Government of India
Gandhian outlook and techniques, New Delhi, 1953.
Homage to Mahatma Gandhi, New Delhi, 1948.

Gregg, Richard B.
A discipline for nonviolence, Ahmedabad, Navajivan Press, 1941.
The power of nonviolence, Ahmedabad, Navajivan Press, 1938.
Which way lies hope? Ahmedabad, Navajivan Press, 1952.

Heath, Carl
Gandhi, London, Allen & Unwin, 1944.

Holmes, John Haynes
The Christ of today, Madras, Tagore & Co., 1922.
My Gandhi, New York, Harper & Brothers, 1953.

Hoyland, John S.
Indian crisis, New York, Macmillan, 1944.
The Cross moves East, London, Allen & Unwin, 1931.

Indian Opinion
Golden Number (Passive resistance movement in South Africa, 1906-14), Natal, Phoenix, 1914.

Jones, E. Stanley
Mahatma Gandhi: an interpretation, London, Hodder & Stoughton, 1948.

Jones, M. E.
Gandhi lives, Philadelphia, David Mckay Co., 1948.

A Selected Bibliography

Kalelkar, Kaka
Stray glimpses of Bapu, Ahmedabad, Navajivan Publishing House, 1950.

Kripalani, J. B.
The Gandhian way, Bombay, Vora & Co., 1938.
The latest fad, Allahabad, 1939.

Kumarappa, Bharatan
On tour with Gandhiji, Aundh, 1945.

Lester, Muriel
Entertaining Gandhi, London, Ivor Nicholson & Watson, 1932.
Gandhi—world citizen, Allahabad, Kitab Mahal.

Mira
Gleanings, Ahmedabad, Navajivan Publishing House, 1949.

Natesan, G. A.
Mahatma Gandhi—the man and his mission, Madras, 1943.

Nehru, Jawaharlal
An autobiography, London, John Lane, 1936.
The discovery of India, Calcutta, Signet Press, 1941.
Eighteen months in India, Allahabad, Kitabistan, 1938.
Mahatma Gandhi, Calcutta, Signet Press, 1949.
The unity of India, London, Lindsay Drummond, 1941.

Polak, H. S. L.; Brailsford, H. N.; Lord Pethick-Lawrence
Mahatma Gandhi, London, Odhams Press, 1949.

Polak, Millie Graham
Mr. Gandhi—the man, London, Allen & Unwin, 1931.

Prabhu, R. K.; Rao, U. R. (Eds.)
India of my dreams, Bombay, Hind Kitabs, 1947.
The mind of Mahatma Gandhi, Bombay, Oxford University Press, 1945.

Prasad, Rajendra
Gandhiji in Champaran, Madras, S. Ganesan, 1928.
Mahatma Gandhi and Bihar, Bombay, Hind Kitabs, 1949.

Pyarelal
The epic fast, Ahmedabad, Navajivan Press, 1932.
A pilgrimage for peace, Ahmedabad, Navajivan Press, 1950.
A nation builder at work, Ahmedabad, Navajivan Press, 1952.
Gandhian techniques in the modern world, Ahmedabad, Navajivan Publishing House, 1953.
Mahatma Gandhi, the last phase, Ahmedabad, Navajivan Publishing House, 1956 and 1957 (2 vols.).

Radhakrishnan, S. (Ed.)
Mahatma Gandhi, London, Allen & Unwin, 1939.

Ramachandran, G.
A sheaf of Gandhi anecdotes, Bombay, Hind Kitabs, 1946.

Reynolds, Reginald
India, Gandhi and world peace, London, 1931.

Rolland, Romain
Mahatma Gandhi, London, Allen & Unwin, 1924.

Sheean, Vincent
Lead, Kindly Light, New York, Random House, 1949.

Shridharani, K.
War without violence, New York, Harcourt Brace & Co., 1939.

Tagore, Rabindranath
Mahatmaji and the depressed humanity, Calcutta, Visva-Bharati, 1932.

Tendulkar, D. G.
Mahatma, life of Mohandas Karamchand Gandhi, Bombay, Vithalbhai K.
Jhaveri and D. G. Tendulkar, 1951, 1952, 1953 and 1954 (8 vols.).

Tendulkar, D. G.; Rau, Chalapathi M.; Sarabhai, Mridula; Jhaveri, Vithalbhai K.
(Eds.)
Gandhiji: his life and work, Bombay, Karnatak Publishing House, 1944.

Visva-Bharati Quarterly
Gandhi Memorial Peace Number, Santiniketan, 1949.

Walker, Roy
Sword of gold, London, 1945.
The wisdom of Gandhi, London, Andrew Pakers Ltd., 1943.

Yagnik, Indulal K.
Gandhi as I know him, Delhi, 1945.

French

Rolland, Romain
Mahatma Gandhi, édition nouvelle augmentée d'une postface, Paris, Dela-
main et Boutelleau, 1924.
Mahatma Gandhi, édition nouvelle, revue, corrigée et augmentée, Paris, Dela-
main et Boutelleau, 1929.

Vulda, Laura
L'Inde sous Gandhi, Aix-en-Provence, Les Éditions du feu, 1931.

A Selected Bibliography

Gandhi, Mohandas Karamchand
>In *Larousse du xxe siècle,* publié sous la direction de Paul Augé, Paris, Larousse, 1928-33.
>*M. K. Gandhi à l'oeuvre,* suite de sa vie, écrite par lui-même; traduit de l'anglais par André Bernard, 6e éd., Paris, Rieder, 1934. (Collection *Europe.*)

Privat, Edmond Théophile
>*Aux Indes avec Gandhi,* Paris, V. Attinger, 1934. (Série *Orient,* n° 11.)
>Nouvelle edition, 1948, publiée par La Concorde, Lausanne.

Landeau, Marcel
>*Gandhi tel que je l'ai connu,* Paris, 1938.

Samios, Eleni
>*La sainte vie de Mahatma Gandhi,* préface de Jean Herbert, 3e éd., Gap, Ophrys, 1947. (Collection *Krishna.*)

Kaplan, Alexandre
>*Gandhi et Tolstoï; les sources d'une filiation spirituelle,* préface de M. l'abbé Pierre, Nancy, Imprimerie L. Stoquert, 1949.

Drevet, Camille
>*Mahatma Gandhi,* Strasbourg, Le Roux, 1951.

Sheean, Vincent
>*Le chemin vers la lumière,* traduit par Claude Elsen et Jacqueline Sellers, Paris, Plon, 1951. (Collection *L'épi,* nouvelle série.)

Fischer, Louis
>*Vie du Mahatma Gandhi,* traduit de l'américain par Eugène Bestaux, Paris, Calmann-Lévy, 1952. (Collection *Précurseurs de génie.*)

Spanish

Gandhi, Mohandas Karamchand
>In: *Enciclopedia universal ilustrada europeo-americana,* Barcelona, Espasa-Calpe, 1905-33.

Rolland, Romain
>*Mahatma Gandhi,* traducción del francés por el Dr. Salomón Margulis, Buenos Aires, S.A.D.E., 1942.

Andresco, Victor
>*Mohandas Karamchand Gandhi, el gran político indio,* Madrid, Casa Goni, 1948.

All Men Are Brothers

Recent biographies in English

Ashe, Geoffrey
Gandhi, Stein and Day, 1968.

Erikson, Erik
Gandhi's Truth, On the Origins of Militant Nonviolence

Horsburgh, H. J. N.
Nonviolence and Aggression, A Study of Gandhi's Moral Equivalent of War

Nanda, B. R.
A Biography of Gandhi, Barron's, 1969.

The Collected Works of Gandhi, published by the Indian Government are available from Greenleaf Books, South Ackworth, New Hampshire 03607. Greenleaf has a very large collection of books by and about Gandhi. Write for their free listing.

Other works:

Bondurant, Joan
Conquest of Violence, The Gandhian Philosophy of Conflict, U. of California, 1965 (new edition expected in 1973).

Mahadevan, T. K. and G. Ramachandran,
Gandhi, His Relevance for our Times, World Without War Publications, 1971.

Brief Chronology of Events in Gandhi's Life

1869, October 2	Mohandas Karamchand Gandhi born
1883	Marries Kasturbai
1888, September 4	Sails to England to study law
1891, September	Called to the Bar, returns to India
1892	Practices law at Rajkot and Bombay, not very successfully
1893, April	Leaves for South Africa for the first time; acts as a legal consultant
1893, May-June	Experiences racial discrimination and decides to fight against racial prejudice in South Africa
1896	Returns to India to organize support for Indians in South Africa
1896, November 30	Returns to South Africa with wife and children
1897	Petitions, writes letters, calls upon British authorities to end discriminatory laws.
1899	Forms Indian Ambulance Corps during the Boer War
1901, October	Returns to India
1902	Practices law, seeks Indian support of South African Indians
1902, November	Recalled to South Africa to fight against anti-Asiatic legislation in Transvaal.
1903	Enrolled as Attorney of Supreme Court of Transvaal
1905	Opposes Bengal Partition, appeals to British colonial officials to treat India as an "integral part of the Empire."
1906	Announces for Indian Home rule. Declares disinterestedness in worldly goods; takes vows of celibacy for life.
1906, September	Organizes Indian opposition to Transvaal Asiatic Laws; addresses a mass meeting of Indians at Johannesburg which takes an oath of passive resistance.
1907, January	Writes *Ethical Religion*
1907, March	New protest meetings held by Indians against the Asiatic Registration Act passed in Transvaal.
1907	Petitions, addresses mass meetings, leads passive

	resistance, pickets and visits Smuts in Pretoria in opposition to the Registration Act.
1908, January	Gandhi adopts the word "Satyagraha" in place of "Passive Resistance" to describe his nonviolence.
1908	Sentenced to two months' imprisonment for failure to leave Transvaal.
1908	Gandhi agrees to voluntary registration if the Registration Act is repealed, is physically attacked by those who believe he has betrayed the Indian cause.
1909	Continues Satyagraha campaign against the Registration Act in Transvaal. Visits England, seeks to influence British opinion.
1909, November	Writes *Hind Swaraj* or *Indian Home Rule*
1913	Indian marriages in South Africa invalidated by Supreme Court Judgment. Gandhi defers plans to return to India.
1913, May	Gandhi promises Satyagraha campaign if South African government does not repeal marriage law.
1913, September	Campaign begins, Gandhi's wife is arrested.
1913, October	Gandhi urges a strike by miners, leads a march into the Transvaal.
1914, January	Suspends Satyagraha campaign following agreement with Smuts.
1914	Returns to India
1914, May 20	Founds Satyagraha Ashram at Ahmedabad, India
1917	Fights successfully against indentured Indian emigration
1918, January	Takes up cause of textile laborers in Ahmedabad; initiates Satyagraha in Bombay district.
1919, April	Inaugurates all-India Satyagraha movement
1919, April 11	Arrested in Delhi, escorted back to Bombay, violence occurs in several towns.
April 13	Troops fire on an unarmed crowd killing over 400 people. Gandhi declares three day penitential fast, suspends Satyagraha.
1919, October	Assumes editorship of *Young India*
1919, November	Presides over all-India Khilafat Conference at Delhi
1920, September	Indian National Congress at Calcutta accepts his

	programme of non-cooperation to obtain redress of Punjab and Khilafat wrongs.
1921, April	Leads complete boycott of foreign cloth
1922, February	Gives notice to Viceroy of intention to launch Satyagraha campaign in Bardoli (Gujarat).
1922, March 10	Arrested for sedition and sentenced to six years imprisonment, March 18
1924, February 5	Released from prison
1924, September	Fasts twenty-one days for Hindu-Moslem unity
1925, November	Begins writing final version of autobiography
1928, December	Gandhi moves in favor of Independence if Dominion status is not granted by the end of 1929
1929, December	Lahore Congress declares for complete independence at Gandhi's insistence.
1930, February	Launches Civil Disobedience movement
1930, April 6	Intentionally breaks salt laws
1930, May	Gandhi arrested and imprisoned. Civil disobedience follows all over India.
1931, March	Gandhi and Irwin (Viceroy of India) reach agreement
1931, August	Sails for England to attend Second Round Table discussion
1932, January	Arrested six days after his return from England
1932, September 20	Begins a fast unto death in jail to secure abolition of separate electorates for Harijans.
1932, September 26	Breaks fast as the demand is accepted.
1933, February 11	Founds the weekly paper *Harijan*
1933, May 8	Begins twenty-one day fast for self-purification, suspends Satyagraha campaign.
1933, July	Informs government of Bombay of his decision to revive the Civil Disobedience movement. Arrest follows.
1933, August	Goes on fast on being denied facilities to carry on anti-untouchability propaganda
1933, November	Commences Harijan-uplift tour
1934, September	Announces his retirement from politics to engage in developing village industries, Harijan service and education through basic crafts.
1934, October	Inaugurates All-India Village Industries Association
1937, October	Presides over Educational Conference calling for education through craft labor

1939, March	Commences "fast unto death" to secure adherence to promise of government reform.
1940, October	Sanctions individual civil disobedience in wartime. Suspends Harijan and allied weeklies.
1941, December	Asks to be relieved of leadership in Congress by Working Committee
1942, May	Appeals to British Government to quit India, arrested in August
1943, February	Fasts for twenty-one days.
1944, February	Kasturbai Gandhi dies
1944, May	Gandhi unconditionally released from prison
1944, September	Gandhi-Jinnah talks regarding Pakistan
1945, April	Gandhi argues for equality and freedom for India as a condition of peace. Also asks for a just peace for Germany and Japan.
1946, January	Tours Southern India arguing against untouchability and Hindustani propaganda
1946, February	Harijan and allied papers revived
1946, June	Congress Working Committee decides to accept Interim Government scheme.
1946, August	Viceroy of India announces invitation to Congress to form Provisional Government
1946, August	Gandhi opposes partition of India
1946, August	Great Calcutta Killing
1946, September	Congress forms an interim government
1946, October	Noakhalli Massacre
1947, January	Mountbatten, new Viceroy, arrives in Delhi
1947, April	Gandhi and Jinnah issue joint appeal for peace
1947, May	Congress Working Committee accepts Partition in principle over Gandhi's opposition.
1947, June	Indian leaders accept Mountbatten partition plan, Gandhi opposes
1947, July	Independence of India Bill passed
1947, August 14	Gandhi hails August 15th as a day for rejoicing for the independence of India; but deplores the birth of Pakistan
1947, September	Fighting breaks out in Kashmir
1947, December	Kashmir dispute referred to the United Nations
1948, January	Gandhi fasts for communal peace in Delhi, January 12 to 18
January 30, 1948	Gandhi assassinated on way to evening prayers.